Zeitgenössische Musikwissenschaft

Series Editor

Jan Hemming, Institut für Musik, Universität Kassel, Kassel, Hessen, Germany

Die zeitgenössische Musikwissenschaft hat in den letzten Jahren einen immensen Innovationsschub erfahren. Sie widmet sich der ganzen Bandbreite von Themen und Methoden und überwindet die Grenzen zwischen (sogenannter) Kunstmusik und populärer Musik oder zwischen den althergebrachten Teilbereichen der Historischen- und Systematischen Musikwissenschaft sowie der Ethnomusikologie. Dies eröffnet neue intra-, inter- und transdisziplinäre Perspektiven in konstruktivem Austausch mit Cultural- und Gender Studies, Empirical Musicology oder Digital Humanities. Die Reihe Zeitgenössische Musikwissenschaft löst namentlich die Reihe Systematische Musikwissenschaft ab und macht sich weiterhin zur Aufgabe, durch Veröffentlichung von Überblickswerken, Monographien und Diskussionsbänden innovative musikwissenschaftliche Ansätze zu präsentieren.

Herausgegeben von
Jan Hemming
Kassel, Deutschland

Contemporary musicology has undergone enormous innovations in recent years. It now addresses a complete range of topics and methods and crosses the borders between (so-called) art music and popular music or between the traditional realms of historical, systematic and ethnomusicology. This opens up new intra-, inter- and transdisciplinary perspectives in close exchange with Cultural and Gender Studies, Empirical Musicology or Digital Humanities. The series Contemporary Musicology follows up the series Systematic Musicology and continues presenting innovative musicological approaches by publishing textbooks, monographs and discussion volumes.

Edited by
Jan Hemming
Kassel, Germany

More information about this series at https://link.springer.com/bookseries/16520

Leo Feisthauer

Theorizing Music Videos of the Late 2010s
A Prosumer's Study of a Medium

J.B. METZLER

Leo Feisthauer
Kassel, Germany

Dissertation at the University of Kassel, Faculty 01
Author: Leo Feisthauer
Date of disputation: May 28th, 2021

ISSN 2662-9089 ISSN 2662-9097 (electronic)
Zeitgenössische Musikwissenschaft
ISBN 978-3-662-65048-6 ISBN 978-3-662-65049-3 (eBook)
https://doi.org/10.1007/978-3-662-65049-3

© The Editor(s) (if applicable) and The Author(s), under exclusive license to Springer-Verlag GmbH, DE, part of Springer Nature 2022
This work is subject to copyright. All rights are solely and exclusively licensed by the Publisher, whether the whole or part of the material is concerned, specifically the rights of translation, reprinting, reuse of illustrations, recitation, broadcasting, reproduction on microfilms or in any other physical way, and transmission or information storage and retrieval, electronic adaptation, computer software, or by similar or dissimilar methodology now known or hereafter developed.
The use of general descriptive names, registered names, trademarks, service marks, etc. in this publication does not imply, even in the absence of a specific statement, that such names are exempt from the relevant protective laws and regulations and therefore free for general use.
The publisher, the authors and the editors are safe to assume that the advice and information in this book are believed to be true and accurate at the date of publication. Neither the publisher nor the authors or the editors give a warranty, expressed or implied, with respect to the material contained herein or for any errors or omissions that may have been made. The publisher remains neutral with regard to jurisdictional claims in published maps and institutional affiliations.

Responsible Editor: Marta Schmidt
This J.B. Metzler imprint is published by the registered company Springer-Verlag GmbH, DE part of Springer Nature.
The registered company address is: Heidelberger Platz 3, 14197 Berlin, Germany

Acknowledgments

I would like to profoundly thank Prof. Dr. Jan Hemming and Prof. Dr. Christoph Jacke for encouraging and supervising this work. I thank Sascha Jeschonneck, Julia Alcamo, Prof. Dr. Claudia Bullerjahn, Dr. Holger Schwetter, Tim Koglin, Martha Herbold, Matthias Krüger, Astrid Stricker, Annika Rink and the participants of the Examinations Colloquium at the IfM Kassel for constructive feedback and helpful discussion and Johanna Feuerhake for legal advice. Furthermore, I want to thank Katharina Duve, Timo Schierhorn, UWE from Auge Altona, and Dave Meyers for the interviews.

Contents

1	**Introduction**	1
2	**Summarizing the Research Status**	9
	2.1 Defining Music Videos?	9
	2.2 A Short History of Music Videos From 1980–2014	13
	2.3 Renaissance	20
	2.4 A Critical Discussion of Existing Literature	23
3	**Reconsidering Contemporary Music Videos**	29
	3.1 Changed Behavior of Reception and Consumption	31
	3.2 Content	38
	3.2.1 Kendrick Lamar—Humble \\ You Gotta See This	45
	3.3 Aesthetics	52
	3.3.1 Jamie xx—Gosh \\ Dystopia and Numbness	64
	3.4 A Democratized Art Form	70
	3.5 The Future of Music Videos?	72
	3.6 Conclusion	76
4	**Prosuming a Music Video in the Late 2010s**	79
	4.1 Motivation	81
	4.2 Technical Conditions	87
	4.2.1 Björk—Iosss \\ Pushing the Limits Back to the Roots ...	90
	4.3 Context, Canons, and Inspiration	94
	4.3.1 Deichkind—Wer Sagt Denn Das? \\ Everything is a Remix	102

5	**What is Music Videos' Cultural Impact ?**	107
	5.1 A Short Theoretical Context	114
	5.2 Observing Culture	119
	5.2.1 The Chainsmokers—#SELFIE \\ The Mirror in the Mirror	119
	5.2.2 Joyner Lucas—I'm Not Racist \\ Sit Down, Be Humble!	123
	5.3 Generating Culture	128
	5.3.1 Childish Gambino—This Is America \\ Dance the Riot Away	133
	5.3.2 BTS—Fake Love \\—Real Industry	140
	5.4 Appropriating Culture	146
	5.4.1 Coldplay—Hymn for the Weekend \\ An Interesting Cocktail	148
	5.4.2 Appropriating the Internet Universe Due to Lack of Own Cultural Heritage	154
	5.5 Observing/Appropriating/Generating YouTube	157
6	**Conclusion**	163
Bibliography		169

Introduction

I have always been fascinated by music videos. Born in the early 1990 s, I still got to experience MTV in its latest state of being a hot spot in music and popular culture. At the same time, mobile phones acquired the ability to display videos and USB sticks could be handed around to share bigger files. I remember watching Sum 41 and Blink 182-clips on schoolyards and collecting music videos on a folder on my desktop.

Some years later, I started making short films on my own and music videos for other bands. My perspective got augmented from just being a consumer to seeing things as a producer: I became—typical for my generation—a prosumer, something that I will discuss at length as one of the main arguments of this work.

Most of the time, there was initially no or only a very limited budget available for the productions. Nevertheless, my team members and I always had great ambitions regarding the dimensions of the video. We were regularly inspired by new music videos and tried to use the technical, human, and financial resources available to us as efficiently as possible. We were often forced to rely on DIY methods and the free cooperation of technical companies, pyrotechnicians, location owners, and many more. To our satisfaction, we were very often rewarded by success and a growing network.

Although the videos did not go viral, they always represented a success for us for our own further work and also in the audience, who appreciated the handwriting of the videos and gave us a lot of support.

At university, I studied music and took up making music videos seriously, and now, this research on music videos in their current form offers me an opportunity to take a step back and to address the topic from an academic viewpoint. So I must disclaim that the point of view from which I write this work is thus shaped by my own biography and my experience in the field of producing music videos.

This PhD dissertation is based on theory formation. Its goal is to **formulate a status quo** of the music video medium in the late **2010 s** and analyze if mentionable stylistic trends or innovations are establishing and if so, if these findings demand **new impulses for the scholarly debate** so far. I am thus investigating methods and structures that routinely create order for social and cultural phenomena in practical activities—in my case, in music videos. Following a wide array of disciplines, perspectives and approaches, this work is designed to **contribute to a developing understanding** of the medium and its evolution.

Next to musical and cinematic analyses that are both descriptive and hermeneutic, the study is methodologically located in the interpretative paradigm[1], which includes social constructivism, ethnomethodology, symbolic interactionism, and has its roots in the Chicago School. Their shared basic assumption is that people act towards things based on the meaning that these things have for them. This meaning is created in an interpretative process with other actors and can be changed, varied, and stabilized. To reconstruct the creation of meaning (and thus reality), a subject-oriented view of the actors and content is required. One could argue that music videos are interpretative methods themselves that make sense of the world of the social entity's members. Trying to understand music videos, in our case, and explaining their meanings is the method that ethnomethodology employs.[2] Rather than a theory that announces in advance what is true or correct (which a priori would be pointless and downright impossible, concerning the high pace at which the medium is evolving), I find it more fruitful to theorize 'without guarantees'[3] and with a 'necessary modesty of theory'[4], as Stuart Hall put it.

Since I have a personal history as a musician and both a consumer and producer of music videos, this subject-oriented view on the topic, or in other words—understanding music videos in their context through the experiences of the researcher—shall be the fundament of my academic practice. Moreover, this personal experience or personal empiricism is also the particular feature of this work, compared with other academia on the topic, which was often written with a purely theoretical background. Although I am not analyzing my own artistic work, a producer's perspective shall be profitable for the scientific debate.

---

[1] Wilson (1970), *Normative and Interpretative Paradigms in Sociology*, 57–79, Keller (2009), *Das Interaktive Paradigma—Eine Einführung*.

[2] Kurtişoğlu (2014), *Ethnomethodology in the use of Ethnomusicology and Ethnochoreology*, 285.

[3] Hall (1996), *The problem of ideology: Marxism without guarantees*.

[4] Hall (1992), *Cultural studies and its theoretical legacies*, 286.

1 Introduction

I will show that since from around the year 2014, music videos have been going through a significant evolution, **a Renaissance,** as I call it. Just as European culture of the 15th and 16th century was reviving the artistic achievements and style of Roman and Greek antiquity, the current music video market also revives its past golden age, which can be set during the 1980 s and 90 s. After a period of stagnation and disinterest in the early 2000 s, music videos nowadays are much more than just an advertisement for a specific song and even more than just a visual product to accompany music. The music video has become an independent art form with a vast and interactive audience, making it a, if not the most, **democratic** one. Traditional art forms have somewhat hierarchical standards of aesthetics, which then enforce traditional notions of power and the 'conventional hermeneutic pecking order', as J. Maggio calls it[5]. However, in the music video world, every artist, from high-selling popstars to independent, local bands, mainly deals with the same platform of distribution and the same task to create a combination of sound and image worth watching (see Setion 3.4).

Furthermore, I want to analyze the **interaction of culture and music videos and their role as a supertextual**[6] **constant** in an ever-growing multi-media world.

This diagnosis entails an array of consequences music videos pose in their cultural environment: The most important one is that they represent something I would like to call a 'cultural melting-pot' that offers a field of research of various cultural aspects in a concentrated and somewhat definable form. I will analyze and discuss this argument in chapter 5 to theorize music videos' impact on media and society. Music is said to be a universal language[7] that can express emotions across disparate cultures. That term goes back to like Henry Longfellow, Arthur Schopenhauer, and E.T.A Hoffmann[8] and has been controversial ever since[9]. However, I find it exciting to conceptually transfer art forms into other forms (such as understanding music as text) and then find new impulses for the discussion. In this context, I want to propose the perception of music videos as a tool and a **language of pop- and internet culture** that is vividly negotiating its technical and cultural environment and everything internet culture brings forth. I base this on the understanding of language as a communication system used

---

[5] Maggio (2007), *Comics and Cartoons: A Democratic Art-Form*, 237.

[6] Vernallis (2013), *Unruly Media: YouTube, Music Video, and the New Digital Cinema*, 2.

[7] E.g. Cooke (1959), *The Language of Music*, https://news.harvard.edu/gazette/story/2019/11/new-harvard-study-establishes-music-is-universal/

[8] Higgins (2012), *The Music Between Us: Is Music a Universal Language?*, 2.

[9] E.g. Ibid., Letts (1997), *Music: Universal language between all nations?*

by a particular community.[10] If viewed as a structural system where signs are governed by specific rules of combination to communicate meaning, it becomes plausible that certain codes such as aesthetics, narration, pictures, symbols, etc. in combination with itself or the music, convey meaning. However, unlike in the traditional structuralist model, the sign's meaning does not necessarily need to be fixed; it might also be negotiable. How this interdisciplinary perception of music videos might be fruitful for the discourse, I will theorize more deeply in later chapters.

The third focus of this work will be the closer analysis of the **prosumer's role in current music videos**. The 'prosumer' is a term blending the words producer and consumer and was first introduced back in 1980 by futurologist Alvin Toffler[11] and later picked up by various scholars, mainly in the context of IT issues as in 'The Digital Economy' from 1994 by Don Tapscott. In chapter 4, I spend time with the concept of prosumerism, which I will show to be central to today's music video world.

I notice that academia yet struggles to cover music videos adequately. Even Mathias Bonde Korsgaard says in his book from 2017 that scientific literature has yet to keep up with the ever-evolving development of music videos, which has become one of the most important online media.[12] Statements like these encouraged me to make music videos the subject of my scholarly work, expanding my own experience as both consumer and producer into an academic framework.

I must clarify that one cannot speak of any kind of unity regarding 'the contemporary music video' that could be compared to that of another period. There have been progressive and influential videos at any point of music video's history. And today—just as there have been back in the days—there also is an immense number of videos that deliver no evolution, progression or interesting phenomena whatsoever. Already in 1987, E. Ann Kaplan noticed the problems with analyzing music videos appearing in an ever-growing plurality[13]. Since then, the situation has by no means become easier to overview. All one can do is describe their own views and experiences and refer to existing literature that discusses similar observations. This is why my analyses and the findings focus mainly on the medium music video rather than particular videos. Nevertheless, in chapters 3

---

[10] https://www.lexico.com/en/definition/language,
https://www.collinsdictionary.com/dictionary/english/language.

[11] Toffler (1980), *The Third Wave*, 282.

[12] Korsgaard (2017), *Music Video After MTV*, 3.

[13] Kaplan (1987), *Rocking around the clock. Music Television, Postmodernism and Consumer Culture*, 54.

1 Introduction

to 5, I do in-depth analyses of several music videos to exemplary show certain capabilities and characteristics of contemporary videos and discuss specifics theories on prosumerism and cultural impact on their basis. The corpus of music videos mentioned throughout this work is mainly selected abductively, that is, as a starting point or evidence for the theories other scholars or I postulate. In the epistemological concept of abduction, which goes back to the American philosopher Charles Sanders Peirce, a result concludes a rule and a case, which can then be deductively derived and inductively verified in other cases. Abduction is, therefore, a conclusion with comparatively high fallibility and merely suggests that something may be. Nevertheless, according to Peirce, it is the only approach that can draft new rules or draw conclusions from something incomprehensible or new at first.[14] All of the chosen music videos illustrate the particular phenomena that I discuss in this work. Some videos already were subject of former scholarly work, some are among the most popular videos ever made, and some are relatively unknown but still are part of the music video world and thereby its nature. I wrote all of the nine in-depth analyses in this work in the context of one specific subtopic. The justification for including them in the corpus was the assumption that these nine videos, considering the subtopics, were essential and possibly deductively transferable to the discourse. A list of the 106 videos mentioned in this book is attached at the end. Other authors may have used different videos or followed different rules in their selection of videos, which is part of my constructivist approach.

Since there is a broad variety of aspects of the music video world that I will discuss in this work, the methods of analyzing the actual videos are not limited to just one approach. They range from more conventional film analyses such as technical deconstruction and exegetical studies to transdisciplinary processes that focus on facets beyond the actual video, such as socio-cultural impact and internet culture. Especially during the latter, I am oriented towards the questions about the mass communication process music clip proposed by Christoph Jacke in 2003[15], which in my opinion are still applicable. They pursue the motives and meanings of different participants in the fields of production, distribution, reception, and further processing and are oriented transdisciplinary, which allows a broad and universal discussion of the cultural product.

I plan this work to be **interactive** to a degree: I will quote many music videos of different styles and view numbers and, in the PDF version, direct the reader

---

[14] Reichertz (2012), *Abduktion, Deduktion und Induktion in der qualitativen Forschung*, 276–286.

[15] Jacke (2003), *Kontextuelle Kontingenz*: Musikvideos im wissenschaftlichen Umgang, 35.

to the YouTube videos via hyperlinks. Some readers might not be as deep into the matter as I got during my research. By giving the facility to watch the underlying music video themselves as they read my thoughts on them, I want to help understand my perspectives and arguments and spark the reader's own mind and ideas while reading the text. I partly follow George Thoma et al. here and their idea of the 'Interactive Publication'[16]. In their already aged paper of 2010, they proposed a similar approach:

> The increasing prevalence of multimedia and research data generated by scientific work affords an opportunity to reformulate the idea of a scientific article from the traditional static document, or even one with links to supplemental material in remote databases, to a self-contained, multimedia-rich interactive publication.[17]

Some of the methods that they suggest of how to achieve this are outdated today. Still, the idea of providing a multimedia document when writing about a multimedia subject seems nothing but logical to me. Apart from links to the videos themselves, there will be many stills from particular videos. I aim to fulfill the desirable attributes of an 'Interactive Publication', formulated again by Thoma et al., to make the document a research tool itself. According to them, the reader should be able to:

> (a) view any of these objects on the screen, and importantly, without losing context within the text; (b) link from one object to another; (c) interact with the objects in the sense of exercising control over them (e.g. start and stop video); (d) reuse the media content for analysis and presentation.[18]

This book is about a rapidly evolving matter as the music video world constantly moves on and offers new perspectives and facets to think and talk about. That means that while writing this, I have to keep observing the market and possibly add or even rewrite some passages as their viability or currency might have changed over time. Nevertheless, this work is designed to illustrate the medium's current status quo and deliver a modern and holistic analysis of music videos in a specific time span.

I will name view-numbers of videos on YouTube in some instances, simply for the reason that a tremendous quantitative resonance is a sort of a cultural impact, too, and I want to discuss music videos within their reach. Even though view numbers can be unreliable, and I am aware of the existence of bots for

---

[16] Thoma et al. (2010), *Interactive Publication: The document as a research tool.*
[17] Ibid., 1.
[18] Ibid., 2.

generating clicks, they sometimes are my point of departure. Not because they are saying anything about the videos' quality. In the examples I give, aspects like public discussion or the incitement of high view numbers for the users to click on the video themselves back up the justification to take their reach on YouTube into account. And last but not least, they are an important commercial factor for the industry as we will see.

Choice of words and referencing

Klaus Beck[19] and Roland Burkart[20] differentiate between transmission, processing, and storage technologies (or first-order media) and communication media (or media of second-order), which are part of a mass media public[21]. Regarding the latter, I conform to a definition of media that Werner Faulstich formulates in reference to Ulrich Saxer (1991): *A medium is an institutionalized system around an organized communication channel of specific capacity with social dominance.*[22] The keywords communication and social dominance, are well suited as starting points for further reflections that come up in the course of the work on topics such as music videos as a language, ad music videos' impact on culture and society.

The last facet, which I would like to take up in the terminology concerning the 'medium', are the so-called 'media offers' as part of the compact media concept according to Siegfried J. Schmidt, synthesized from the components of communication instruments, media technologies, social system components, and media offers.[23] The media offers emerge from the interaction of the three preceding factors as concrete products, such as books, television programs or, in this case, music videos. But Christoph Jacke remarks that it is a matter of the scientific treatment of music clips in particular as 'more than media offers'[24]. After all, music clips only become observable and analyzable in complex networks of relationships from legal, economic, social, political, and other contexts, as he writes, just as my approach in this work is.

---

[19] Beck (2006), *Computervermittelte Kommunikation im Internet*, 12.

[20] Burkart (2002), *Was ist eigentlich ein ‹Medium›? Überlegungen zu einem kommunikationswissenschaft-lichen Medienbegriff angesichts der Konvergenzdebatte*, 20.

[21] Gerhards/Neidhardt (1990), *Strukturen und Funktionen moderner Öffentlichkeit. Fragestellungen und An-sätze*, 20–25.

[22] Faulstich (2002), *Einführung in die Medienwissenschaft. Probleme—Methoden—Domänen*, 26.

[23] Schmidt (2008), *Der Medienkompaktbegriff*, 144–145.

[24] Jacke (2003), *Kontextuelle Kontingenz—Musikclips im wissenschaftlichen Umgang*, 34.

I will generally use the term 'music video', but also speak of 'clip' or 'video' synonymously. Even though scholars like Martin Lilkendey or Christoph Jacke do distinguish these terms and point out the technically correct use of the word 'video'[25], those arguments are understandable to me but at the same time far from the current discourse, given that the storage medium video (a first-order medium, as Beck and Burkart define it) is replaced by more modern technologies and practically non-existent anymore. And even if so, they may be marginalized, which is why I stick to the term that is most commonly used in the contemporary debate, that is 'video'.

When speaking of 'we', I do not formulate absolute truths that count for everybody. I use it when I speak from the perspective of an abstract collective that forms the audience of music videos and that I am part of, such as the collective of prosumers or sometimes even the collective of the general recipients. I differentiate between 'I' and 'we' because there are many systems and medial concepts discussed in this work founded on sociability and made for collective, rather than individual, consumption.

When speaking about a particular music video, I will italicize its title and add its year of release. This, on the one hand, highlights the topic of what this work is about and, on the other hand, provides additional information that puts the video into a cultural-historical perspective. Referring to songs rather than music videos, I will enclose them in quotation marks. For example: *Alright* (2015) by Kendrick Lamar means the music video for the song 'Alright'. Along the chapters, I will mark certain terms and keywords **bold** to add an orientational guideline for the reader and an overview of the most important theses of this work.

---

[25] Ibid., 27.

Summarizing the Research Status 2

In order to be able to understand the phenomenon music video, I first want to take a look at some definitions by different authors of existing literature and then dedicate a subchapter to the historical evolution of music videos. They are at every moment influenced by society and technology to such an extent that they basically must be interpreted and discussed all over again every few years. However, this does not mean that literature from the past forty years or so has lost its value. Still, it is an appeal to academia to go back into the complex matter over and over to avoid missing the medium's current development and impact. That is why I believe that one can understand today's status better if given a historical and theoretical context.

2.1 Defining Music Videos?

A fundamental but viable approach to the interaction of music and image is to be found in Carol Vernallis' classic work 'Experiencing Music Video—Aesthetics and Cultural Context'. If a variety of visual and musical material is brought together in a music video, Vernallis argues, these materials seem to interact, they *'seem to enter into conversation with one another, offering commentary, calling one another into question and even [...] deriding or discrediting the others'*[1]. We must thus hypothesize that **through the synthesis of both media, a semantic augmentation of the original material** is happening, which in its new context is to be interpreted under new circumstances. The artist and theorist Peter Weibel in the year 1987 said something similar: he described music videos as a contemporary-popular form of visual music, which is a dynamic art form that combines **visual**

---

[1] Vernallis (2004), *Experiencing Music Video*, 192.

© The Author(s), under exclusive license to Springer-Verlag GmbH, DE, part of Springer Nature 2022
L. Feisthauer, *Theorizing Music Videos of the Late 2010s*, Zeitgenössische Musikwissenschaft, https://doi.org/10.1007/978-3-662-65049-3_2

and musical material in a way so that they interact and jointly create an effect, which only one of them on its own never would have achieved.[2] This effect is also used by film music, where a soundtrack is added to the visual material to give it a certain mood or feel it would not have without it. Or, as the iconic film music composer Bernhard Hermann (Alfred Hitchcock) puts it, music in film becomes '*the communicating link between the screen and the audience, reaching out and enveloping all into one single experience*'[3].

But why this augmentation in the first place? Why would anybody create a new context for a song that perhaps was composed and performed without any visual image in mind and would work on its own? The inherent sense of purpose of music videos was criticized and even denied since the beginning of their existence. E. Ann Kaplan or Lothar Mikos, for instance, are talking about 'self-reflexive floods of images'[4]. As many theorists saw it, music television was a superficial jumble of nonsense and spectacle—nonlinear, non-narrative, incoherent, and illogical.[5]

Into the first half of the 2010 s, the fact was widely accepted that music videos first and foremost were **advertisements for the song** in order to sell it or promote an album. For example, these definitions are to be found in Andrew Goodwin's 'Dancing in the distraction factory' from 1992 and still in Axel Schmidt's 'Viva MTV!' from 2009, which both are well-known publications. This understanding gets disputed progressively in more recent works, but also in the early days, the discussion about the discrepancy between advertisement and art was held. A good example is Pulp's *Babies* (1992), which begins with the text '*a promo video is simply an advertisement for a song*' and satirizes then prominent conventions by blending in texts like '*lip-sync*' or '*narration*' whenever these elements appear in the video. Ironically, two years later, the song was re-released because of growing popularity with a new video, which had a much more commercial and conventional style and more adapted aesthetics and therefore can indeed be interpreted as 'simply an advertisement for a song'[6]. I don't want to value one version over the other but demonstrate the tension field of artistic expression and commercial rules music videos have always struggled with.

---

[2] Weibel (1987), *Von der visuellen Musik zum Musikvideo*, 119.
[3] Smith (2002), *A Heart at Fire's Center: The Life and Music of Bernard Herrmann*, 122.
[4] Mikos (1993), *Selbstreflexive Bilderflut. Zur kulturellen Bedeutung des Musikkanals MTV*
[5] see, in particular, Fiske (1986), *MTV: Post Structural Post Modern* and Kaplan (1987), *Rocking around the clock. Music Television, Postmodernism and Consumer Culture.*
[6] Halligan (2016), *A promo video is simply an advertisement for a song?*, 406.

2.1 Defining Music Videos?

Martin Lilkendey in 2017 defines music videos as a *'musical short film by the entertainment industry, in which a popular song is played and on a visual dimension is brought up narratively, performatively or associatively.'*[7]. He moves away from the pure advertising functionality of the clip. However, he still sees the song as the origin and requirement for the audiovisual product and names the popular entertainment industry as the author for music videos. By saying that, he neglects clips outside the world of pop music, as in the context of classical or contemporary avant-garde music, but also videos made by amateurs or videos that don't necessarily have a song as a starting point. Examples for the latter are The Lonely Island (USA) or Ylvis (Norway). Both groups produce the song and a very sophisticated video as one concept, while the songs' contents most times are incredibly ironic and exaggerated. In Ylvis' *Language of Love* (2016) for example, the protagonist first falls in love with an only Korean-speaking woman that he does not understand and then with a seal and they conversate primarily in seal sounds. The video is subtitled almost throughout, and so the song works practically exclusively in its visual context. In these cases, the imagery plays an equivalent role to the music and completes the humor and the song's general concept.

A more progressive and up-to-date approach to the definition of music videos is taken, again by Carol Vernallis, in the 'Oxford Handbook of New Audiovisual Aesthetics', which was published four years before Lilkendey's book. Here, Vernallis respects the current development in reception and production and describes the music video not only from within itself but with the background of its context and its effect on the viewer:

> We used to define music video as a product of the record company in which images are put to a recorded pop song in order to sell the song. **None of this definition holds any more**. On YouTube, individuals as much as record companies post music video clips, and many prosumers have no hope of selling anything. [...] a clip might look like a music video, but the music be neither prior nor preeminent. [...] Clips can occur in any duration and format.[8]

These are new observations, and they cover facets that weren't considered by the previous definitions I quoted. They stress the complex variety of the product music video and complicate the attempt to formulate a universal and still viable definition. Despite that variety, what remains is the search for common aspects

---

[7] Lilkendey (2017), *100 Jahre Musikvideo—Eine Genregeschichte*, 24.
[8] Richardson et al. (2013) *Oxford Handbook of New Audiovisual Aesthetics*, 438.

of all music videos. For that, Vernallis (2004) and Korsgaard (2013) use Ludwig Wittgenstein's model of family resemblance. It is usually applied to describe characteristics of objects, which cannot be sufficiently captured with taxonomic or hieratic classification because there are too many fundamental differences. Instead of considering only one universal characteristic, a variety of features is taken into account that might not appear simultaneously and in the same way. Terms may also be blurry and be based on paradigmatic uses. Gordon Baker summarizes in his reference work about Wittgenstein's philosophical investigations that an analysis is not necessary to describe and use those terms.[9] Applied to the discussion on formulating a definition of music videos, that model alleviates it by taking away the pressure or, say, the mandatory nature of having a definition at all for being able to make progress in research. According to Andrew Darley, music videos are examples of 'displayed intertextuality' (a parameter that seems significantly underestimated to me) that **frustrate attempts at categorization along traditional lines**[10]. Maura Edmond names three new characteristics of contemporary music videos that are 1.) the searchable and on-demand nature of online exhibition, 2.) an amplified variety, and 3.) a greatly expanded definition of what might be considered a music video.[11] Carol Vernallis thinks about how one could formulate this expanded definition might be and follows:

> We might thus define music video, simply and perhaps too broadly, **as relation of sounds and image that we recognize as such**.[12]

Although she does not stop here, I find this proposition interesting despite its seemingly tautological nature. While it without question is very broad, it helps us talk about audiovisual products that resemble conventional music videos but actually are made as advertisements, satirical statements, etc. and stresses the increasingly blurred lines between 'genres' in the medial world. I will come back to this idea and review if it is applicable or if it might be helpful for a contemporary discussion of music video after all.

Vernallis comes to the conclusion of understanding music videos in an 'interpersonal' method. That is, she suggests considering **music and imagery as**

---

[9] Baker (1980) *Understanding and Meaning. An Analytical Commentary on the Philosophical Investigations*.
[10] Darley (2000), *Visual Digital Culture: Surface play and Spectacle in New Media Genres*, 115.
[11] Edmond (2014), *Here We Go Again: Music Video After YouTube*, 312.
[12] Vernallis (2013), *Music Videos Second Aesthetic?*, 438.

partners, as spouses even in couples therapy. According to her, analysts might then ask questions such as:

> What kind of behavior does this persona exhibit, what attitudes, dispositions, traits, and ways of functioning? Are there examples of pushing, shoving, or mutual admiration? [...] We can assume there are issues of dominance and subservience, passivity, and aggression. [...] Some **new entity or quality emerges from the couple's relationship**, and we respond more to that quality than to either individual of the pair.[13]

This supports the claim by Peter Weibel that music and imagery interact and jointly create an effect, which only one of them on its own never would have achieved. And furthermore, it also illustrates nicely how both the musical and the visual layer become a whole that can only be judged and understood as one and not apart from each other. Staying in the metaphor, let's imagine our couple of music and visuals together at a dinner party. If it is going to be a great night and all the other couples will like our couple is neither determined by the individual characters, nor by the clothes one or the other is wearing but how they perform as a couple. Do they know each other, can they laugh with each other and make all the other couples say 'Oh, it's always nice to have them at a party!' or are they constantly interrupting each other and just make everybody feel awkward?

This understanding of the two elements as equal parts of the final music video that form a new, independent product is essential for me and is a premise for this work.

2.2 A Short History of Music Videos From 1980–2014

In scientific literature, one would often read **attempts to find and point the finger on the roots of music videos** more than a hundred years ago. To begin with, there is the classical opera, and other theatrical performances of music, later on cinemas would play a significant role in the search for the historical background of the music video. Walt Disney's *Fantasia* (1940), being the first cinematographic dramatization of classical music for sure was groundbreaking and greatly influential on other works to come. Also, films like Love Me Tender (1956), starring the singing Elvis Presley and The Beatles' A Hard Day's Night (1964), would experiment with film and music and are often mentioned in the discourse. In the 1970 s the first videos emerged which widely match the conceptual standards of music

---

[13] Ibid. 440.

videos we have today. An artist to be noted is the British photographer and director Keith MacMillan, who produced over 600 music videos between 1977 and 1981, among others for Paul McCartney, Kate Bush, and Blondie[14]. You will find various sources defining Queen's <u>Bohemian Rhapsody</u> (1975) as the first proper music video[15], which was basically a concert-clip with some more experimental segments in which the cover-arrangement of 'Queen II' was visually processed and animated. Some other sources name <u>Video Killed the Radio Star</u> (1981) by the Buggles the first music video ever, which polemically was the first video ever to be broadcasted on MTV[16]. From our perspective today though, the search for the birth of the music video is rather idle and only of historical interest because it does not contribute to our current understanding of music videos. Still, that date, **August 1st, 1981**, when MTV got on air, indeed is **a milestone in the history of the music video, as we know it today.**

In the late 1970 s, in the course of recession, the American music industry was facing a massive drop in sales, which was why new ways of advertisement had to be found to prevent a continuing decrease of sales numbers. John A. Lack, Leader of WASEC (Warner Amex Satellite Entertainment Group), the shortly before founded joint venture of Warner and American Express, together with broadcast expert Robert W. Pittman developed the music video channel MTV (Music Television)[17]. Music videos had gotten their own exclusive broadcasting platform. In the beginning, there were some complications concerning reach and repertoire, which in the first days consisted of just 120 clips and was only to be received in a couple of households with cable TV in New York[18]. On top of that, MTV was accused of homophobia and racism, an understandable allegation: In the beginning, the channel refused to play Afro-American rhythm and blues and even Michael Jacksons <u>Billie Jean</u> (1982) was only broadcasted after protests by his label[19].

1984 for the first time ever, the MTV Video Music Awards, an honoring for the best music video of the year, which over the years have become a worldwide event, were held. The first video to receive this price was The Cars' <u>You Might Think</u> (1984). In three years, MTV had come a long way, already having a viewership of 22 million people between twelve and thirty-four years and a weekly

---

[14] Lilkendey (2017), *100 Jahre Musikvideo—Eine Genregeschichte*, 79.
[15] E.g. Schlemmer-James (2006) *Schnittmuster*, 60.
[16] Filmlexikon Uni Kiel—Musikvideo.
[17] Weiß (2007), *Madonna revidiert—Rekursivität im Videoclip*, 17.
[18] Lilkendey (2017), *100 Jahre Musikvideo—Eine Genregeschichte*, 80.
[19] Ibid. p. 82.

2.2 A Short History of Music Videos From 1980–2014

income of advertisements of over a million dollars. The channel had become a highly influential institution in the music industry and pop culture.

The history of music videos can't be told without mentioning the innovations and the overall impact of Michael Jackson. He (and his production teams) early saw music videos' great potential and got famous for many of his videos: Most of all *Thriller* (1982) which set new standards for special and visual effects or *Black or White* (1991) with its legendary dance choreographies and the world's first use of morphing technology in music videos. Furthermore, Hollywood directors would often be recruited for Jackson's videos. For example, John Landis directed *Thriller* and *Black or White,* and Martin Scorsese was engaged in *Bad* (1987). In 1995, Jackson set the record for the most expensive music video of all time with *Scream* (1995, directed by Mark Romanek), costing seven million dollars. In those glory days, the initially intended purpose of music videos being an advertisement for the song was fulfilled. For instance, after the release of Michael Jackson's *Billie Jean*, ten million records were sold that could be traced back to the advertising effect of the video[20]. The careers of stars like Madonna owe a lot to MTV because they served the concept of a visual-musical projection of culture, while at the same time MTV profited from driving forces like those celebrities[21]. This principle not only applied to musicians, but also artists from various other backgrounds. For instance, Keith Haring got employed for designing costumes for Grace Jones' *I'm not Perfect* (1986) and Andy Warhol as director for The Cars' *Hello Again* (1984).

In that time of experiments and wealth, filmmakers and directors could establish themselves as progressive visionaries that would **influence the medium sustainably**. Names to be noticed among others are for sure Chris Cunningham (e.g. Placebo, Madonna, Aphex Twin), Michel Gondry (e.g. Björk, Radiohead, The White Stripes) and Hype Williams (e.g. Tupac Shakur, OutKast, Dr. Dre). The latter, who still is directing music videos today, has had a significant impact on the aesthetic tradition of Hip-Hop, like shots with dancing women and expensive cars in the background or the MC rapping into the camera in front of his gang. Those shots, for example, made it into a variety of Hip-Hop-videos and are to be also seen in early clips by Williams like *No Diggity* (1996) by Blackstreet.

These years, from around 1983 until 1997, are often described as '**the golden age of music video**'[22], a term that I will come back to often in this work. Music

---

[20] Bódy (1986), *Vom kommerziellen zum kulturellen Videoclip*, 39.

[21] Neumann-Braun (1999), *Viva MTV!—Popmusik im Fernsehen*, 12.

[22] E.g. Rosiny (2013), *Tanz Film: Intermediale Beziehungen zwischen Mediengeschichte und moderner Tanzästhetik*, 182.

videos established themselves as an individual medium and began to influence the rest of the media world. The so-called 'music-video-look' or also 'MTV-aesthetics'[23], meaning for example the fast cutting 'on the beat', inspired many movies and TV series like 'Top Gun', 'Miami Vice' or 'The Fast and The Furious'[24] (Fig. 2.1).

Fig. 2.1 Blackstreet—No Diggity, Min. 02:34, Min. 04:01

Until the mid-90 s, MTV was, with few exceptions like the 'Saturday Night Life'-show, a pure music video channel. In the second half of the decade, it began to fill 25% of its program with non-music content and initiated its way to becoming a lifestyle- and entertainment channel. Already in the year 2000, compared to 1995, 40% fewer music videos were broadcasted[25]. In this time, **MTV and with it the music industry passed its zenith** and from then on experienced a substantial decrease in interest and attention. The successful music video director Khalil Joseph, who, for instance, produced Beyoncé's visual album[26] *Lemonade* (2016), describes the situation as follows:

> *I stopped watching music videos sometime in the mid-nineties, when the music industry went wonk, and most of the artists I admired started producing perfunctory visual tracks that felt like last-ditch marketing tools rather than expressive companions to their audio tracks.*[27]

---

[23] E.g. Korsgaard (2017) *Music Video After MTV*, 149.
[24] Ibid.
[25] Lilkendey (2017), *100 Jahre Musikvideo—Eine Genregeschichte*, 83.
[26] A visual album is a whole record that is released with music videos in order to gain even more possibilities of expression than just the music and the artwork. The Beatles *A Hard Day's Night* (1964) or Pink Floyd's *The Wall* (1979) are possible early example for this form.
[27] https://www.newyorker.com/culture/culture-desk/kahlil-josephs-emotional-eye (acc. April 21st, 2019)

2.2 A Short History of Music Videos From 1980–2014

Music videos **seemed to have trivialized themselves.** But a new milestone was set just a few years later. According to the online database mvdbase.com in the year 2005, there was an increase of around 600% in released music videos. This is mainly due to the online video platform **YouTube**, which launched in this year. The other reason is to be traced back to the sinking cost of video equipment so that private persons could make their own videos, which only a few years before was only possible for big media companies (Fig. 2.2).

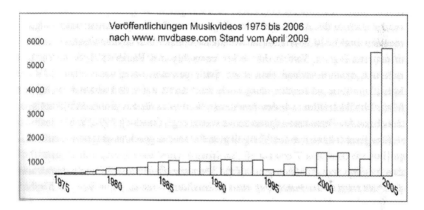

Fig. 2.2 Publications of music videos between 1975 and 2006 according to mvdbase.com[28]

Since then, YouTube is, without doubt, the most important platform for music videos, and for that shall be focused here briefly, while I will analyze it more deeply in the context of today's reception of music videos in Section 3.1. According to own statements, YouTube was founded free from commercial interest by a group of friends to not have to send big video files via e-mail. They didn't expect the overwhelming response for the platform by other users, which led to Google's decision to overtake it for around 1,5 billion dollars only one year after YouTube launched[29]. Like MTV or other media platforms, YouTube also had problems initially, mainly copyright issues, which led to various charges and

---

[28] Vieregg (2008), *Die Ästhetik des Musikvideos und seine ökonomische Funktion*, 85. This source by far does not show all of the released clips, because it refers to its own database, nevertheless it demonstrates a representative trend.

[29] http://www.nbcnews.com/id/15196982/ns/business-us_business/t/google-buys-youtube-billion/#.WsOs_38uDIU (acc. March 11th, 2019)

legal disputes. It was also criticized and marginalized as 'youth culture' for the banality of content (*'Nothing seems too prosaic or narcistic for these videographer monkeys'*[30]), which by proclaiming 'Broadcast Yourself'[31] was part of the platform's concept[32]. People filmed themselves while singing, shopping, dancing or even sleeping, and by that, the platform evolved to a hot spot of innovative participatory culture. This field of tension between self-promotion, authenticity, and attention economy offered ideal circumstances to give bands and artists a forum to express themselves in a new way accessible for everyone and, often only as a second step, to bring themselves to the market[33]. An early example of a band that used that new environment par excellence is **OK Go**. The US-American band released their video <u>Here it Goes Again</u> (2006), which was also frequently quoted by scholarly literature[34], in which they perform a sophisticated choreography on six treadmills in a single shot of a seemingly cheap camera. In very little time, the video got viral because of its simple originality and earned the band a broad audience around the world. They carried on their tradition of handmade, creative aesthetics in videos like <u>WTF?</u> (2009) and <u>This Too Shall Pass</u> (2010) and could establish themselves today as a reference in creative and entertaining music video making.

Paula Hearsum distinguishes the different video platforms and their successes, also referring to their functionalities[35]. While MTV had only a 'dual functionality', consisting of listening and watching, YouTube could offer a **'multiple functionality'** of listening, watching, rating, reading, commenting, and sharing. That new possibility of participation allowed great successes, like the DIY videos by OK Go, but at the same time made linear entertainment television with a dual functionality less and less attractive. In that time, MTV had passed on its significance for the music scene and was broadcasting almost exclusively reality- and lifestyle shows, until the point that in 2010 they canceled their slogan 'Music

---

[30] Keen (2008), *The Cult of the Amateur—How Today's Internet is Killing Our Culture and Assaulting Our Economy*, 5.
[31] 'Broadcast Yourself' was the slogan until 2012, when the platform got rid of any form of slogan.
[32] Marek (2013), *Understanding YouTube*, 17.
[33] For further information on YouTube see e.g. Burgess/Green (2009); *YouTube. Online video and participatory culture.* Polity Press, Cambridge and Marek (2013): *Understanding YouTube—Über die Faszination eines Mediums*, transcript, Bielefeld.
[34] E.g. Korsgaard (2017), 97, Richardson (2013), 443, 490.
[35] Hearsum (2013), *The Emancipation of Music Video*, 491.

2.2 A Short History of Music Videos From 1980–2014

Television' in order to react to the programs' reorientation[36]. Regional music video channels like MTV Germany even were shut down in 2013 and 2018.

In 2008, the US-American pop singer Lady Gaga set a next major milestone in music video history. She released her debut album 'The Fame' and presented herself from the beginning on as an eccentric piece of art somewhere between glamour, camp, and erotica. She celebrated that during concerts and other public appearances, such as when she walked the MTV Video Music Awards' red carpet in a dress made of meat, but also to a great extent in her music videos. At the latest, with her second video _Poker Face_ (2009), she could establish her aesthetic brand of flamboyant costumes, dance choreographies, and pop culture. In 2009/2010 followed the double video _Paparazzi/Telephone,_ directed by Jonas Åkerlund and with a summed-up running time of 16:43 minutes. In the first video, Gaga kills her lover or husband; in the second one, Beyoncé bails her out of jail, just to get on a Tarantino-esque rampage of poisoning a whole lot of other people. Carol Vernallis, in an article from 2011, compares these videos to Michael Jackson's _Thriller_ because of their common topic of the protagonists' ambiguity and concludes that Gaga and Åkerlund are departing from the traditional narrative and are taking what can be described as the **'next step' in music video storytelling**[37]. Also in 2010, Gaga set the record for being the first artist to reach the one billion views mark with her videos combined[38]. Jonas Åkerlund, who had been in the business since the early 1990 s, said in an interview on YouTube about the situation back then:

> I was just about to give up on music videos and then Lady Gaga showed up in my life and made it exciting again. She was the first artist that I met who said: 'we don't care about MTV, we can do it any way we want, we will use the internet as a platform to get it out there'! [...] After years of MTV and censorship telling me what to do and how to do it [...] I wasn't really creative at all. So, here's a young new artist with great music and lot of talent that inspired me to go to a new level of music videos.[39]

Since 2009, **vevo** (short for video evolution), a joint-venture video hosting service among the three major record companies Universal, EMI and Sony (since 2016 also Warner) has become the most significant music video host on YouTube, naming itself 'the world's leading all-premium music video and entertainment

---

[36] http://meedia.de/2010/02/09/mtv-streicht-music-aus-dem-logo/ (acc. June 19th, 2019).
[37] Vernallis (2011), _Storytelling on the ledge—Lady Gaga's Paparazzi and Telephone,_ 155.
[38] http://www.bbc.co.uk/newsbeat/article/11626592/lady-gaga-beats-justin-bieber-to-youtube-record (acc. January 30th, 2019).
[39] https://www.youtube.com/watch?v=Xb40vZmdc5g, 5:45 min.

platform'[40]. Like MTV, the channel network, in the beginning, had **copyright issues** in various countries, which is why many music videos, especially in Germany, weren't available. This lawsuit was ended in 2013, which led to a significant increment of overall-view numbers.

To sum it up, after music videos in the 1980 s and 90 s were in a period of experimentation and could establish a new mainstream medium, they went through a low in the early 2000 s, caused by the structural change and decreasing common interest. MTV vanished more and more and was no longer a warrant for commercially successful distribution of music videos. In the literature, some say that the year 2005 and the launch of YouTube represent the last milestone that initiated the 'current age of music videos'[41]. However, I can't agree with that. It is true that, through its sudden omnipresence, YouTube led to a boom in production and consumption but nevertheless did not immediately bring innovative ideas to form a new identity of the medium. Artists had yet to discover and explore the new possibilities the platform would offer, and the market and the audience had to adapt. From around the year 2010 on and majorly influenced by Lady Gaga, pompous volume productions, some also in the short-filmish tradition of Michael Jackson etc., got en vogue again. It is difficult to put the finger on a specific date or year when music videos were on their low point or passed a new milestone. Especially regarding the quality, one cannot make any universally valid judgments, for there were pioneering examples on any platform and in any year. I would suggest though, to define the time when **music videos were made internationally available through agreements on distributing licenses** and vevo, more precisely the time between 2009 and 2013, **as the beginning of the new era of music videos** that lasts until today. Music videos must always be analyzed within the context of their reception (see Section 3.1), which is why the aspect of global accessibility and the involved acceptance of YouTube as the principal music video platform seems reasonable to me as a critical turning point.

2.3   Renaissance

As I mentioned in the introduction, I attribute the evolution of music video a significant development, a Renaissance. In the last chapter on music video's history, there is already noticeable evidence for such a process. In this subchapter, I

---

[40] www.vevo.com (acc. October 20th, 2019).
[41] See e.g. Hearsum (2013), *The Emancipation of Music Video*, 492.

2.3 Renaissance

briefly want to emphasize this claim and explain my choice of words and discuss the arguments on it.

It is known that the Renaissance describes a period of time beginning in the late 15th century, in which, spreading from northern Italy, European artists, writers, and philosophers occupied themselves with the reincarnation of antique knowledge and art. The German philologist Klaus Hempfer writes in that context and quotes the Italian humanist from the Renaissance, Marsilio Ficino, about a **'return of a golden age'**[42]. Here, parallels to Claudia Rosiny and her interpretation of the 'golden age of music video' in 'Tanz Film' are visible. It gets even more apparent in an article by Gerd Blum, who is quoting Giorgio Vasari, who in the year 1550 for the first time used the term 'rinascita', Italian for Renaissance. He writes that the antique scheme of **growth, bloom, decay, and new genesis** is underlying the triad of Antiquity, Middle Ages, and Rinascita[43].

This very scheme can be transferred analogously to the history of the music video: the growth and bloom of the 1980 s and 90 s were followed by a decay of the next decade and now by a new genesis, which was initiated by global accessibility and the involved new attention music videos gained from it. In his book from 2017, Mathias Bonde Korsgaard also claims that we are experiencing a 'second golden age of music videos'[44]. Thus, he makes direct reference to the terminology as used by Ficino.

In online journalism, the term of a new 'golden age' is also well used. US-American journalist Danielle Scruggs in an article in the online magazine artsy.com writes about the current times being 'the golden age of black music video'. She points out numerous examples, among others videos by Beyoncè, Jay-Z, and Kamasi Washington, all of whom, for Scruggs, contribute to this glorification and imitate or reviving works of famous and iconic artists. These include famous photographers like Gordon Parks and Roy DeCavara, who were active in the American civil-rights movement and whose works are now for example being picked up in videos like *Element* (2018) by Kendrick Lamar, but also contemporary painters or filmmakers like Lynette Yiadom-Boakye and Julie Dash. Scruggs concludes:

> [...] thanks to the insistence of these musical and moving image pioneers on honoring the legacies of artists who have come before them, the most evocative and challenging

---

[42] Hempfer (1993), *Renaissance—Diskursstrukturen und epistemologische Voraussetzungen*, 10.

[43] Blum (2010), *Zur Geschichtstheologie von Vasaris Vite (1550)*, 273.

[44] Korsgaard (2017), Music Video After MTV, 2.

> *images of black life today can be found in another medium that's being consumed by mass audiences: the music video.*[45]

A new contextualization is being described, not as remixing or sampling, but as a conscious return to and reviving of past cultural achievements while at the same time advancing it in the new context. Klaus Hempfer points out that the significant novelty of the Renaissance in the Italian 15th century, compared to previous retrospective trends, was that it understood itself also as a breakup with the period immediately preceding it[46]. It was about abandoning established conventions and mindsets. This also applies to recent developments in music videos. Sarah Boardman, in an interview with The Guardian, compares videos from the years 2013 to 2016 and sees significant differences and trends:

> *However, unlike a few years ago, when the likes of Robin Thicke and Miley Cyrus were going for the shock factor*[47], *artists are taking artistic, inventive approaches. When they* do *try to provoke outrage – as with Kanye West's 'Famous' [2016] or Rihanna's 'Bitch Better Have My Money' [2015] – it's a step beyond 'Blurred Lines' or 'Wrecking Ball'.*[48]

And finally, there are the music video directors themselves, such as Jonas Åkerlund, who was quoted in the previous chapter. There he spoke about his decreasing interest in music videos around the year 2008 and complained about the restrictions imposed by MTV and how he found new excitement in the new environment of YouTube (*'After years of MTV and censorship telling me what to do and how to do, it I was just about to give up on music videos'*). Dave Meyers, who is directing many music videos for extremely famous musicians such as Billie Eilish, Taylor Swift, Travis Scott, etc. and who did an interview with the author from 2018, can agree to the terminology of a 'Renaissance':

> *[Some] years ago, [music videos] were cultural events. Then the industry collapsed. Videos suffered. YouTube gave a new avenue of consumption. And from that birthed a different style of cultural events.*

---

[45] https://www.artsy.net/article/artsy-editorial-golden-age-black-music-video (acc. February 2nd, 2019).

[46] Hempfer (1993), *Renaissance—Diskursstrukturen und epistemologische Voraussetzungen*, 12.

[47] She refers to the videos *Blurred Lines* (2013) and *Wrecking Ball* (2013), that both make use of the ‚shock-factor', as Boardman writes, obtained mainly by nudity.

[48] https://www.theguardian.com/music/2016/jul/28/how-pop-music-video-got-weird-again (acc. February 5th, 2019)

I have to clarify that this diagnosis is based not only on absolute numbers of video releases or on an absolute quality of music videos from one period of time to another. That is, I am not arguing that at some point, there have not been made music videos or that between year x and year y, all music videos were of inferior quality compared to the ones today. As I said, there have been progressive and influential videos at any point in music video's history. Music videos were never really gone. However, what has changed though, is the global passion and affection that both producers and consumers of any kind have of music videos and that facilitates a whole new treatment of the subject in its social and medial context. This clearly results from the observations from the last two chapters.

Although the diagnosis of a Renaissance seems obvious and is necessary to have in mind since it lays a certain foundation for this work, the following chapters are not written with an idea of constant comparison. In other words, while current music videos undoubtedly stand at a certain point that is certainly influenced by its history and heritage, they nevertheless shall primarily be analyzed synchronically, put in structuralist terms.

2.4 A Critical Discussion of Existing Literature

According to Renate Müller & Klaus Behne, existing literature can be divided roughly in two sections: On the one hand, the analysis of the product itself and, on the other hand, the one of its effect and reception[49]. The product's analysis is once more divided into three sub-sections that are a) the aesthetic-historical dimension, b) the formal-classificatory dimension, and c) the critical mass-medial analysis of the medium. Especially the latter segment was covered in the 1980 s and 90 s with various publications like 'Videoclips—Die geheimen Verführer der Jugend?'(German: Videoclips—The secret seducers of the youth?) (1991) by Michael Altrogge und Rolf Amann, in which the authors analyzed empirically if heavy-metal videos constituted dangers for children and adolescents (they did not).

The formal-classificatory section also is present since the 1980 s and, facing the heterogeneity of the material, has set itself the task of finding methods and criteria to summarize music videos in larger groups and thus to **find a model for a categorization**. Michael Shore, back in 1985, formulated a three-category model, similar to the definition mentioned above by Lilkendey, in which he divides music videos into the categories 'performance', 'narrative' and 'mixed forms'.

---

[49] Müller & Behne (1996), *Wahrnehmung und Nutzung von Videoclips*, 12.

- *There are straight lip-synched performance clips. [...]*
- *There are high concept clips full of image overload and deliberately ambiguous narrative tangents that only occasionally resolve to constitute a semblance of a plot. [...]*
- *In between, there are various hybrids of the two polarities, clips that mix the performance with conceptualized plot or performance with flashes of associative imagery.*[50]

This sort of model intends to cover all the manifestations of videos and therefore seems valid and is accepted and used by various scholars. While there are variations with the terms 'performance' and 'concept/narrative' in some publications, they remain the basis of most typologies[51]. For example, Johannes Menge in 1989 assigns all music videos to only the two poles 'performance-clip' and 'concept-clip', while the latter, according to his description, contains mainly narrations[52]. Concept clips also are sometimes understood as abstract 'art-clips'[53] with no performance, narration whatsoever.

Generally speaking, it can be observed that a large part of scholarly literature up until the 1990 s was occupied with classification and thoughts on the involved risks for certain consumers and the comparison to previous artforms. The latter is described by Ulrich Wenzel in his article ‚Pawlows Panther—Zur Rezeption von Musikvideos zwischen bedingtem Reflex und zeichentheoretischer Reflexion'[54] from 1999. He points out that scholars agree that music videos resembled one another in the absence of traditional artistic measurements like they held in novels or movies. As a consequence though, this conclusion's evaluation was dominated in two extremes: For some, this abandonment of traditions was a highly problematic loss; for others it was just a postmodern, subversive critique[55]. To sum it up, researchers in that era seemingly **had to take sides** in the discussion and judgment over the rapid development of a new medium.

Diane Railton & Paul Watson divide the research into similar fields as Müller & Behne: On the one hand, postmodernism's preoccupation with notions of **semiotic excess**, assemblage, self-reflexivity, and fragmentation, while on the other hand, music videos were used to interrogate the relationship between

---

[50] Shore (1985), *The Rolling Stone Book of Rock Video*, 99.
[51] Vieregg (2008), *Die Ästhetik des Musikvideos und seine ökonomische Funktion*, 49.
[52] Menge (1989), *Videoclips: Ein Klassifikationsmodell*, 191.
[53] Rötter (2000), ‚Videoclips und Visualisierung von E-Musik', 269.
[54] In: Neumann-Braun (1999): *Viva MTV!*, 45–73.
[55] Wenzel (1999), *Pawlows Panther*, 45.

2.4 A Critical Discussion of Existing Literature 25

music and cultural politics, especially the cultural politics of race and gender.[56] Throughout the history of scholarly analysis of music videos, **gender**, which can be assigned to Müller & Behne's second section, the reception of music video, has always been very present. Especially the depiction of women, which has been often stereotyped and objectified in Rock and Hip-Hop-videos, triggered a discussion in society and literature as well. Early examples for this are 'Race and gender in music videos: The same beat but a different drummer' by Jane D. Brown and Kenneth Campbell (1986) and 'How rock music videos can change what is seen when boy meets girl: Priming stereotypic appraisal of social interactions' by Christine and Ranald Hansen (1988). Both are empirical works that analyze the percentual representation of race and gender in music video television and the capacities of gender roles in music videos. The issue of gender representation and feminism in music videos is still around in younger years, although significantly less covered than in the late 20th century and mainly in shorter articles. Examples are case studies such as Amy Dworsky's '(Miss) Representation: An Analysis of the Music Videos and Lyrics of Janelle Monae as an Expression of Femininity, Feminism, and Female Rage' (2019) and Gooyong Kim's 'Neoliberal feminism in contemporary South Korean popular music' (2019) or psychological analyses such as 'Adopting the Objectifying Gaze: Exposure to Sexually Objectifying Music Videos and Subsequent Gazing Behavior' (2018) by Kathrin Karsay et al.

Looking into publications and also according to Danish culture and communications scholar Mathias Bonde Korsgaard not only the widespread interest in music videos decreased but also the scholarly engagement went down from the second half of the 1990 s on. He even names Andrew Goodwin's holistic and progressive analysis of MTV and music videos' essence 'Dancing in the Distraction Factory' from 1992 as the ending of a **first substantial wave of scholarly literature** about music videos that, with few exceptions (e.g. Kevin Williams' 'Why I (Still) Want My MTV: Music Video and Aesthetic Communication' (2003), Carol Vernallis' 'Experiencing Music Video'(2004) and Joachim Strands 'The Cinesthetic Montage of Music-Video: Hearing the Image and Seeing the Sound' (2008)) hasn't been followed in that extend **until the 2010 s**. I want to add Keazor & Wübbena's 'Video Thrills the Radio Star' (2007) to that collection for its great bandwidth and global approach to analyzing music videos of that time. In those years of seeming disinterest, if we may call them that, a general pessimistic

---

[56] Railton & Watson (2011), *Music Video and the Politics of Representation*, 9.

opinion towards music video can be noticed. Still in the book 'Imageb(u)ilder—Vergangenheit, Gegenwart und Zukunft des Musikvideos'[57], published by Keazor et al. in 2011, **the question if**, due to sinking budgets, regressing music television and the upcoming smartphones, **music videos were 'dead'** is posed multiple times[58]. Korsgaard then observes a new increase of scientific interest in the context of the medium's development, which, especially through YouTube, had made significant progress[59]. Gina Arnold's 'Music/Video—Histories, Aesthetics, Media' (2017), a work by multiple authors from different disciplines and ongoing research by Carol Vernallis are to be named as central to this recent segment of academia on music videos.

Nevertheless, the academic coverage of music videos has always been incomplete and overshadowed by certain insecurity. Music videos are highly complex products of audiovisual art. As E. Ann Kaplan noted, they straddle a border between advertising and art, and on top of that, the analyst must also **feel comfortable with addressing a variety of disciplines**. That includes at least music, image (including the moving bodies, cinematography, and editing), lyrics, the relation among them[60], and in some cases also the aspect of marketing. Considering this, one can imagine that there is and has been quite a dearth of music-video scholarship. Railton & Watson criticize both journalistic and scholarly literature also for the lack of institutionalization of music video studies:

> In their own ways, then, both cultural journalism, in absenting [music videos] from its purview[61], and the academy, in making its analysis dependent on something else [at the very least the respective song or the promotional function], replay and confirm the idea that music video is, in itself, a weightless, trivial phenomenon.[62]

This analysis of scholarly treatment stresses the observation of seeming disinterest by Korsgaard. He himself published the book 'Music Video After MTV: Audiovisual Studies, New Media, and Popular Music' in 2017, one of the most recent and comprehensive works on the topic. In this, he writes about a 'second

---

[57] German: Past, present, and future of the music video.
[58] E.g. Keazor & Wübbena (2011), *Imageb(u)ilder*, 16.
[59] Korsgaard, "Music Video Transformed" in *The Oxford Handbook of New Audiovisual Aesthetics*, 501.
[60] Vernallis (2019), academia.edu/39528324.
[61] This critique is to be considered in its time of creation. Nowadays it does not hold up anymore, since many sites, blogs and channels have picked the topic in recent time.
[62] Railton & Watson (2011), *Music Video and the Politics of Representation*, 5.

2.4 A Critical Discussion of Existing Literature

golden age of music videos'[63]. This is an important thesis, and having found this, Korsgaard points out that *'it is clear that more work needs to be done'*[64] in order to **keep up with the rapid developments the medium is undertaking** and to fill the discrepant gap between music video's unbridled popular success and the lagging scholarly interest.

What also seems problematic to me is the lack of topicality in many scholarly works that additionally has to do with time-consuming processes of publishing, which is why I plead for online publishing rather than in the form of conventional print publishing. In 2018, for example, an article by Henry Keazor about music video aesthetics for handheld devices was released[65]. The latest music video discussed was from 2014, all the others were even older. Thus, most of the described phenomena were outdated again by 2018 and other developments had taken their place, which is also the case in many other works, especially monographies and articles of print magazines. This is why I chose to pick the timespan of roughly the last five years and discuss the music videos as a medium rather than the specific characteristics of individual videos. Thereby I want to provide an overview of the medium in one particular era that is **as compact and dense as possible** and thereby as valuable as possible for contemporary scholars and those to come in the future. Apart from that, my personal background as a filmmaker evokes distinctive motivations and approaches to the topic that contribute to a vivid and progressive discussion of music videos.

One last fact to mention when writing about existing literature is that researchers obviously always have been dependent on the respective broadcast media of their time. Matthias Weiß, for example, collected his own library of music videos, which he recorded from television during 1984 and 2004 and still used it in 2007, two years after the launch of YouTube[66]. So, analyzing and comparing a certain number of videos was connected to quite a lot of effort. Today, YouTube as the primary source for music video is simultaneously blessing and curse. Although one has access to almost every video ever made, it is hard to focus on only one particular subject because there are infinite videos that appear and can relativize or even disprove observations made on other clips and thus make music videos a never-ending research area.

---

[63] Korsgaard (2017), Music Video After MTV, 2.
[64] Ibid., 200.
[65] Keazor (2018) Portable music videos? Music video aesthetics for handheld devices. In: Volume!: la revue des musiques populaires, 14:2.
[66] Weiß (2007), *Madonna revidiert—Rekursivität im Musikvideo*, 15.

In the following chapters of this work, I will approach the medium from different perspectives, trying to consider what it means to keep up with the medium's rapid development. To discuss the interaction of culture and music videos and their role as an integral constant in a pluralizing multi-media world (see Section 3.5), I will mainly follow the analysis of music videos' effects and reception and dive into historical-aesthetical aspects. When analyzing the possible understanding of music videos as a 'language' as noted in the introduction, I will work interdisciplinarily, consulting literary studies and linguistics.

Reconsidering Contemporary Music Videos 3

After going into the history and the economic and distributive conditions, which lead to the point of view from where we see contemporary music videos today, in this chapter, I want to explore the medium's more recent and current developments to provide a historical context for further analyses in chapter 4 and 5. I will look into aspects of technology, changed behavior of consumption and production, and content and aesthetics. The observations are based on a range of contemporary music videos (that is, primarily from 2015 on) and analyze if there are **mentionable developments or innovations establishing in reception, aesthetics and content** and if so, if these findings demand new impulses for the scholarly debate so far.

The pure quantitative popularity of music videos has gone through the roof. At the latest since South Korean Rapper Psy hit the then magical one-billion-views mark in 2012 with his video *Gangnam Style*, being followed by many other artists, new standards for music video consumption had been set. Or as Gina Arnold puts it: '[Gangnam Style] *signifies a global turn in both the reach and the significance of music videos, bringing a new visual energy to the world of cultural artefacts.*'[1] Indeed, music video's association with linear television nowadays may be labeled as a pre-historical, prototypical phase in the medium's development. YouTube and social media seem to have become much more fitting to the music video than any cable network ever was. Railton & Watson argue that this is not only due to the sheer size and growth of the platforms but the fact that '*the products themselves are increasingly designed for dissemination on multiple platforms [...] which both imply and impel different modes of consumption*'[2]. One certainly has to keep in mind that music videos represent by far the leading genre

---

[1] Arnold et al. (2017), *Music/Video—Histories, Aesthetics, Media*, 246.
[2] Railton & Watson (2011), *Music Video and the Politics of Representation*, 143.

© The Author(s), under exclusive license to Springer-Verlag GmbH, DE, part of Springer Nature 2022
L. Feisthauer, *Theorizing Music Videos of the Late 2010s*, Zeitgenössische Musikwissenschaft, https://doi.org/10.1007/978-3-662-65049-3_3

regarding view numbers on YouTube. For example, vevo in the beginning of 2019 had 25 billion monthly views[3].

But it's not only the pure demand for videos, which is on an all-time high. Also, the artists' longing for appreciation of their videos through fans and critics seem to orientate themselves according to previous successes by e.g. Michael Jackson or Madonna. Dave Meyers, a successful music video director, who will be quoted more extensively later, speaks in this context of music videos as **'cultural events'**[4]. This is a term that also other scholars use like for example James Montgomery, who commented Lady Gaga's *Telephone* (2010) on MTV with: *'You will remember where you were when you first saw it' and that its release was 'Gaga's passport to the rarest of pop stratospheres, up there with the Madonnas and the, gasp, Michael Jacksons'*[5]. Or Armond White, who wrote in the New York Press that *Telephone* was **'more exciting than any feature-length American film** released so far this year' and held it as a 'medium landmark'[6].

At the same time, according to Sarah Boardman, leader of the music division at Pulse Films, which was for instance involved in videos for Beyoncé, there is a seemingly contrary development on the economic side. In an interview with 'The Guardian' from 2016 she points out that the is a growing gap in budgeting music videos, which wasn't existent in the past:

> *At the moment, you have no middle in budgets – you have £30,000 for the majority of artists, then you have £200,000 for [Justin] Bieber or Carly Rae Jepsen, for a big pop star, but there's nothing in between. You used to get £50,000, £60,000, £70,000, £90,000 quite often. Now you have good, credible artists and they're getting £30,000 or £40,000, and it's really difficult to make something stand out for that sort of money.*[7]

I will examine how all these developments, if existent, may add to the question of this chapter, how an appropriate discussion about music videos must be held in our times.

---

[3] https://www.vevo.com/ (acc. February 4th, 2019).
[4] See appendix, Interview with Dave Meyers.
[5] http://www.mtv.com/news/articles/1633772/20100311/lady_gaga.jhtml (acc. March 18th, 2019).
[6] http://www.nypress.com/article-21128-going-gaga.html (acc. April 22nd, 2019).
[7] https://www.theguardian.com/music/2016/jul/28/how-pop-music-video-got-weird-again.

3.1 Changed Behavior of Reception and Consumption

As I pointed out in the discussion on existing literature, music videos were often discussed with an obligatory link to MTV, its most important distribution platform until the early 2000 s. That means that the context of reception is of a significant importance for the production of music videos and their effect and shall also be analyzed in this chapter, for it has changed quite dramatically since the 1990 s.

A seemingly significant premise when comparing different periods of music video consumption is the availability of the videos themselves. Like I mentioned in 2.3, there wasn't any possibility to just play specific videos or to repeat them in the days of MTV. The only way to evade the linear program was to record the channel and then make own libraries of video cassettes or, later, DVDs. However, this was rather time- and money-consuming, so that not many people would have the privilege to play their own program. This linearity experienced a significant shift towards user-defined, non-linear patterns with the rise of online video platforms. Everybody now can watch any video, follow recommendations of friends, blogs, or algorithms of the particular platforms and have the freedom to surf self-determined through the offered videos. And there is one more key development that affects music videos in both reception and consumption, and that is the role with the social web that came along the Web 2.0. The medial public, now represented by a communication space in the social web, is no longer solely characterized by texts and images, as it was the case in the internet of the 1990 s. By facilitating the opportunity to communicate and multiple functionalities, as Paula Hearsum calls them, **both the users and the respective platforms become actors** simultaneously. Especially YouTube becomes gallery and arena concurrently.[8] This allows a whole new dimension for music videos' identity that one has to keep in mind and that I will cover in-depth in chapters 4 and 5.

I want to take a step back in the history of music consumption, namely to the phenomenon of severe recession in sales since the 1990 s. Suppose you take a look to sales of the Recording Industry Association of America (RIAA) and compare it to the results of Section 2.2, in which I spoke about a 'first golden age' of music videos during the 1980 s and 90 s. In that case, the concept of music videos being advertisement products for the songs starts to make more sense. We notice **an analog development in the music market and music video importance**: until the turn of the millennium, there was a massive music market growth (Fig. 3.1).

---

[8] Cseke (2018), *Protest, Kunst und Theater auf YouTube*, 92, 93.

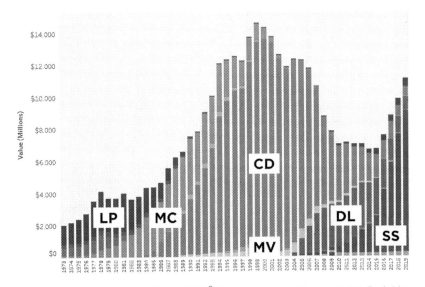

Fig. 3.1 US sales between 1973 and 2019.[9] Colors represent different media: Dark blue: LP/EP, light blue: cassette (MC), orange: CD, yellow: music videos (physical) (MV), violet: download albums and singles (DL), green: streaming-services (subscription and on-demand) (SS)

But since the year 1999, according to the worldwide International Federation of the Phonographic Industry, the revenues dropped by around 25%. Again, a parallel between music videos and their effect as advertisements is clearly noticeable. The decreasing interest in the videos matches exactly the dropping revenues. In 1999, physical sales accounted for nearly 100% of the income, in 2016 barely 34%. With almost 80%, digital distribution made up for the most significant economic share. The largest portion is covered by paid subscription models such as Spotify, Apple Music etc. However, ad-supported On-Demand-Streaming (which is the concept of music videos on YouTube) first showed up in the list with a share of 1,6 percent in 2011 and with 8,2 percent of the market was a branch almost worth one billion US-Dollars in 2019. Back in 2004/2005, physical music videos never exceeded a share of close to five percent of the market (Fig.3.2).

Of course, YouTube still is a commercially driven platform owned by the world's second most valuable brand, Google. That means that while music videos

---

[9] https://www.riaa.com/u-s-sales-database/ (acc. October 10th, 2020, labelled by author).

3.1 Changed Behavior of Reception and Consumption

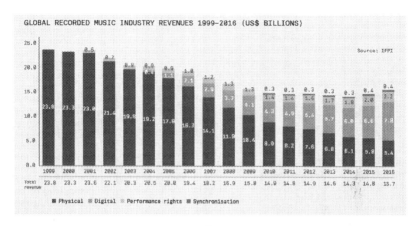

Fig. 3.2 Global music revenues 1999–2016[10]

enjoy the freedom of choosing whatever content (apart from violations of terms of use such as nudity, violence etc.), aesthetic and format they want, they underly a commercial system. Just like on MTV, ads still play a significant role there. Users can monetarize their videos and thereby place ads of five to twenty seconds to play before them. The money is then shared between the user and YouTube.

Interesting to note in this context is the growing number of so-called '**audio-only clips**' on YouTube, which means singles that don't yet have their own music video[11] but nevertheless get released on the artist's official channel. An example of this phenomenon is the official Eminem channel. Between December of 2017 and September of 2018, he released eight such clips, of which three were followed by a 'real' music video within more or less a month[12]. He achieved between 6,6 million and 235 million views on just the individual audio-only clips. With this method, the platform YouTube can be used to spread the song and to generate views, even if there is no video at all. This lets the artist and the record company earn twice on a platform with just one actual song. According to data released by the RIAA in 2017[13], YouTube pays out roughly **$1.50 for every 1,000 views.**

---

[10] IFPI Global Music Report 2017, 11.

[11] Usually the only image of the video is a picture, most times the cover of the associated album or single.

[12] https://www.youtube.com/user/EminemMusic (acc. August 6th, 2019).

[13] https://www.riaa.com/medium-five-stubborn-truths-youtube-value-gap/ (acc. August 23rd, 2019).

By those calculations, $246,000 would have gone to Eminem (and his production companies) for the 164 million views of 'River (Audio) feat. Ed Sheeran' at the time of writing, and a similar amount again for the official music video to come two months later. Lyor Cohen, YouTube's global head of music and a former longtime label executive, estimated revenue of roughly twice that amount, but that depends on many variables, like overseas income and whether an artist agrees to certain kinds of ads.[14] Since YouTube earns by those ads as well, the platform is interested in keeping their users on it for as long as possible, watching as many videos as possible.

Here, the algorithms for recommendations come into play. As in other search engines and social media platforms, they are potent tools of artificial intelligence that are designed to optimize the user experience on the site. They analyze the user's behavior on the platform and generate recommendations based on searches, watched videos, etc. YouTube is surprisingly transparent considering their technical details about their algorithms and explained them in two articles from 2010 and 2016:

> In general, there are two broad classes of data to consider: 1) content data, such as the raw video streams and video metadata such as title, description, etc., and 2) user activity data, which can further be divided into explicit and implicit categories. Explicit activities include rating a video, favoriting/liking a video, or subscribing to an uploader. Implicit activities are datum generated as a result of users watching and interacting with videos (Fig.3.3).[15]

These recommendations thus are a significant factor in how videos earn clicks. Other sources are subscriptions on YouTube itself or other social media platforms where the video is announced and trending charts. Trending videos must not necessarily fit the user's profile but are watched by a significant number of other users during a specific time. If music videos make it in the trending videos, which is often the case, they are usually video releases by more famous artists. However, YouTube's algorithms to a certain degree, are a 'black box', as for example the New York Times calls them[16]. Since they are processes and choices made by computers, not every case is entirely understandable. The Norwegian band boy pablo explains the development of their video _Everytime_ on the pop culture magazine complex.com: The video only got a few thousand views in the

---

[14] https://www.billboard.com/articles/business/8511114/taylor-swift-me-music-videos-digital-age-economics (acc. February 14th, 2019).

[15] Davidson et al. (2010), *The YouTube video recommendation system*.

[16] https://www.nytimes.com/2019/06/14/opinion/youtube-algorithm.html (acc. August 7th, 2019).

3.1 Changed Behavior of Reception and Consumption

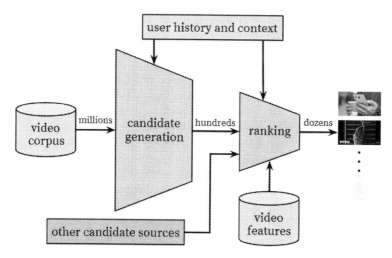

Fig. 3.3 Recommendation system architecture demonstrating the 'funnel' where candidate videos are retrieved and ranked before presenting only a few to the user[17]

first few weeks when they uploaded the video (similar to everything else they had put out at the time). A little while later, a post on Reddit gave it a bump to about 25,000 views. But then everything went really fast when it started showing up in everyone's 'recommended' tab, and the view counts soared into the hundreds of thousands.

> *The real boost hit [...] as a result of YouTube adding the video as a recommendation on people's front page, if you had watched videos with similar music. [...] So the YouTube algorithms were in our favor for some reason. From there, we started getting 40–50,000 views per day, which has a direct correlation with all the streaming services boy pablo's music is available through. So in a matter of just a few days, all of boy pablo's songs are performing way better than normal.*[18]

Apart from these economic-infrastructural components of the music industry that have changed over time, other questions are arising when facing the metamorphosed way we consume media today. How is the ubiquitous mass of products

---

[17] Covington et al. (2016), *Deep Neural Networks for YouTube Recommendations*
[18] https://www.complex.com/pigeons-and-planes/2017/10/boy-pablo-everytime-youtube-algorithm-interview (acc. September 9th, 2019).

(again videos in our case) affecting our relation to specific artists? Do we consume music or music videos while watching YouTube? That is, do we have altering preferences for music (audio only) and music videos? Clearly, in the time of MTV, viewers were consuming videos beyond their actual musical taste, as well, but it was part of MTV's concept, having to be the only channel and covering everything there is. Today, however, **we curate** (to a certain extent, taking algorithms in account) **our program ourselves**. To give viable answers to these questions, one would have to draw up statistics, which I cannot provide in this work. But in my opinion, these questions obviously stand for the pluralization of media that leads to a **pluralization of taste or style or, at the very least, interest**. This is a phenomenon known for quite some time[19], but that has intensified with Web 2.0 and streaming hosts, and that is crucial when talking about the reception of current music videos.

For Sarah Boardman, if a relation between viewer and artist still is existent, the indirectness to the stars or, more precise, the **participation in their lives**, is central for the aesthetic product of the music video:

> It isn't quite the P. Diddy[20] world that it used to be. You see fewer videos where people are in golden palaces with tigers and yachts, because you've probably seen how they live on a day-to-day basis anyway.[21]

The life of the pop stars, especially in the teenie-pop segment, has become significantly more direct. Platforms like Instagram and TikTok and the overall 'selfie society' deliver various (pseudo-) private insights to the lives of the stars and at the same time demystify them to a certain degree. **Virtual closeness** has equally become a substantial part of stardom. On Taylor Swifts' Instagram channel, one can see a variety of backstage- and even 'home'-videos, in which the singer talks to the viewers like they were old friends. Like that, she can reach particularly very young fans at every time and around the globe and builds trust and attachment at the same time. Popstars of the 1990 s as opposed could basically only rely on TV appearances, which only a very small part of the fans could watch only in specific timeslots.

But it's not only the world of pop music that has shifted in its fan-idol-relationship. Many rappers no longer live in a glamorous world of luxury cars

---

[19] E.g. Polhemus (1997), In the Supermarket of Style, in Redhead et al. (eds.) The Clubcultures Reader. 148–151.

[20] P. Diddy (aka Puff Daddy) is an US-american rapper, who especially during the late 90 s and early 2000 s lived a stereotypically luxurious lifestyle.

[21] https://www.theguardian.com/music/2016/jul/28/how-pop-music-video-got-weird-again.

3.1 Changed Behavior of Reception and Consumption

and expensive clothing, unreachable for the fans—they are part of a democratic and open world. Whether it is Kendrick Lamar, who presents himself a leader of the Black-Lives-Matters-movement in *Alright* (2015) and on the artwork of the correspondent album 'How To Pimp a Butterfly', or Joyner Lucas, who in *I'm Not Racist* (2017) stages the conflict between black and white in the United States between two protagonists in an intimate theater-esque video. Or whether it is Drake, who in *God's Plan* (2018) walks through Miami and as giving away the whole video budget of almost one million dollars to people seemingly in need or donating it to institutions like the fire department. Virtually staged like an emotional TV-Show, Drake embodies a tangible superstar, a Samaritan even if, or maybe in his case, just because he is currently one of the best-paid musicians in the world.

Finally, I want to revise the idea of music videos being an advertisement for a song once again. With the popularity of TikTok and Instagram Stories, it is clear we are living in an age of short-form video, which has replaced long music videos as promotion tools. For example, a DIY-Guide by the prevalent online music-publisher cdbaby claims:

> *The same tenants of YouTube success apply to short-form video – frequency, posting on a schedule, measuring engagement – but instead of you needing to make a big investment of time or money making a long video, all you really need now is 15 seconds, some interesting imagery, and a good song or message.*

They advise the musicians to repurpose longer videos like music videos, live streams, or concert videos and chop them up into bits for short Instagram posts, Instagram Stories with overlaid text or lyrics, 8-second looped video for Spotify's Canvas feature, TikTok clips, teasers for an upcoming release, or 15-second video ads.[22]

The promotion of a musician and his work, especially for younger audiences, nowadays takes place on social media platforms and must fit into a high-paced timeline. Musicians, therefore, use short visual products for advertising purposes. A complete music video rarely appears in social media feeds; usually, only teasers are posted for the full version, which can then be seen on YouTube. This fact underlines the development that musicians today use music videos as stand-alone products. However, this is no evidence to me that the music video form is under siege. I will discuss this further in Sections 3.2 and 3.5.

---

[22] https://diymusician.cdbaby.com/music-promotion/how-to-make-quality-video-content-quickly-and-cheaply/ (acc. July 29th, 2020).

This chapter has shown that not only the discussion about the reception of the music video is to be kept up, but also the one about the construction of the video itself in the context of its reception, a fact I will take into account during the analyses to follow.

3.2 Content

What could be practical consequences from these developments observed in the previous chapters and how are they affecting the music videos' content? Again, generalizations are hard to formulate, which is why I will work exemplarily in this subchapter.

According to Goodwin and Vernallis, the **content of music videos is intimately related to their music genre**[23]. There, a music genre is described as a category that identifies a piece of music as belonging to a set of conventions. A team from the Cornell University around Sarah Gross developed a tool to automatically generate, from an input music track, a music video made of segments of YouTube music videos which would fit this music.[24] In this method, based on the definitions by Goodwin and Vernallis and an extensive analysis of their own database ('≈1000 MVs of the most popular artists on YouTube'), four genre categories are established for their algorithm. Music videos of these four groups present the following visual characteristics:

Pop/Indie: Close-ups on the singer, dance routines, less conceptual scenes due to focus on the artist

Rock/Metal/Alternative: Musical performance, concert performance, more conceptual scenes

Hip-Hop/Rap/RnB: Sports clothing, black performers, singer close-ups, less conceptual scenes due to focus on artist, sexualized woman, street environment

Electronic/House: Dance routines, very conceptual except for DJ concert performances, representations of people partying, natural environment

This sort of definition and categorization makes it fairly easy to talk about music videos, but I want to question such models and define the term 'genre' briefly in order to use it adequately in the following chapters. Jeong-Won Sin, Head of Sales in Digital Distribution at Universal Music and scholar, also states that

---

[23] Goodwin (1992), *Dancing in The Distraction Factory: Music Television and Popular Culture*. Vernallis (2004), *Experiencing Music Video: Aesthetics and Cultural Context*.
[24] https://arxiv.org/abs/1905.12245 (acc. February 14th, 2019).

genres serve to categorize works in classes of other related works and genre-theory has the task to build and to justify these categories.[25] This definition from 2014 is somewhat questionable but still interesting to read from somebody from the music business. It shows that still in younger years, the industry relies on this conventional definition of genres. However, I believe that genres, as conceived in the model above, cannot really be distinguished anymore. Regarding Gross' model, see for example Billie Eilish—*when the party's over* (2018), Slipknot—*All Out Life* (2018), Joyner Lucas—*I'm Not Racist* (2017), and Salvatore Ganacci—*Horse* (2019) for videos that do not match their proposed genre. Especially in Section 5.5, I will discuss mechanics and examples of trans-stylistic inspiration and appreciation. Furthermore, the phrase 'Genre is Dead' also has already established itself in popular culture and is even the title of an online music magazine[26]. What about other definitions, then? Fabian Holt stresses the focus on *understanding* genres rather than *defining* them. He argues:

> *Definitions and categories serve practical purposes and tell us something about how people understand music. But we should be suspicious because they create boundaries, because they have a static nature, and because they have political ramifications and draw attention away from more important matters.*[27]

David Brackett is also skeptical about genres as static groupings of empirically verifiable characteristics and offers a broad definition of genre as '*associations of texts whose criteria of similarity may vary according to the uses to which the genre labels are put.*'[28]

So, at least for the frame of this work, **let us understand 'genre' merely as a specific aesthetic that in a certain period of time has a considerable number of users and followers.**

Besides all plurality and non-conformity, there is still one noticeable parameter that seems to be present in all parts of the medial world, in music, film, advertising, or music videos: **authenticity**. In the media world, it is mandatory, it is hyped, and it is ambiguous. In the context of media-creation on the internet, it describes first and foremost the quality of making one's product stand out of the mass by giving it a certain dimension of 'realness', of 'honesty' and 'originality'. However, in the 'era of postmodern arbitrariness, authenticity evolves to a place

---

[25] Sin (2014), *Du bist, was du hörst—Musiklabels im als Wegweiser im digitalen Zeitalter*, 130, 133.

[26] https://genreisdead.com/

[27] Holt (2007), *Genre in Popular Music*, 8.

[28] Brackett (2016), *Categorizing Sound: Genre and Twentieth-Century Popular Music*, 4.

nostalgic desire'[29] and is supposed to guarantee something 'unique' in the medial oversupply we face every day, finally leading to sympathy or willingness to buy. Authenticity is a delicate matter, though, as Hans-Joachim Hinrichsen points out. He observes that whoever is using the term today regarding any form of art may reveal himself as hopelessly naïve[30]. Despite the terms' trivialization, its concept is so often found in music and culture that it seems sensible to me to utilize it to look at trends developing on a formal level.

What are examples of different music videos pursuing authenticity? Firstly, the portion of music videos of the last years that do not limit their length to the song is growing, and the mediums' general limits and norms are getting more and more relative. Artists use the extra time and broken-up norms to present their artistic ideas in alternative ways that the song and the stage would not offer. And the viewers seem to be very open to this. A good example of that is Lady Gaga's _G.U.Y._ (2014). The song was released with two video versions.

On the one hand, the official, twelve-minute-long video with lots of extra-plot and even extra music, one week later on the other hand, a second version got released, which is only the actual length of the song (some four minutes). Five years later, at the time of writing this, **the long version had about 25% more views than the song-only version**. This shows that if there is an offer providing an extended creative vision of the artist, which goes beyond the supposedly advertised music, the viewership may very well be **willing to consume music videos as their own art form**. In the music and media market, authenticity is advertised as a mighty good worth pursuing (there are hundreds of tutorials on how to be authentic on YouTube), and that seems to become more and more critical in shaping music videos; in _River_ (2018, 6.55 min.) by Eminem feat. Ed Sheeran, the song continuously gets disrupted by scenes from a scripted documentary about a love story with Eminem and his partner and interviews with Eminem himself, talking about the song's plot. In Eminem's _Framed_ (2018, 05:31 min.), the song also gets interrupted, this time by scenes from a scripted Breaking-News show that is commenting on the video's plot. In Romano's _Copyshop_ (2017, 10:42 min.) again there are inserts of him talking about his past and thereby contextualizing the lyrics, followed by a four-and-a-half-minute-long interlude that musically does not belong to the actual song, where one follows the protagonist through the nights of Hong Kong. In all these examples, the artists reveal a lot of themselves, trying to illustrate a character that goes beyond the mere performing artist.

---

[29] Rössner/Uhl (2012), _Renaissance der Authentizität—Über die neue Sehnsucht nach dem Ursprünglichen_, 9.
[30] Hinrichsen, (2012), 159.

3.2 Content

Lady Gaga presents herself as a walking piece of art, whose entire environment is thought aesthetically, Romano tries to prove that he really incorporates the persona he is on stage in the real world, and Eminem shows himself, even if scripted, private, and vulnerable. In their own ways, they all offer the audience the opportunity to experience their idols in an authentic communication ensemble

Another example for music videos going beyond their supposedly advertised products (as in the quote 'a promo video is simply an advertisement for a song') while pursuing authenticity is advertising itself. I want to quote Spike Jonze's (known for movies like 'Being John Malkovich', 'Her' and 'Jackass', but also music videos) clip for the fragrance KENZO World from the year 2016, in which the actress Margaret Qualley is dancing frantically through what seems to be a theater's foyer. What makes it so interesting is that it, by traditional measurements, would not be considered a music video. The song it plays for three minutes, 'Mutant Brain' by Sam Spiegel & Ape Drums, does not get mentioned in the video title but only in the video's info box[31], accompanied by a Spotify link. On the fragrance's official website, too, only Spike Jonze, Margaret Qualley, and the choreographer get mentioned, neither the song nor the musicians. So, **what exactly is this video?** Just a very long advertisement? A music video that doesn't appreciate its musical contributor sufficiently?

I think Carol Vernallis' thoughts of music videos *'as relation of sounds and image that we recognize as such'* may help here. What aspects and components are there in the clip that we recognize as music video-specific? (Fig.3.4)

- Firstly, there is the fact that a whole pop song almost uninterruptedly gets played without being overlaid by other sound noises and hence is the video's primary audio track
- The length of 03:48 minutes is a widespread format for traditional music videos
- Dance is linked to music since its beginning and has also always been an essential part of music videos
- The protagonist's movements and the video's edit are aligned with the music

With these findings alone, one does notice that the filmmakers are very well aware of the music, and it's not only accessory to the visual component. This seems to be the distinctive characteristic compared to other long advertisement clips. In 'Coco Mademoiselle' by Chanel (2011, 03:20 min.), James Brown's 'Man's World' is underlying the video, in 'Go with the Flaw' by Diesel (2017,

---

[31] Video title and info box both referring to YouTube.

Fig. 3.4 *KENZO World* features a partly narrative structure, which means a recognizable but straightforward plot with a beginning and ending: The protagonist is uncomfortably listening to a speech in the middle of people she seemingly doesn't want to be with. She then leaves the room and starts to dance through the building, shoots laser-beams from her hands and at the end flies through an eye of flowers that stands for the iconic flacon which is shown afterward

02:10 min.) it's Edith Piaf's 'Je ne regrette rien'. In both clips, however, the relation of music and image is much more arbitrary than in *KENZO World*. Also, both decided to use very popular songs that are already known in many other contexts, which adds another critical point to the list of recognizable features a music video can have: the exclusivity in the relation between music and images. For the audience, 'Mutant Brain' most probably is exclusively connoted to Kenzo, and, if they saw the video without knowing the brand or having their own experiences with the fragrance, vice versa. However, Chanel and Diesel will not achieve such an original audiovisual link. Furthermore, *KENZO World* resembles to a great

3.2 Content

extent the official music video of Fatboy Slim's 'Weapon of Choice' (2000), also directed by Spike Jonze. Here, the actor Christopher Walken dances and flies with similarly eccentric movements through an empty hotel lobby. The color grading[32] and the camera work are somewhat comparable, as well. The Kenzo clip thus does not make use of different aesthetics than one would expect in a music video. And, last but not least, apart from the Kenzo-logo at the beginning of the video, it does not reveal to the viewer, what this video is all about until the very end of the clip, when the flacon is finally displayed.

Moreover, it is interesting to see the concatenation of inspirations and imitations surrounding this video that are softening the medium's limits and definitions once again; *KENZO World* leaves its borrowings from *Weapon of Choice* evident. Hence, already here the first intentional transgression between both media, advertisement, and music video is happening. The next step, back again to music video, can be seen in Taylor Swift's *Delicate* (2018) that again shows obvious parallels to *KENZO World*. There, Swift dances through a foyer with similar movements as Qualley, having as a consequence that she and the director Joseph Kahn are being accused of plagiarizing Spike Jonze[33]. More important than having found a final definition of this example being a music video or not, is to acknowledge **borderline cases** like this in the context of the ubiquitous influence of music videos and use them to build a **valid basis for discussion** of the subject.

This Kenzo advertisement hasn't stayed a unicum. In March 2018, Spike Jonze shot another dance music video to promote Apple's HomePod using Anderson.Paaks's ''Til it's over'. These clips are mainly distributed via YouTube because a four-minute slot in regular TV or cinema would be too expensive and, in some cases, wouldn't legally count as advertisement anymore. By treating the spot like a music video, the companies can enjoy the benefits and possibilities such a long video offers, including the viewing habits and algorithms that YouTube implies. It is also this exclusive and non-linear release that pushes the advertisement closer to the modern concept of a music video.

It sure is difficult to claim that it was authenticity that Kenzo and Jonze were pursuing with their clip and that it is a forming factor of our present time to differentiate it from previous periods. However, it seems to me that while some years ago, external factors like clothing, appearance, and choice of words were essential for depicting authenticity, today, the personality and the artist's individual brand counts more than ever.

---

[32] Color grading is the final coloring process in post-production.
[33] e.g. https://www.youtube.com/watch?v=RuW3eDH8VF0 'Taylor Swift Accused Of RIPPING OFF "Delicate" Video from Perfume Ad?'.

Another vivid example of this is Young Thug's *Wyclef Jean* (2017), in which a presumably authentic presentation of the artist is achieved in quite a different way, namely that he himself is practically not shown at all. The video consists of so-called B-roll-fosotage, which means behind-the-scenes-material, improvisations, and even stock footage. The whole video is commented with text-inserts by the director Ryan Staake, who tells the viewer about the process of making the project and 'how the whole video fell apart'[34]. According to the video, Young Thug never showed up for the shoot, so the crew basically could only shoot test material with the models and the set, which is what the final now consists of. Even audio messages from Young Thug are played, in which he tells the director his ideas for the video and that the crew later tried to implement. Even if the viewer counts on him finally to appear in the video, he doesn't, making him somewhat mysterious and amusing. Even the online magazine Noisey two days after the video release posted a making-of of the video, in which a reporter is also confused by Young Thug's non-appearance. *Wyclef Jean* illustrates two things very well: On the one hand, the current generosity concerning content standards in very popular (at the time of this analysis, the video has over 34 million views on YouTube) music videos. The many text inserts and audio messages heavily distract from the music and lyrics and make the video a distinctive artistic product. And on the other hand, this depiction unconventionally evokes an authentic and sympathetic image of the artist as a nonconformist creative person, who has very clear, even if partly weird, plans for his videos, but then doesn't show up for unknown reasons for the extremely expensive shoot (according to the video it cost over 100.000 dollars). Considering that one has to assume that video was staged with all its supposed problems and that the making-of by Noisey was a well-set PR campaign, the concept of pursuing authenticity still performs very well.

I conclude that the circumstances and the conditions music videos are facing have changed dramatically and they all must compete for **standing out of the mass**, for the **viewers' sympathy and their attention**. Be it achieved through technological innovation, particularly spectacular video or just through supposed authenticity. The ratio between the idea and production effort has changed: **an original idea seems to prevail the money that is behind a project**—This interacts with the fact that budgets for music videos are getting smaller and smaller and that many bands also have great success with no-budget videos (see boy pablo—*Everything*). A very practical outcome of this development is the decrease of videos with traditional forms of presentation, particularly the pure 'performance-clip' appears ever more seldom.

---

[34] Young Thug—*Wyclef Jean*, Min. 01:16.

3.2.1 Kendrick Lamar—Humble \\ You Gotta See This

Closing the subchapter about content in music videos of the late 2010 s, I want to show and examine the above-mentioned phenomena and the theses I have put forward on the basis of a case study. I will analyze the music and lyrics and from then move on to the video and try to deconstruct it in technical, textual, and exegetical manner in order to demonstrate how its content shapes the final product.

Kendrick Lamar is often said to be one of the most innovative rappers in recent history, even beyond the circle of his fans[35]. This is also proven by the numerous awards he has received in recent years, including the Pulitzer Prize in April 2018, which that year was awarded to a hip-hop artist for the first time. *Humble* was released on Kendrick Lamar's YouTube-vevo channel on March 30, 2017, and at the time of writing, has over 720 million views less than a year later. In 2017, it won the MTV Video Music Award and a Grammy, both for the 'Video Of The Year'.

The distributional range of the video alone is remarkable. All other music videos on his channel have far fewer hits, the second most-viewed clip, *All The Stars*, a collaboration with SZA, is far behind with only 259 million clicks. This also makes it one of the most-watched Hip-Hop videos ever, Drake's *Hotline Bling* is even more successful with almost 1.6 billion hits. This extremely high popularity is also supposed to be the main reason why I would like to examine this video of him in particular.

The most essential characteristics of the music are its extreme reduction, the absence of a harmonic structure, or instead of harmonies at all, and the pronounced repetitiveness. The minimalistic beat of the song consists of a backbeat drumbeat in 4/4 time, which uses the classic clap and hihat sounds from the Roland TR-808 and some differently sampled sounds. It is characterized by the syncopated bass drum movement that remains the same throughout the song except for some hihat variations (Fig. 3.5).

Fig. 3.5 Drumbeat in 'Humble'

---

[35] https://www.fastcompany.com/40401628/kendrick-lamar-wants-to-stay-humble-but-this-is-a-video-to-brag-about (acc. July 8th, 2020).

The most important and distinctive instrument is the piano, most likely the software emulation 'The Grandeur' of a Steinway D grand piano by Native Instruments. This virtual instrument is a very common one and is also easily accessible to private users. In 'Humble', it plays a one-bar riff throughout the song, which is interlocked with the drumbeat, primarily as single notes and as a variation with an additional higher octave. Besides the voice, the only other instrument and musical element is a sawtooth synthesizer, which plays a simple riff on an a#" from time to time (see Fig. 3.6) (Fig.3.7).

Fig. 3.6 Piano-riff in 'Humble'

Fig. 3.7 Synthesizer-line in 'Humble'

The missing bass is filled up by the bass drum, which consists of several samples layered on top of each other, one of which has a very long decay in the sub-bass range, creating a constant drone. This highly reduced beat leaves a lot of room for Kendrick Lamar's distinctive nasal voice, both compositionally and in terms of frequencies. He fills this space with a very clear, well-structured rap on a 16th note-level, not virtuoso in technique, but still in lyricism and the energy with which he virtually forces every word on the listener.

> *You gotta see this, we gonna witness, way, yeah, yeah!*[36]
> *Ay, I remember syrup sandwiches and crime allowances*
> *Finesse a nigga with some counterfeits*
> *But now I'm countin' this*
> *Parmesan where my accountant lives*
> *[...]*

---

[36] This 'prologue' varies from the album version of the song. There the line is: 'Nobody pray for me, even a day for me, way, yeah yeah!'—an indication of the audience's involvement in the work.

> *Sit down*
> *(Hol' up lil' bitch, hol' up lil' bitch) be humble*
> *[...]*
> *I'm so fuckin' sick and tired of the Photoshop*
> *Show me somethin' natural like afro on Richard Pryor*
> *Show me somethin' natural like ass with some stretchmarks*
> *Still will take you down right on your mama's couch in Polo socks, ay*
> *[...]I don't fabricate it, ay, most of y'all be fakin', ay*
> *I stay modest 'bout it, ay, she elaborate it, ay*
> *This that Grey Poupon, that Evian, that TED Talk, ay*
> *Watch my soul speak, you let the meds talk, ay*
> *If I kill a nigga, it won't be the alcohol, ay*
> *I'm the realest nigga after all, bitch, be humble*[37]

The video was directed by Californian filmmaker and photographer Dave Meyers and 'The Little Homies', a pseudonym for Kendrick Lamar himself and his manager Dave Free, who together work on all of Lamar's music videos. Dave Meyers has been producing music videos since 1997 for various musicians from very different genres[38]. In addition to *Humble*, he had great success in 2017 with videos such as *Swish Swish* by Katy Perry and *Havana* by Camila Cabello, both of which achieved way over half a billion clicks each. After he had produced a short commercial for Lamar's previous album 'To Pimp A Butterfly' and a music video for SZA, a soul singer from the same label, he was given the job for *Humble*.[39] This video also features a prominent reference to the directors in the very first shot, even before the song itself begins (see fig. 3.8).

All the sets, costumes, and images are so strongly conceptualized and metaphorized that it is impossible to speak of a purely performative lip-sync video. The video makes use of some 'practical-in-camera' effects, that is, effects that are already created during shooting and not by computer animation in post-production. For example, Lamar can be seen several times on a bicycle in a 360° video that is shaped into a 'little world', a sphere (see fig. 3.8). This effect can be achieved with appropriate cameras, for example, the GoPro Fusion, which records a 360° image from which the desired image can later be calculated.

---

[37] Duckwarth, Williams, Hogan—Aftermath/Interscope (Top Dawg Entertainment) 2017.

[38] For example: Britney Spears—*Lucky* (2000), Céline Dion—*I'm Alive* (2002), Korn—*Twisted Transistor* (2005).

[39] See Appendix—Interview with Dave Meyers.

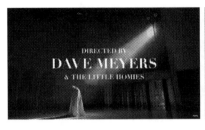 

Fig. 3.8 *Humble*, Min. 00:07 and 00:42

Furthermore, a glitch effect is used various times (for example at 01:28 minutes), where several cameras film the same subject next to each other and from slightly different perspectives. In editing, they cut very quickly between the cameras, which results in a kind of torn image, but the movements, in this case, Lamar's lip movements and gestures, remain fluid. The last practical effect is a camera robot, which is used from minute 01:57. More precisely, it is a computer-controlled robot arm on which the camera is mounted. This allows very fast, precise camera movements that could not be achieved by hand or other mechanical tools.

In addition, several art-historical or pop-cultural intertextualities can be identified, some of which are already present in the lyrics. Already the very first shot is a homage to the series 'The Young Pope' by Paolo Sorrentino (see fig. 3.8), Leonardo da Vinci's 'The Last Supper' from around the year 1490 is also re-enacted with Lamar's 'Gang'. (see fig. 3.9). It should be noted here that this painting is one of the most important works of Renaissance art due to its use of perspective. The directors are probably less concerned with this fact than with reference to one of the most famous depictions of Jesus Christ but facing the context of this work and the idea of a Renaissance of the music video, it still is worth mentioning. In minute 2:11 the text mentions 'Grey Poupon', a mustard brand whose commercial from 1983 is quoted in the film (see fig. 3.10) and in the scene from minute 01:57, Lamar himself, with his clothes and attitude, references Steve Jobs. (see fig. 3.9)

In addition to these religious metaphors, Lamar also stages himself as a wealthy hedonist who plays golf well-dressed or throws money around quite boldly and has it counted by lightly dressed women. The reference to 'Grey Poupon', a somewhat more expensive Dijon mustard, which was sold and initially advertised in the USA in the 1980 s, and which is picked up on both textually and visually in the music video, is also metaphorical for wealth and

Fig. 3.9 *Humble*, Min. 02:06 and 01:16

Fig. 3.10 Grey Poupon Clip (1983) and *Humble*, Min. 02:12

style that is widely used in hip-hop and about the use of which own studies have already been conducted.[40]

Many of the pictures play with sacral, religious, and even messiah-like motifs and connotations, especially in the context that Kendrick Lamar was already repeatedly titled 'The Saviour of Rap' after his album 'To Pimp A Butterfly' (2015)[41]. Lamar in papal garb in a single beam of light, Lamar on the bicycle around which the world revolves, Lamar as Jesus Christ himself at the Last Supper, Lamar in the midst of nodding bald men who appear like a sworn group of monks chanting his mantra 'Sit down, bitch, be humble!'. Even the scene in which Lamar stands in bright white clothing between men with burning ropes around their heads (see fig. 3.11) can be referred to the biblical passage Luke 3,16: 'He will baptize you with the Holy Spirit and fire'. Lamar will lead his disciples to the right way, in the background, on a container, other men who may

---

[40] https://www.youtube.com/watch?v=jOgPk5T1xi0—Why rappers love Grey Poupon.
[41] E.g. https://www.shortlist.com/entertainment/music/kendrick-lamar-the-saviour-of-hip-hop/79605 (acc. July 9th, 2020).

have already gone through the ritual are dancing. Another possible interpretation would be to understand the scene as a symbol of the fire of Pentecost, of the Holy Spirit descending on the people: 'And there appeared to them tongues, parted and as of fire, and sat upon each one of them', as it says in the Acts of Apostles 2, 3.

Fig. 3.11 *Humble,* Min. 01:04 and 01:42

With its distinctive visuals, the video underlines Lamar's life as a high-flyer, as a wealthy, infallible leader of faith (as Steve Jobs was for the disciples of the Apple movement at the time), but at the same time, it is repeatedly interrupted by the lines 'Sit down, bitch, be humble!'. It would seem reasonable to interpret this call towards his fans, disciples, or critics to be humble before Lamar. This would give the music video an extremely arrogant and selfish style in the context of his glorious self-dramatization. But this does not fit in with Kendrick Lamar, the intelligent rap and the video's topics and dramatization, which is why the mantra should rather be understood as a reminder to himself, to always remember his origins and home town Compton and to be humble himself before his new, famous life. At minute 02:18, the stable, magnificent image is suddenly refracted; Lamar is seen rapping from outside a suburban house at night, police light falls on the house facade. A reference to the crime and police violence against African Americans, a theme he devoted himself to especially in his previous album 'To Pimp A Butterfly', which led him to great fame and recognition. And at the same time, the slogan 'Be Humble!' in the hip-hop tradition can be understood as a subtle diss against other rappers, such as Drake, who calls himself "6god", or people like the American president, the upset society, or anyone else to whom humility would be advised. Contrasting all the self-aggrandizement, Lamar is sitting in the hair salon next to the women who count his money in other scenes in another scene. An unusual self-portrayal among rappers, once again the self-confident protagonist, is contrasted with a normalizing break.

3.2 Content

A scene that is discussed very extensively and controversially online comes at minute 01:44 on the text:

> *I'm so fuckin' sick and tired of the Photoshop*
> *Show me somethin' natural like afro on Richard Pryor*
> *Show me somethin' natural like ass with some stretchmarks*

The screen is split, with Lamar on the left and a female model on the right. As the woman crosses the centre of the picture, one notices that the left part of the picture shows the 'natural', the right part the put on, made-up version of the person. On the right side, she is heavily made up and costumed, on the left side, she wears regular clothes, does not wear make-up, and her hair is not coiffed. One can see skin impurities and a figure that does not entirely correspond to the western ideal of beauty. It is worth mentioning that Lamar does not change when he changes sides, another nod to his depiction of untouchable perfection (Fig.3.12).

Fig. 3.12 *Humble*, Min. 01:46 and 01:56

Then you see a buttocks that also does not correspond to this ideal of beauty and Hip-Hop video norm. Lamar denounces the idealized fake society here, with the desire to get something real, natural, like an iconic Afro or natural female body, contrasting all the retouched, hypocritical content. Reactions in the context of feminism are not far off, both from users who praise it for this supposedly progressive statement and those criticizing it for still objectifying the female body and using the same aesthetics as the mainstream it accuses[42]. In my opinion, however, no 'feminist' ambitions whatsoever are identifiable; Lamar and Meyers

---

[42] http://theconversation.com/the-false-feminism-of-kendrick-lamars-humble-75596 (acc. July 9th, 2020).

act in the tradition of Hip-Hop and rival its dusty and too often copied conventions rather than making a civil rights statement. Kendrick Lamar as the revolutionary, the visionary and not as the moralizer who jumps on already existing currents and social concerns such as women's rights movements.

I find that Lamar is very much aware of the tradition in which he moves. In the music, which is in no way inferior to the qualities of old-school rap, and also in the video. One can say that he takes the conventional content of Hip-Hop videos, which were made iconic by Hype Williams and others, and consistently develops them. The half-naked women counting his money are almost a parody of themselves, the scenes in which Lamar raps in front of his gang into the camera are also ironized and exaggerated by allusions to Steve Jobs or Jesus Christ. The 'P-Diddy-Lifestyle' is present through text passages and scenes with golf, money and Grey Poupon, at the same time, it reflects it critically. An examination of his own biography takes place, not only with his roots in Compton ('I remember syrup sandwiches and crime allowances') and later fame ('But now I'm coutin' this parmesan where my accountant lives'), but also with Hip-Hop, which of course represents a large part of Lamar's life.

With this example, I demonstrated how a contemporary music video can use a variety of techniques and motives to create a distinctive, original content and not just accompanies the song but lets the video become a whole new work of art by itself.

3.3 Aesthetics

When it comes to analyzing music videos' aesthetics, a common notion in the literature are the so-called 'MTV-aesthetics' that, again, relate to, for example, fast cuts and cutting 'on the beat'[43]. One must add that already in 2007, Marco Calavita argued that the 'MTV' in 'MTV-aesthetics' serves a symbolic function, since already then the vast majority of music videos were screened in channels other than MTV.[44] Either way, at first sight, **there seem to be specific codes that define music videos' aesthetics**. What they might represent and how they appear and evolve in current videos is what I want to examine in this chapter.

To begin with one example, I want to note the phenomenon in our time of extremely fast-paced and competing music (video) consumption, that sometimes

---

[43] E.g. Korsgaard (2017) *Music Video After MTV*, 149.
[44] Calavita (2007), *"MTV Aesthetics" at the Movies: Interrogating a Film Criticism Fallacy*, 1.

3.3 Aesthetics

(teasers for) music videos by default appear muted in social media or YouTube-feeds. If the users are not interested in the video in the first place, it has to attract them only with its visuals to get them to turn on the sound and give their full attention to the video. After all, this is an important fact to consider and also to oppose the common perception that *'without the actual music, there really is no music video'*, as claimed for example in Daniel Cookney's article 'Vimeo Killed the Radio Star'[45]. Our competence regarding the named aesthetics lets us recognize the video as a music video, even if there is no band performing on instruments nor a singer lip-syncing. In our classification, we rely on experiences and conventions that music videos keep bringing to the market. A competent audience capable of distinguishing the aesthetics of different media is vital for this development. In the following, I want to look at which aesthetical concepts and developments are characteristic of contemporary videos.

> *Whereas the music video initially sought to look like a concert, now the concert in some cases attempts to look like a music video.*[46]

This is a statement by Mathias Korsgaard from the year 2017, and it is by all means understandable. Music consumption most rarely happens without a visual component. Be it music video, album or single covers or the live performance. Artists are aware of that and it seems that the self-perception of some musicians has changed over time and especially the musical genre of Hip-Hop presents itself as a hub for multi-talented artists that aspire much more than just be perceived as good rappers or even gifted musicians.

The US-American Rapper Tyler, The Creator, who on almost all of his videos has views in the eight digits, goes so far in an interview with Larry King in the year 2017, as to say, he doesn't want to see his name in line with other rappers, but with well-known movie directors like Wes Anderson and Quentin Tarantino[47]. Both are very famous for their individual and iconic aesthetics. This statement is clearly noticeable in videos like <u>*IFHY*</u> (2013), where he made use of a dollhouse-like set, which is also often used by Wes Anderson in movies such as 'The Life Aquatic with Steve Zissou' from 2004. In *IFHY* obvious parallels regarding set, camera works and color palette to Andersons movies are visible.

Tyler, the Creator thus is pursuing a more holistic principle of his personality as an artist. The world we live in gets more dynamic, colorful, and cinematic every day. Aminé, another US-American Rapper with a somewhat (!) similar

---

[45] Arnold et al. (2017), *Music/Video—Histories, Aesthetics, Media*, 225.

[46] Korsgaard (2017), *Music Video After MTV*, 159.

[47] https://www.youtube.com/watch?v=kC3y_9PNaoM&t=174s (Min. 8:20).

style to Tyler, The Creator says, he is making his own (often very elaborated and well known) videos because he sees them as 'audition tapes for bigger things'[48]. Both Tyler, The Creator and Aminé are young, and their success to a great extend is self-made, mainly through music videos gone viral. **The connection of sound and image is by now implicit** which is why many artists, like Tyler, the Creator or Aminé, present themselves not 'only' as musicians. In other words, the idea of a musician is often a priori linked to a visual component of his or her artistic work. This results in music videos that are much more conceptual than performative and that often add a distinctive narrative to the song. The aesthetics appear particularly self-conscious, which means for example: strong, over-the-top colors, jumping deliberately between looks and moods, embracing the unpleasant as in long, awkward shots, and making use of shock factors and ironic trash.

There are more examples from other musical genres as well: The above-mentioned OK Go, for example, are much more famous for their videos than for their music itself. In order to cope with ever-growing demands to their ideas, they regularly take sponsorships from brands that get mentioned in the videos. For *Upside Down & Inside Out* (2016), a Russian airline provided a plane and the crew for zero-gravity shots and for *Obsession* (2018), a producer of printing paper got them a massive amount of paper they used for 567 printers on set. It is to be noticed that a visual idea and the implementation of the project itself is in focus. The actual song moves more and more to the background and only provides a thematic frame for the visuals and rhythmical cues for editing, which makes it rather replaceable. And still, OK Go keeps being a solid reference for artistic practice in the music video world.

An example for another video-brand, but quite in the opposite direction, are the videos of the funk-band 'Vulfpeck'. Like their most famous one Dean Town (2016), their official videos simply show them playing the particular song live, most times in a studio-like atmosphere, that at the same time are the official album versions. The interesting thing here is that, like with OK Go, there is a strong gradient of quality between audio and video, but quite the other way around: Vulfpeck are very sophisticated musicians, playing very elaborated music, while the videos are done in an extremely and intentionally amateur-like quality that can be interpreted as an understatement or the pursuit of a unique and 'authentic' image (Fig.3.13).

This became their visual brand of embracing the visually poor and, at the same time, the understatement in which they frame their music. This concept actually

---

[48] The Making of Aminè's "Spice Girl" Music Video https://www.youtube.com/watch?v=0r_QXiXFk4Y.

3.3 Aesthetics

Fig. 3.13 Vulfpeck—<u>Lost My Treble Long Ago</u> and <u>Dean Town</u>

can be retrieved a lot in the jazz-esque community, as for example with the US-electro-funk-band Knower. What we have here, is a new concept and chronology of music videos and album music. While in most occasions, the way to go is: 1. The idea for a song, 2. Song gets recorded, 3. The idea for a video, 4. Video gets produced, 5. The music video is released, OK Go apparently works like this: 1. The idea for a Video, 2. The idea for a Song, 3. Song gets recorded, 4. Video gets produced, 5. The music video gets released. Bands like Vulfpeck again work much quicker: 1. The idea for a song, 2. Song gets recorded/Video gets produced, 3. Music Video gets released.

<u>Excursus: Dilettantism in High-Scoring Music Videos or Aesthetical Authenticity</u>
What do the following three videos and many others all have in common?: Ed Sheeran feat. Justin Bieber—<u>I Don't Care</u> (2019), Young Thug—<u>Wyclef Jean</u> (2017), Ariana Grande—<u>Monopoly</u> (2019). They all represent a trend happening on the current music video landscape that embraces what I want to call dilettantism in professional music videos, a trend that poses a counterweight to the big and cinematic productions that are getting released more and more. They are characterized by either cheap camera and camerawork and/or very unsophisticated visual effects like faulty working green screens or low-resolution stock footage etc. At the same time, all of these artists are some of the biggest selling names on the current market. So, why don't they just use state-of-the-art technique and equipment and produce highly sophisticated videos and why are people satisfied with such videos and don't demand the latter? From my perspective, this mainly has to do with prosumerism, which I will discuss in-depth in the next chapter, and I would suggest two possible opinions that may or may not rule each other out:

1.) This first one assumes that **big production companies simply adopt the aesthetics** that are around and popular with the many videos by less sophisticated prosumers. Usually, these bands make their technical weakness their brand, their unique selling point and through virality or other factors may be successful with it. Examples for this are the early OK GO, Norwegian boyband boy pablo or the German performance collective HGich.T. If now an artist or a company that otherwise is known for big and expensive productions appropriates these aesthetics, it may be criticized artistically and conceptually for its lack of own ideas, but it is a sure sign for the market's orientation towards its surrounding circumstances. Put differently, on YouTube, and thus for music videos, the amateur content seems to have significant influence on the market.

2.) **Weak effects are relatable to prosumers.** Because, when starting to get used to postproduction software, one will have to complete several attempts to get the desired results right and not have them looking cheap and faulty. By embracing precisely that, the artists and directors of the named videos take the amateurs side and narrow the gap between established and exclusive production companies and the fan that understands something about postproduction and understands phrases like 'we'll fix it in post'[49] (*Wyclef Jean*, 02:52 min.). And there is one further dimension to it: real 'magic' in audiovisual products, for example, reacting with the 'Wow-factor' of 'How did they do this?', has become very rare due to the prosumers' ever-growing expertise[50]. When it comes to VFX (Visual Effects) and other effects and the artist wants to produce something unexpected for the viewer, he or she has the choice between two things: either actually coming up with something innovative, elaborate, and (in most cases) costly, or make use of more common effects, whose functioning is widely known among internet users (like for example green-screens) in an ironic and deliberately dilettante way. In the latter cases, these effects, or at least the process of post-production we are talking about, experience a significant evolution: They no longer only are tools to get across an action or expression the artist wants to convey, a signifier, one could say if talking about music videos as a language and thereby helping oneself with linguistic terms. They become the concept itself, the signified, represented by themselves. In that manner, the **effects become potential content without 'just' being used to express superordinate aesthetics and content**. An example: Conventional green-screens are used to place a character in a specific scenery to tell the story, let's say Frodo and Sam in the heart of Mount Doom that does not actually exist and therefore has to be created digitally in order to tell the story.

---

[49] When something on set is not working correctly but there is no time or way to repeat the scenes until they are right, a common phrase is: 'We'll fix it in post(-production)', meaning that the problem will be solved somehow digitally and most times rather unpleasantly.

[50] see Section 4.2.

3.3 Aesthetics

However, in music videos, the producers like to embrace the usage of cheap VFX and make that the content of the video, as in *I Don't Care,* for example (Fig.3.14) (Fig.3.15).

Fig. 3.14 Frodo in front of a green screen

Fig. 3.15 Ed Sheeran feat. Justin Bieber—*I* (in Mount Doom)[51] *Don't Care,* Min. 01:53

As I will examine more deeply in Section 4.2, visual effects nowadays are easily accessible tools of the trade, and why shouldn't the art world keep making its tools art, as it has done before? Kazimir Malevich, Agnés Martin, or William

---

[51] The Lord of the Rings—The Return of the King, DVD, New Line Cinema, WingNut Films, 2003.

Turnbull are examples of artists who painted white on white or even left the canvas blank and thereby included their material to work with into their artistic expression. For film artist Stan Brakhage, celluloid was more than a simple steppingstone in the process of creating and screening a film, but a (physical) medium to be explored in itself.'[52] Dada and Fluxus are further references for this concept. Having this in mind might explain this initial observation of dilettantism in pro-videos that at first glance seems contradictory or arbitrary.

Back to the main text. It is, however, not only the niches that promote innovation in music videos: established names of the music industry like the rapper Kanye West are contributing to the more extreme-getting visualization of music, too. In 2016 he pushed the boundaries of superstar-music-videos with *Famous*(Fig. 3.16).

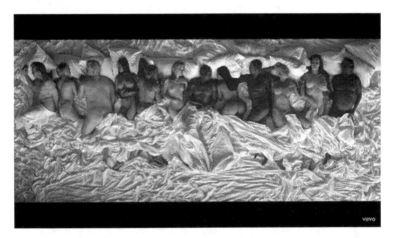

Fig. 3.16 Kanye West—*Famous*, Min. 08:45

The video is over ten minutes long and shows West himself, lying next to eleven (hyper-realistic wax figures of) naked celebrities, among them for example Taylor Swift, Donald Trump, Kim Kardashian, and George W. Bush. In the middle part of the video, there is a five-minute-long section without music, in which the camera is slowly moving across the seemingly sleeping bodies in dimmed light. The audience's rating of the video on YouTube is remarkable, which is to

---

[52] https://www.youtube.com/watch?v=-3rSP3-iWvs Stan Brakhage | The Untutored Eye, 01:36 min.

3.3 Aesthetics

time of this analysis with 34 million views and around 800.000 ratings at below 50%, which for a music video by a world-star is extremely low and equally rare. It is noteworthy that a critical debate on provocations and transgressions is happening and products, at first sight, don't just get accepted. However, at the same time, West lowers the pain threshold of acceptance and broadens the expectance for upcoming videos, not only for himself, but for the entire music video market. The importance of the two factors **acceptance and expectance** referring to the aesthetic outcome of a music video can also be exemplarily seen in *This Is America* (2018) by Childish Gambino, which I will examine more deeply in Section 5.3.1. Here the music video again becomes a venue for the discussion on gun-control and the Black-Lives-Matter-movement and uses a much more dramatic aesthetic as in for example Kendrick Lamar's *Alright* (2015). Twice in the video, there are explicit shootings, it has an overall very intimidating atmosphere, and depicted riots get contrasted with almost schizophrenic happy dance and the supporting music (Fig. 3.17).

Fig. 3.17 Childish Gambino—*This Is America*, Min. 00:52

Already three days after its release, it counted over 31 million views and was #1 trending in multiple countries. This heavy response the video got demonstrates that seriousness and partly disturbing images as expression of political concern is accepted by a broad audience and has arrived in mass-culture.

Another aspect that affects more individual aesthetics in music videos is **the role of the directors**, who seem to become more important or, more specifically, prominent in the videos. On the one hand, especially in the amateur segment, they face great chances of reaching a much bigger audience as they would with short films or other purely visual products. Furthermore, the financing of their ideas' implementation is given through the bands or in the professional segment, through the record company or the label and does not have to be handled on the filmmakers' own. So, **music videos offer fertile ground** with fortunate circumstances on that the filmmakers can fully concentrate on their artistic vision. This very vision is of interest for the band or the label, too. In times of ever-growing and strengthening competition, the own video must stand out from the mass. The yearning for authenticity thus is also to be found here. In the following two examples, the directors get named very early on in the video. Be it because of the directors' pure reputation, on which they counted in Imagine Dragons' *Thunder* (2017, dir. Joseph Kahn[53], fig. 3.19), or indeed the directors' unique and individual vision, giving the music a further, artistically sublime component and therefore being appreciated, like, among many others, in the case of Jamie xx's *Gosh* (2016, dir. Romain Gavras, fig. 3.19) (Fig. 3.18)

Fig. 3.18 Jamie xx—*Gosh*, Min. 00:09 and Imagine Dragons—*Thunder*, 00:13

This is a more recent development. In 2008, Sebastian Vieregg wrote about directors being consciously left in the background, except for a few Hollywood stars like Martin Scorsese or John Landis, to attribute more of the creative performance to the artists and thus give them the attention[54]. He continues by saying that artists and directors were downright discouraged from investing themselves

---

[53] Joseph Kahn is a successful music video director, who is cooperating with some of the biggest names of the industry. Nevertheless, only his name isn't a guarantor for unconditioned success; some of his work gets criticized, for instance his video for Taylor Swift's *Delicate* (2018), because it resembles to a crucial amount a previous video for *KENZO World (2016)* by Spike Jonze.

[54] Vieregg (2008), *Die Ästhetik des Musikvideos und seine ökonomische Funktion*, 23.

3.3 Aesthetics

in innovations because with proven stylistics, the chance was greater to get into broadcast's rotation[55]. Since those rules due to the video platforms' evolution do not count anymore, this decision sometimes seemed to have taken a 180-degree turn. The curation is made by the user him- or herself and is not anymore determined by the video's commercial success, but by their individual presentation and content. The realization of collaborations with external artists being potentially profitable in every way and the openness to let the own art be part of a new piece of art, of which one no longer is the exclusive creator, are getting more popular every day. At the same time, revealing a big team behind the video grants it a higher and more cinematic liability: Rolling credits at the end of music videos, even if only a few minutes long, have become noticeably popular, as to be seen for example in every Aminé-video or Coldplay's *Adventure of a Lifetime* (2015). The individual aesthetics and with it the originality of a video gain importance and its creator equally get appreciated for his contribution.

Peter Weibel in the year 1987 speaks about the aesthetics of music videos as a blend of avant-garde. *The clips we see are images of images and echoes of sounds, we already heard yesterday*[56]—This statement more than 30 years old seems to be passed over today, almost shifted to its opposite. Music videos are keen to place themselves in the tradition of innovation as a progressive medium, not only close to, but representing the pulse of time. Film historian William Moritz states: '*MTV music videos are committed to experimental film.*'[57]. Such statements seem to be experiencing a whole new relevance today.

In Section 2.1, I mentioned the thesis of the music video being a contemporary form of visual music, proposed by Peter Weibel. According to prominent composers of this genre like Dieter Schnebel or Oskar Fischinger, a significant element of it is that the visual component is already incorporated in the composition and not, as in many music videos, forced onto the music. Thus, Weibel's thesis today possibly is more fitting and important than ever before; musicians and record companies are thinking more visually, both on aesthetical and commercial level, up to the point that filmmakers are already involved in the songwriting process and that songs ideas that go along with promising video ideas get preferred.[58] A single without a video will barely receive adequate attention and the video at the same time offers an almost infinite world of opportunities, to express the artistic vision as vivid and multi-facetted as possible.

---

[55] Ibid. 93.

[56] Weibel (1987), *Von der visuellen Musik zum Musikvideo*, 119.

[57] Moritz (1994), *Bilder-Recycling. Die Wurzeln von MTV im Experimentalfilm*, 26.

[58] Interview with Auge Altona and the author. See appendix.

Summing up, what are music videos' aesthetical trends in the late 2010 s after all? I think it is fair to say that there are none and countless at the same time. The dimensions music videos are produced and consumed via the internet ensure an extremely wide variety of 'genres' that all have their own innovative and influential codes, and all are to be taken seriously. This extreme pluralization leads to difficulties in attempting to define music videos at all, as we have seen, and also in trying to point the finger on specific aesthetical directions for there are so many. However, what I can observe and want to lay out, is the expansion and development of two visual extremes.

On the one hand, that is partly due to technical advances; there are big and cinematic productions such as *Gosh* (2016) by Jamie xx or *Bad Blood* (2015) by Taylor Swift. No expense or effort is spared to achieve movie-like aesthetics, actions, and massive and impressive images. In Section 4.2, I will go deeper into the technical conditions that also facilitate this development.

Fig. 3.19 *Gosh* and *Bad Blood* are examples for elaborate and cinematic music videos

On the other hand, there is a considerable number of videos charging ahead that embrace trash, camp or simply 'the weird'. Historically seen, this is no particularly new development as these videos can be seen in the tradition of artists like Aphex Twin, Grace Jones, Björk and many others who have explored the unconventional and disturbing expressional possibilities of music videos decades ago. Nevertheless, in my opinion, this 'trend' also is expression of our 'saturated digital world'[59] and a statement about how certain topics today may only be treated. I will take *HATEFUL LOVE* (2016) by the Russian rave-collective, as I understand it, Little Big as an example. For the band, the tools of the conventional debate on violence, masculinity and power do not seem fruitful anymore, which

---

[59] E.g. Buckingham (2007), *Youth, Identity and Digital Media*, 78, Pink & Leder Mackley (2013), *Saturated and situated: expanding the meaning of media in the routines of everyday life*.

3.3 Aesthetics

is why they stage the discussion in the form of grotesque visuals that are as obscene as they are rebellious (Fig. 3.20).

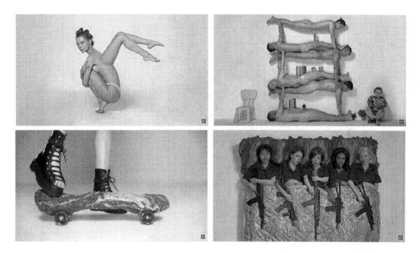

Fig. 3.20 *HATEFUL LOVE* is mere depiction of weirdness and camp as with digitally mutated people, half naked women holding guns and licking ice creams of meat underlying extremely violent and sadistic lyrics

Satire, in many cases, seems to be the only plausible approach, even, and most times just because the topic is serious and over the years has been covered seriously. We see this throughout all musical genres and issues: in the Swedish rave-DJ Salvatore Ganacci's *Horse* (2019), he revenges innocent animals from being punched in the face. In the US-rapper-duo's Run the Jewels *Nobody Speak* (2016), a political debate in a parliament escalates into a slapstick fight with flying chickens and running pigs. And in *Heiße Luft* (2016) by the pop-rock band Wir bringen kalten Kaffee mit, the issue of right-wing populism is treated by an escalation between two trailer-park neighbors that end up blowing each other up with bazookas. This is just to name a few examples that illustrate the strong influence satire has on the current music video world.

This chapter has attempted to sort and arrange the somewhat unmanageable field of contemporary music video aesthetics. What becomes clear is that, despite certain existing codes and conventional 'recipes', there are no rules at all in designing a music video and that the market is an original creative outlet for any imaginable idea and taste.

3.3.1 Jamie xx—Gosh \\ Dystopia and Numbness

Here again, I want to close this subchapter with an in-depth case study: 'Gosh' is a song by the British electro-musician Jamie xx who gained bigger attention with the group 'The xx' and established himself in the electronic music scene. The song was first released in 2015 on his second album 'In Colour'. The music video directed by the French Romain Gavras, who earlier produced videos for Justice and M.I.A. and others, was released in October of 2016 on Jamie xx's vevo-channel. It is to be noted that around 18 months earlier on his regular YouTube channel, a second video for 'Gosh' was uploaded. It is not unprecedented that multiple videos get produced for just one song. Earlier examples are 'Wuthering Heights' (1978) by Kate Bush or the above-mentioned 'Babies' (1992) by Pulp. However, in both those cases, they released the second versions in the context of new song releases, either regional or under a new label. Despite that, in both cases, the two video versions are not fundamentally different in their concepts. With 'Gosh', there does not seem to be any external reason for the two videos. Furthermore, they vary significantly in content and overall aesthetics. The first video, directed by Erik Wernquist, uses large-scale, spherical images to narrate the approach of a space probe to a Mars-like planet and hints at its colonization. However, it shall not be discussed further in this chapter.

Even the song itself is slightly modified, its structure was adjusted, resulting in 30 seconds of more music than in the first version. There were also high-cut filters used in two segments of the song that are not to be heard on the album version.

The song is very reduced to some few musical elements. The most important and recognizable one is the driving and busy drumbeat that is layered out of various sounds. Together with bits of speech that are sampled from the BBC 1 show 'One In The Jungle Da 2nd Lick Unbroadcast Pilot' from 1995[60], it builds the entire musical structure in the first two minutes of the song.

Oh my gosh
Easy easy!
Hold it down, hold it down!
Oh gosh
Oh my gosh
Yes, UK massive!

---

[60] https://www.whosampled.com/sample/346515/Jamie-xx-Gosh-DJ-Ron-MC-Strings-Unbroadcast-%27One-in-the-Jungle%27-Pilot/ (acc. July 7th, 2020).

3.3 Aesthetics

> *Throughout the UK and beyond*
> *In Ireland, France, BelgiumIn Ireland, France, Belgium*
> *Wherever you can pick this up, man*
> *Many thanks for still keeping the vibe alive!*

In the second part of the song, the speech disappears and a bass-synthesizer playing a simple ostinato on E♭, A♭, and B♭ as well as a solo-lead-synth join in. The latter at first plays very reduced and over time develops motives that get more and more to the musical foreground and become downright ecstatic as the song reaches its last third or so. From these musical elements results a chord structure of E♭ minor and A♭ major (Fig. 3.21)(Fig. 3.22).

Fig. 3.21 Drumbeat from 'Gosh' (simplified)

Fig. 3.22 Bassline from 'Gosh'

The video depicts a dystopic scenery in a gray color palette and bleak atmosphere (an interesting contrast to the album title 'In Colour'). It was shot in the Chinese Hangzhou, Zhejiang, where parts of Paris were recreated in very detail. There are whole blocks, parks, and even a smaller version of the Eiffel Tower. Since the 1990 s, there are plans to replicate western cities like London, Paris, or Jackson Hole, Wyoming, in China. However, all of them had little success and today are mostly uninhabited, making them surreal, almost haunted places, which again is attractive to filmmakers.

Although the shots in the video are very spectacular and feature up to 400 extras, that were casted from a martial-arts-school and then costumed uniformly[61], there is no use of CGI (computer-generated images), green screen,

---

[61] Behind the Scenes of *Gosh*: https://www.youtube.com/watch?v=R6CH18yyQyE.

or other VFX throughout the video. Romain Gavras relied on the extraordinary location, the physical performance, and elaborated use of a video drone.

The video has a strong symbolic character and uses many almost placative metaphors: The protagonist, a person with albinism and African ancestry dressed entirely in white, is to be understood as a messiah. In the opening scene, he is in a room, something between a casino and a brothel full of questionable people that seem to be under the influence of drugs and all wear VR glasses. The protagonist is the only one not wearing such glasses; he is the only one who can 'see'. In the next shot, he is on a balcony in daylight, surrounded by hundreds of his disciples standing on other balconies of the same building but cannot see their messiah.

Fig. 3.23 Jamie XX—*Gosh,* Min. 00:12 and 00:45

Moving on in the video, the protagonist meets three new characters on a staircase (maybe a nod to Led Zeppelin's 'Stairway to heaven'), equally people with albinism and dressed in white but much more passive and secondary in their depiction. I understand them as his angels; they also have golden teeth, similar to a golden tongue, thus, they spread the true word. Between these scenes, the swarm of disciples rushes through the empty streets towards the Eiffel Tower. They all wear dark uniforms but have their hair dyed blonde, maybe to resemble their messiah as much as possible. The protagonist, along with his angels, is driven to the site in a Subaru Impreza WRC. The driver also is dressed in white but wears a mask. He is a priest; one has to think of the Ku-Klux-Klan, he could be anybody and nobody at the same time, but still, he is also a carrier of the faith. The Subaru became iconic in the 1990 s by the successes of rally driver Colin McRae. It is powerful and makes its way through all terrain, even over water (see fig. 3.23) and according to Matthew 14, 29–31, he who has faith will walk on water (Fig. 3.24).

The angels have their eyes closed, they do not need to see, for they know they are on the right path, the path of god. The car's doors are wide open, like

3.3 Aesthetics

Fig. 3.24 *Gosh*, Min. 01:36 and 02:46

inviting all people to join the chariot on the right path. However, the messiah does not seem to be cheerful or even certain. When he arrived at the transcendent ceremony site, he is almost overrun by his disciples, who orbit him in a mantra-esque ritual. They even shout praises like battle cries audible through the music, but they never look directly at him. This blind will to follow him is not what he wants, he knows that his disciples are doing the wrong thing, but he cannot stop them. The ritual excludes the messiah; the crowd sinks into its uniformity and the certainty of having found a figure that they can follow. The protagonist does not transcend, only the camera lifts up in the air at the end of the video and leaves the ceremony and the helpless messiah back on the ground amid a fake and soulless scenery. The music also reaches its climax in density and intensity at this point. The lead-synthesizer develops its melodies in higher and higher registers and complements the plot. The fake Eiffel Tower remains an antenna towards the sky in front of a sunset over a post-apocalyptic city. The music thins out, and the samples of speech one last time suggest a spiritual movement with global extent:

> *Throughout the UK and beyond*
> *In Ireland, France, Belgium*
> *Wherever you can pick this up, man*
> *Many thanks for still keeping the vibe alive!*

As the last event of the video, the camera tilts to the right, one last indication that the story cannot end well or is an illusion (Fig. 3.25).

In the context of the video the title 'Gosh' can be read as a nod to the Second Commandment: ('Thou shalt not take the name of the LORD thy God in vain; for the LORD will not hold him guiltless that taketh his name in vain') The video is imbued with doubt and power(-lessness) and is further supported in this

Fig. 3.25 *Gosh*, Min. 04:32 and 05:18

characteristic by the word fragments 'Oh my gosh!' sampled in the first part of the piece. The aimlessness of the protagonist remains despite his bombastically staged entourage, the video does not provide answers, no absolute truths. On the contrary: the exuberantly applied metaphors and symbols do not hold what they promise, they play with their iconic weight, but in the end, they are only shells that cannot cope with the hopelessness of the scenario.

An interpretation of the catchy chord scheme suggests certain parallels to John Lennon's 'Imagine' verse. This song is a hymn of the peace movement that questions nations, skin colors, and even religion in its role as a trigger for conflicts. Romain Gavras might have found inspiration for a socio-political statement that strongly criticizes religion in itself or at least extreme actions due to spiritual and personal dependence. This thesis can also be supported by an interview with the online magazine dazeddigital from 2010, in which he is asked about the origins of 'nihilistic violence', which he often addresses in other projects, especially in Born Free (2010) by M.I.A. or Stress (2007) by Justice:

> *It's because of the environment. I don't think we are born violent, I think it's just that you have to choose—on one side it's the Yankees and on one side its terrorists, and right now it's all about religion too, and once God is involved it goes to a totally psychotic level, you know? It's like war on acid!*[62]

The use of a religious personality cult in times of hopelessness, as depicted in the video, or even as a reason for violent conflict could thus be negated, entirely in the spirit of John Lennon, albeit less romantically. At the same time, the video also constructs a social scenario that, due to the setting, is reminiscent primarily of Mao Zedong and other political leaders.

---

[62] http://www.dazeddigital.com/artsandculture/article/8250/1/romain-gavras-takes-a-journey-to-the-end-of-the-night (acc. July 10th, 2020).

3.3 Aesthetics

A search for meaning is the central theme of the video. On the one hand, as a treated theme itself: The question of whether (fanatical) spirituality in a world of social and cultural unreliability can be a plausible way (see the opening scene and the fake Paris) is obvious. But on the other hand, the search for meaning is also implicit in the viewer. For Gavras, the reception aesthetics play an important role for his works and for art in general, as the following quote, also from an interview with dazeddigital, shows:

> *When I see a film, I'm more interested in what I take from it than what the guy who made it wants to tell me. Fuck the guy who made it! If he wants to tell me that racism is bad, then I'm really annoyed.*[63]

In general, *Gosh* illustrates clearly how music videos today can take on an equal and even self-determined function compared to the song. The video was produced with a very unique aesthetic. The abstract scenery with no reference to the musician is typical for Romain Gavras. He has an entirely different opinion on the subject of performer vs. protagonist than, for example, the above-mentioned Jonas Åkerlund, for whom both must form a unity:

> *The thing is, I don't necessarily see music videos as a promotional thing. I'd rather kill myself than make a normal music video for YouTube with Bono singing in front of the camera. That's my vision of fucking hell.*[64]

In summary, it can be said that the video consciously gives the song a further level of meaning. The 'semantic expansion of the source material', which is discussed in Section 2.1, is not only achieved by simply adding a visual layer. The strong, extensive imagery places the song in a completely new context and does not do so via thematic references, which the song only scarcely provides, but via its atmosphere and its aesthetics. Coming back to Vernallis' proposed analysis music videos as a couples therapy, one could say that the two partners complement each other astonishingly well and bring out character traits in each other that they would never have realized on their own. The original song 'Gosh' on the album 'In Colour' with its first music video with pictures of space had a completely different identity. However, this new dystopian yet progressive and multi-layered garment fits it very well. Here again, the idea of understanding music videos as a **language** of pop and internet culture comes into play. The codes of the video's aesthetics and narration, its strong images and religious symbols in combination with the music communicate a meaning that the recipients can decode in new and

---

[63] Ibid.
[64] Ibid.

different ways. For example and in addition to my own interpretations, I want to demonstrate two comments by different users under the video on YouTube:

> *[...] I feel like the song/video perfectly embody that inexplicable feeling you get when you're maintaining so much hope for so long without even having a concrete reason to, but you do anyway. [...]* – by Noah[65]
> *[...] I realized we're all just cute little creatures on this earth trying to figure out what we have to do, we all share the same collective consciousness while forming deep bonds with each other. [...]* – by Amber G[66]

This is for sure a manifestation of the diagnosis by Peter Weibel that *'visual and musical material in a way so that they interact and jointly create an effect, which only one of them on its own never would have achieved.'*[67] But what exactly can this effect be? Only a differing aesthetical impression? For me, **both materials jointly create meaning**, which is an important finding for the discussion of music videos as a language.

3.4 A Democratized Art Form

I want to take a step back from the particular videos themselves and take a look at music videos and one factor that makes it especially outstanding and distinctive, which is democratization. As the name already suggests, music videos are interfaces between music and visual art; two worlds that rely on extremely different rules, conventions, and patterns of appreciation. An important one is curation. The judgment of what is 'good' and 'worth watching or paying for' defines the market and thus the public discussion about the artistic discipline. Traditionally, curation in the art world is a highly exclusive and abstract, almost contemptuous matter. Very few and usually very wealthy people define an artwork's value and thereby its public interest.[68] Furthermore, it is dominated by actual exclusivity, meaning that what is in possession of somebody cannot belong to somebody else at the same time. We notice this, for example, in museums where a famous painting is exhibited that might not even appeal to someone's taste, but still is the main attraction, since it is 'the original' Mona Lisa or Guernica or whatever. This is a

---

[65] https://www.youtube.com/watch?v=hTGJfRPLe08&lc=UgyjiqqXbHzSNOXqBUN4AaABAg.

[66] https://www.youtube.com/watch?v=hTGJfRPLe08&lc=UgwSKXTAovzv0lEgIol4AaABAg.

[67] Weibel (1987), *Von der visuellen Musik zum Musikvideo*, 119.

[68] Resch (2018): *Quantifying reputation and success in art*

3.4 A Democratized Art Form

problem, as Stefan Heidenreich states in his essay 'Democratize art!', as the art market does not consider the audience's actual taste and opinions[69] and thereby loses meaning and substance because meaning is not inherent but emerges only from active use. This is a common perception of Romanticism, Wittgenstein, and Cultural Studies. The market itself, says Heidenreich, provides movement, but to generate meaning, one needs remembrance and context.

And on the other hand, we have music. Music is, infrastructurally speaking, set in a completely different dimension: music relies or at least has relied for the longest time of its modern existence, on a high level of self-reflexivity in production and reception that constitute genres[70]. And genres are conventions and expectations that rely on repetition[71], sampling, on codes. Moreover, music is made for the daily consumption of as many listeners as possible and thus copied repeatedly. This lack of pressure for the artists to create something truly original and exclusive and the opportunity for the listeners to build their own opinion and taste over music that they can curate themselves poses a significantly different concept to the art market.

And then finally, there are music videos that combine the two disciplines that **build a bridge** in a way. They extend the discipline of consuming music by a visual component: consuming music now includes consuming visual art, an interpretation of music videos that, as pointed out in the earlier chapters, we might lightheartedly make.

Meaning or the viewer's affinity in whatever character remains the central quality art aspires. Heidenreich discusses this with the term 'beauty', which in German has a more abstract meaning than in English (I would propose meanings like sense or justification). Here, he values personal judgment over possible inherent quality. 'Beautiful is, was is liked' and only through discussing, he says, a social idea of beauty gets generated. Here we are already in the internet's functionalities and mechanisms: YouTube and social media are based on the concept of discussion, of sharing and rating, of feedback and appreciation. Music videos' distribution conditions are predestined for them to become an art form of democratic exchange and valuation. Main keywords of how they use it are 1.) the ever-growing prosumerism that I will dedicate the next chapter to and 2.) the increasing insignificance of the 'mainstream' through pluralization that I will discuss more in chapter 5.

---

[69] Heidenreich (2019), *Demokratisiert die Kunst!*
[70] Hemming (2015), Methoden der Erforschung populärer Musik, 138.
[71] Holt (2007), *Genre in Popular Music*, 3.

Summing up, I see that music videos embody exactly what the art market lacks in participation and democracy. They rather play by the rules of music than by those of art, and by doing so, they create a unique—a better, I want to say—art market on their own. The pure commercial factor is still present—I can notice that at least by looking at the top-segment videos with > 500.000.000 views and corresponding financial incomes. Nonetheless, the overall idea of the music video market today is subversively democratic. Let me list the most important observations, speaking of course qualitatively, not quantitatively:

1. **Music videos are to be understood as art**, just because there is a big enough section of them that understands itself as art.
2. Nobody owns music videos, at least not in the sense museums or collectors own pieces of art. However, I can have the feeling to 'own' a video myself just because I watched it over and over on YouTube and have built a relation to it.
3. Music videos (with very few exceptions), like music, are made for repetitive and universally accessible consumption—that means everywhere and without having to pay for them (directly), and not for exclusive occasions or places.
4. By making viewers use on- and offline social functionalities (like, comment, share, etc. but also talk and discuss in 'real life') to interact with them, **music videos automatically aestheticize their audience's taste, which** then vice versa **shapes the music video landscape itself**. This, on the one hand, serves the concept of prosumerism, which I will delve into in chapter 4 and on the other hand, is mutually dependent on the competent audience that is capable of distinguishing the aesthetics of different media (see Section 3.3).

If the goal is to give (back) art a broad social acceptance and significance, then music videos do very well in contributing to that.

3.5 The Future of Music Videos?

> *As we come across videos set adrift between election news clips, exhortations about how to keep your mate sexually engaged, and the newest fad diets, or click among streams of text, snapshots, and other YouTube links, music videos can now become the anchor rather than the source of discontinuity. Has the form of music video become the supertext?*[72]

---

[72] Vernallis (2013), *Unruly Media: YouTube, Music Video, and the New Digital Cinema*, 2.

3.5 The Future of Music Videos? 73

Carol Vernallis posed this question in 2013. It is a fact not to be neglected that videos that get watched between three or even fifteen minutes contiguously today are not a matter of course. Instagram and Snapchat limit the maximum video length to 60 seconds; advertising and news have to be entertaining and 'newsfeed-fitting', meaning that they mustn't strain the viewers' attention span too much. The fact that music videos even are often watched repeatedly does not necessarily correlate with our current media consumption habits. Compared to the era of MTV and the then-held discussion about trivialization through the music video's briefness and confusion[73], it seems almost ironic that they now count as an accepted carrier of preserved longevity or a new 'supertext', as Vernallis formulates.

But what could an actual future of the music video be like? First of all, pessimistic prognoses will always be part of the discourse. The American musician and producer Brenton Stokes says that music videos have already (now for real) passed their zenith and prophesizes its end being doomed to stagnation due to its own limits:

> We've already experienced the death of music video television upon YouTube's rise to fame since 2005; the death of the music video itself will be stagnation in production quality that is limited by the two-dimensional realm that has cradled it best.[74]

Sunil Manghani, one year later, attested that the music video, being an empty visual product and supplement for the music, seems out of time, unable to hold up with the internet's rapid developments[75], and is in the process of being replaced by the DIY-aesthetic of user-generated videos[76].

In my opinion and especially in the context of previous research and similar prognoses on the topic, statements like these can be marginalized. There is evidence everywhere you look that **both music videos and their cultural status**[77] **evolve all the time:** there are the results of the preceding chapters, new contents that music videos take on, new social roles they are assuming, and new forms of distribution—Thom York's *Anima* (2019), over 15 minutes long and directed

---

[73] E.g. Mikos (1993), *Selbstreflexive Bilderflut. Zur kulturellen Bedeutung des Musikkanals MTV*.

[74] Stokes (2016), *Acoustic Ecology and the Death of the Music Video*, 2.

[75] Manghani (2017), *The Pleasures of (Music) Video*, in: Arnold et al.: *Music/Video*, 21.

[76] Ibid. 39.

[77] By cultural status I refer to the sheer size and diversity of the audience and their willingness to accept music videos in new roles they didn't have 10 or 20 years ago on the one hand and on the other hand the self-confidence and changing roles that music videos attribute to themselves.

by the renowned Paul Thomas Anderson, consists of three songs off the equally named album and was released exclusively on the streaming platform Netflix. By choosing a 'pay-tv' service and not a free one like YouTube, the producers already admitted *Anima* a sincere value and questioned the rule of YouTube being the leading platform to release music videos on successfully and seriously. With Netflix at the moment being the biggest movie and series streaming provider in the game, the choice was certainly a commercial one, too. Besides that though, placing a 15-minute music video next to countless blockbuster movies and series is a bold statement for the future of music videos and their (expected) appreciation. I believe that music videos, perhaps on in new, larger formats, will appear more often on pay-streaming platforms such as Netflix, Amazon Prime etc. This means that music videos will be treated as consistent 'premium content', which is no longer secondary in any way. However, this will initially only be reserved for the very big names in the business with the appropriate financial background and a strong lobby. This phenomenon will be exciting to observe, not only because of the expected quality and scale of these videos, but also as they walk the fine line between an art form that is no longer freely available and thus gains a new reputation, and the rules of commerce that large streaming providers bring with them. Apart from Netflix, Spotify, the biggest music streaming service today, is already moving away from being a pure music provider and is starting to incorporate (music) video content. The platform realizes how important visuals are to audio and that the two go hand in hand, so we are likely to see more music videos being made by these services.[78]

In contrast to Manghani and others, Sarah Boardman is also more optimistic and foresees a brighter future for music videos in a different direction: putting, for example, a focus on virtual reality and having high hopes for it. Furthermore, and partly contrary to the results of this chapter concerning longer videos that go beyond the songs' limits, according to Boardman, music videos will shift in their appearance towards shorter and more social-media-oriented formats[79]. Indeed, you will already find many examples for this kind of evolution, like music videos consisting of Instagram-stories of different channels and later being cut together as one clip[80] or a growing number of bands that choose IGTV (Instagram's video-platform function) as their preferred channel for the video release. Even

---

[78] https://medium.com/@pulsefilms/why-music-videos-are-still-so-important-views-from-inside-the-industry-ebaa7d4758d2 (acc. March 15th, 2019).

[79] https://www.theguardian.com/music/2016/jul/28/how-pop-music-video-got-weird-again.

[80] E.g. https://www.youtube.com/watch?v=t_mN7pKSpqs—DEFLUENCER—Lil'Budget X Manny Marc X Joshi Mizu.

3.5 The Future of Music Videos? 75

the increase in VR-content in basically every region of the medial world, but also in music videos, as prognosticated by Boardman, is already happening. Early approaches like Run the Jewels' <u>Crown</u> (2014) or Reggie Watts' *Waves* (2017) had moderate success, partly resulting from the slow growing popularity and availability of the technology, but also because many times the VR-technology didn't add anything to the video more than the ability for the viewer to look around in a scene, which itself was staged traditionally. More recently, now that the principles and possibilities of virtual reality get more deeply explored, artists like <u>Robot Koch</u> really begin to push VR, both in technological and aesthetical ways, creating a justified new concept of audiovisual media.

Another branch of technology, which we arguably will come across more in the coming years, is artificial intelligence. Already there are services like <u>rotorv ideos.com</u> that are offering music videos for as little as 20 dollars made by algorithms that analyze the song and then, following some parameters the client can set, cut a video from stock footage.[81] Frankly, up to the time of writing this, these computer-made videos (yet) lack a certain originality, and at this stage of technological development, will probably not end up being used by artists who really do care about a visual and individual presentation of themselves. Nevertheless, music videos will always be **pioneers of new media and technology**, as they have been up to this day.

> *But what of the renegades, the rulebreakers of the music video world? Can the next Chris Cunningham break through in this climate?*[82]

This question for the great 'renegades', the pioneers and the rebels like the above mentioned 'auteurs' of the 1990 s that are often named textbook examples for driving forces in the music video history, is understandable. How can they still emerge or even exist in times of the newsfeed, when every next post competes directly with the one before? To what extend will (social-) medial conditions be shaping the coming products, and how much of the artist's own aesthetic vision will be approved and appreciated?

With all due respect for these questions like posed by The Guardian, they are not to be answered sensibly, because, compared directly to the circumstances in the 1990 s, all of the conditions have changed massively. In Section 3.1, I spoke about the relativization of the term 'mass suitability'. To search for a 'breakthrough', like phrased by Boardman, in the current times, in my opinion, is otiose. While back in the days a breakthrough was to make it onto MTV, what

---

[81] See an example of the results here: https://www.youtube.com/watch?v=_1fYl0IauUI.
[82] https://www.theguardian.com/music/2016/jul/28/how-pop-music-video-got-weird-again.

does get counted as a breakthrough today? A success of 500.000 views? Two million views? Or maybe even 100 Million views? There is no single marketplace for music videos like MTV anymore, where the whole range of products is presented and competing with each other. Thirteen years after the launch of YouTube the supply got pluralized in the highest measure, there are no rules for single 'genres' anymore and taste and trend over and over inspire and influence themselves again. This leads to the point that the music videos are not justifiably definable and also not comparable with themselves or at least their former self anymore.

Coming back to Boardman's thesis of music videos shifting towards social media, I want to recall the 'supertext'. If we understand music videos as the constant, I think that not social media forms or even regresses them, but the other way around. **Music videos have outlived many appearances of social media** like myspace, Google +, etc. Even right now we are witnessing the decay of Facebook. Until now, all these platforms have had a shorter lifespan than music videos, but at the same time are **part of their history**. This fact stresses the viability of the idea of the supertext. Even YouTube, like MTV, will probably be replaced by new forms of distribution in the future. However, just by looking at the last forty years of music video history, I am most convinced that they will prevail and accompany major technological and infrastructural developments rather than be eliminated by them. As Holly Rogers notes, '*it is also important to notice that the music video was not just the result of a televisual revolution in the 1980 s* [and will probably not be terminated by an online evolution of the 2020 s], *but rather has a long and fruitful history that extends back through both the musical and the visual arts.*'[83]

3.6 Conclusion

In the entire last chapter, I tried to describe the thematic complex of the music video, which might seem complicated to overlook at first (or maybe at second) sight, and analyze it in its current historical context. It was pointed out that, facing the ever-growing number of different manifestations, intentions and formats, universal statements about 'the music video' are not to made. An exception is the proposition by Carol Vernallis, quoted at the beginning: '*We might thus define music video [...] as relation of sounds and image that we recognize as such*', which turned out to be eminently viable and applicable. Frankly, that definition might

---

[83] Rogers (2014), *Twisted Synaesthesia—Music Video and the Visual Arts*, 388.

3.6 Conclusion

seem disillusioning due its bulkiness at first sight. But still, it provides a reliable basis, on which the discussion about the topic can be held free from categorization and conventions, which in my opinion is indispensable for a contemporary approach. Music videos have become too important for the music industry. The moving images are too integrated on the internet for it to be treated continually with the scholarly indifference of the last ten or twenty years and the respective outdated premises concerning function and concept.

There is a noticeable trend, in that music videos, compared to the early 2000 s, have a new self-confidence and at the same time abstractly orientate themselves to the delight in experimentation and the 'impact' of the first era of bloom ('cultural events of a different kind', as Dave Meyers puts it). And also, their self-concept as the most agile audiovisual medium, and with that, its influence on pop- and media culture continually gets more present. John Richardson in 2012 states:

> *It is tempting to go so far as to assert that everything happening in audiovisual culture today is somehow related to music video aesthetics. This is a generalization but in some measure true.*[84]

Summing up, the **music video** with its format and its aesthetics **has become more than the dichotomy of moving image and the song** it belongs to, and that define each other. It has become a language of pop and internet culture that the current generation grew up with natively. Hence, it can also be used to convey content and meaning in scenarios beyond music. Be it in advertising, as shown in Jonze's KENZO-clip, movies or satire.

The observations made in Section 2.3, at least on a semantic level, legitimize the use of the term 'Renaissance', which by itself further emphasizes the current importance, or impact I shall say, of music videos and also the need for a revised analysis of the subject. The understanding of the term as an actual comparison to the Renaissance of the 15th and 16th centuries concerning the revival of former ideas and pieces of art certainly still is surprisingly applicable. While there are pretty obvious examples of videos that downright copy clips of the 1980 s, like *Finesse* (2018) by Bruno Mars feat. Cardi B, in which the aesthetics are imitated from the 4:3 aspact ratio to set, color grading and costumes[85], it distills that it is more abstract parameters than the mere look of the 80 s and 90 s that defines the medium's revival. The New York Times in an article of early 2019 also stands up for a new and adequate recognition of music videos, saying that: '*This category*

---

[84] Richardson (2012), *An Eye for Music—Popular Music and the Audiovisual Surreal*, 6–7.

[85] This phenomenon probably is more due to fashion than it is linked to music video industry and appears along the general current 90 s-trend.

should be seen as an opportunity to embrace a whole new breed of musician, one who reflects what has long been true but rarely acknowledged at the Grammys: that the job of a recording artist has changed, and that those now making the most vivid impact are as careful about how they look as how they sound.'[86]

I interviewed Dave Meyers, who is one of the most famous directors of the current music video market's top-segment (e.g. Kendrick Lamar's *Humble* (2018), Billie Eilish—*bad guy* (2019)). I asked him about the difference between music videos from ten years ago and today, in his opinion, more concrete, if and how he would reconsider music videos under a 'Renaissance' premise. His response was the following, closing this chapter about reconsidering contemporary music videos very adequately:

> *Ten years ago, they were cultural events. Then the industry collapsed. Videos suffered. YouTube gave a new avenue of consumption. And from that birthed a different style of cultural events. […] [M]usic changed into a diverse landscape where a quite diverse group of artists with a much wider range of styles now operate and create videos with their unique brand. So, the main evolution -* **we went from a culture of fitting in to a culture of standing out.** *And videos have benefited creatively from that (albeit the budgets aren't the same as they were). So perhaps as a business model it's tougher, but as a creative outlet it's 100 times better.*[87]

---

[86] https://www.nytimes.com/2019/01/30/arts/music/grammy-awards-music-video.html?fbclid=IwAR3xk6zCzIIJ8j1jwpR0_ssPswEgnuF19mmVXY5gLWap51SWqB4Jj_i5F24 (acc. September 15th, 2019).

[87] See appendix, highlighted and corrected orthographically by the author.

Prosuming a Music Video in the Late 2010s

I now want to theorize the more practical sides of music video production in the late 2010s, focusing on the aspect of prosumerism and how it affects the music video world. The term of the prosumer was already mentioned a few times and shall now be sorted out properly. Although the term's morphologic conversion to 'prosuming' or even 'prosumerism' might have a neologistic appearance, it has been done several times before. Albeit it yet shows up only very rarely in the field of media practice, it does much more often in the context of economics, media marketing[1], the rise of the open-source-internet and user-driven platforms, the term gained significance. Prime examples of the latter are projects such as YouTube or Wikipedia. Axel Bruns back in 2008 stressed the central and shaping function of the user for such systems, introducing the similar term of the 'produser':

> Users are always already necessarily also producers of the shared information collection, regardless of whether they are aware of that fact—they have taken on a new, hybrid role, the produser.[2]

Bruns adds an important facet to the discussion with this choice of words, namely that the 'user' just by theoretically being able to contribute to the system is a vital component of it. What he calls the 'shared information collection' refers to the web 2.0 in general. Still, it may also be transferred to YouTube and especially its shared collection of aesthetic and technical knowledge and artistic statements.

---

[1] E.g. Alderete (2017), *The Age of Prosumerism—Some Micro-Economic Analysis*, Costello (2018), *Next step for prosumerism within the rapidly changing agile IT market*, Santomir (2013), *Social Media and Prosumerism: Implications for Sport Marketing Research*.

[2] Bruns (2008), *Blogs, Wikipedia, Second Life, and Beyond: From Production to Produsage*, 2

Salomé Berrocal used the term of the prosumer in the context of social media in 2014. There she says:

> Social networks are clearly a 'prosumption' medium in which prosumers are the loudspeakers that broadcast conversations [...]. In this conversation, the listener not only consumes this content but responds to and reproduces these messages and creates others almost simultaneously.[3]

The phenomenon of the prosumer thus, at least in our context, is linked directly to participatory culture, another key concept that I want to associate with music video production and consumption. Henry Jenkins et al. name **five characteristics that define participatory culture**: 1.) Relatively low barriers to artistic expression and civic engagement, 2.) strong support for creating and sharing one's projects, 3.) informal mentorship, 4.) a belief that contributions matter, and 5.) a sense of social connection.[4] These factors present themselves as viable, especially when illustrated with the case of music videos: points 1–3 and 5 are covered by the infrastructure that YouTube and social media provide—the possibilities for artistic expression are not hindering at all, but rather inviting, as originally formulated by YouTube's slogan 'Broadcast Yourself'. Strong support and mentorship comes through all social media platforms, especially YouTube itself. I will discuss filmmaking tutorials as a key factor for this in section 4.2. And the sense of social connection is within the music video's nature as Sarah Boardman, Head of Music at Pulse Films, puts it: '*A [music] video connects an artist and a listener, as well as connecting a listener to an audience*'[5]. However, Jenkins clarifies in a later work how a platform itself does not evoke participation and also the difference between participation and interaction:

> I do not think technologies are participatory; cultures are. Technologies may [...] facilitate communications [...] and they may encode certain values through their terms of use and through their interfaces. [...]Participation [...] refers to properties of the culture, where groups collectively and individually make decisions that have an impact on their shared experiences. We participate in *something*; we interact with *something*.[6]

The prosumer concept, following Bruns ('*Users are always already necessarily also producers of the shared information collection*'), is applicable to any music

---

[3] Berrocal et al. (2014), *Prosumidores mediáticos en la comunicación política: El 'politainment'*, 66.

[4] Jenkins et al (2006), *Fans, bloggers, and gamers: Exploring participatory culture*, xi.

[5] https://medium.com/@pulsefilms/why-music-videos-are-still-so-important-views-from-inside-the-industry-ebaa7d4758d2.

[6] Jenkins et al (2015), *Participatory Culture in a Networked Era*, 22.

video creator nowadays, also due to the development of distribution in recent years that I pointed out in section 3.2. The share of the audience that creates its own audiovisual products (and, as a result, has an entirely different perspective on the market) is getting bigger and bigger. Concerning all these factors, I find it highly necessary to admit the prosumers an individual scholarly treatment, for which I propose the terms 'prosuming' and 'prosumerism' for media practice.

This chapter by no means is a guide on 'how-to' make a video, but more of a temporally captured observation of how-to make music videos in the late 2010s, one could say. I now try to outline the motivational, industrial, and technical circumstances of making a music video, which prosumers face in their work. Subsequent to the previous chapter, I will also delve into existing canons and intertextuality, which become crucial under the premise that every production is happening in interaction with the reception of existing material. Being a prosumer of music videos myself, I chose the titles of the following subchapters based on what I find most characteristic about a prosumer's work: It all has to start somewhere with a **motivation** of whatever nature. And from there, the **technical conditions** and **how one deals with their inspirations and influences define the practical outcome**.

4.1 Motivation

I want to go back to the initial question of 'Why to make a music video in the first place?'. While I have covered a lot of functionalities and roles music videos can have in our medial world in the previous chapters of this work, I now want to take a closer look on things, regarding the particular motivational reasons and causes of why a music video might turn out the way it does in the late 2010s. For instance, an amateur might have very different objectives to produce a music video than an established and famous artist, a pop singer other ones than an alternative electro-artist, and so forth. In the following, I will propose three different motivations that affect the outcome of contemporary music videos. Transitions between particular motivations obviously are not absolute, and there are mixed types or individual cases that do not apply to any of them.

1. Following conventions

This is the most obvious and universal motivation and it applies to the majority of music videos out there, depending on the interpretation of 'conventions'. One plays by the rules of these conventions by following the existing and popular method of producing a music video subsequent to a song, not even particularly for commercial, promotional or any other economic nor even artistic reasons, but **just because it is common practice**. This covers very much all music videos, which were made for songs that got created without visual components in the first place, as for example Ylvis does. Until here, we do not have to distinguish between amateurs and professional labels or, say, between financing a big production that is supposed to earn money and an amateurish no-budget production. The motivation to make a video because it is usual stays the same. That, of course, can also be a departure that does not exclude other artistic, content-related, or economic motivations to follow. The motivation to obey the market's rules, or simply put, doing it for the money, for instance, is different. I came across the definition of 'music videos as promotion for a song' here and there. While I have shown earlier that music videos have established themselves well beyond the confines of an advertisement, the promotional factor certainly remains central. However, instead of a particular song to sell, some artists today, at least in the professional pop music sector and especially with a younger fan community, use music videos to sell their 'brand'. When **single songs become more replaceable and less significant**, those artists position themselves similarly to a company. An example for this is the US producer and DJ Marshmello. In the description box under *Happier* (2018), there is an array of links, redirecting to merchandising shops, social-media channels, even gaming content with Marshmello and links to all his 17 other music videos. All of that is automatically presented in the users' native language in order to make their experience of getting to know Marshmello as comfortable as possible and to make them consume as much of Marshmello's content and products as possible.

Another reading of 'following conventions' is to **stick to certain perceptions and codes of music videos**, for they comply with common sense and expectations by the industry and the audience. These might include copying actual contents and aesthetics used by existing videos, concepts for pursuing authenticity or triggering certain reactions like shock, surprise, disgust, etc. As I already mentioned in the introduction to this work, there are a *lot* of music videos that in their essence do not offer anything new or evolved, compared to 'mainstream' videos from 20 or even 30 years ago, illustrated for instance by the resemblance of DJ Khaled's *I'm the One* from 2018 and The Notorious B.I.G.'s *Juicy* from 1994 (Fig 4.1).

By no means I want to devaluate these videos in comparison to more innovative videos, they follow a certain practice of music video production that is part of the game, just like any of the more progressive practices. I will discuss the

4.1 Motivation

Fig. 4.1 DJ Khaled, *I'm the One* and The Notorious B.I.G., *Juicy*

aspect of copying and sticking to supposed rules more in section 4.3 and with a background of literary studies.

2. Expressing oneself

Expressing oneself is a vague term and can be related to basically any chosen job, hobby or dedication a person could do, so it needs further clarification. A brief look into academia about creativity shall help: Andreas Reckwitz speaks of a contemporary western society that wants and is supposed to be creative per se. He describes a 'dispositive of creativity' with a simultaneous longing and imperative for creativity.[7] While the need for creativity in the 1960s still was linked to a counter-cultural rebellion against the bourgeois lifestyle, not later than the 1980s, the normative concept of creativity formed a central and driving force in the western society: individuals, organizations, institutions—today, the whole society orientates itself on the creative.[8] Thus, expressing oneself creatively, however one might interpret that, is a **social duty in our current western society** anyhow. What makes music videos stand out from all these other possibilities to 'express oneself' (painting, dancing, acting, walking in the woods, etc.) are their promising opportunities of plausible success and recognition. In earlier chapters, I already covered the economic advantages of music videos and the great expectations and openness the internet and the audience have towards them. The technical conditions, which will be analyzed more deeply in the following subchapter, are yet another parameter that results in extremely inviting circumstances for prosumers and a low threshold to dive into the music video world and find out how the

---

[7] Reckwitz (2014 [2012]): *Die Erfindung der Kreativität. Zum Prozess gesellschaftlicher Ästhetisierung*, 19.
[8] Ibid., 11.

internet's audience responds to one's audiovisual expression. This applies to both amateurs and professionals and manifests itself in amateur videos with peculiar aesthetics gone viral like boy pablo—_Everytime_ (2017) or famous musicians taking an unexpected and daring turn in their music video aesthetics. Examples are Kanye West's _Famous_ (2016) or Ariana Grande's _Monopoly_ (2019) that takes a drastic change in style to trash and amateurism only three months after her very glossy _7 rings_ (2019) came out (Fig 4.2).

Fig. 4.2 boy pablo—_Everytime, 01:42 min._[9] and Ariana Grande—_Monopoly,_ 1:58 min[10]

Another facet of expressing oneself that is a mixture of economic and individual aesthetic intentions is attracting **attention**. A music video enriches a song's likelihood of being shared and allows people to have an opinion on it, although they might neither have any musical knowledge nor comprehension of the lyrics. If the video is convincing, they might even not like the song but still share it. This contributes majorly to music video's dimension of sociability. Let us take Childish Gambino's _This is America_ (2018) as an example. Assuming he had an important issue that he wanted to convey through this song in the most effective and impactful way: with only the song, he wouldn't have come nearly as far as with the graphic and explicit video. The lyrics are quite cryptic, and even though the music has an interesting and innovative touch, it would certainly not have raised too much attention on its own. Put together with the video that is

---

[9] Boy Pablo stage themselves as the other-the-top dear and harmless teenage boys. They just perform their song by a river in the evening light, but the way they always smile at the camera, even though it's in direct sunlight or extremely far away, makes the scenario both awkward and charming.

[10] _Monopoly_ uses self-recorded scenes by Grande with a 90s DV-Camera and footage that seems like a goofy teenage girls' night out. Additionally, it suggests that, judged by the visual quality and platitude of the postproduction that feature emojis, they themselves edited the whole video in the exact mood of the night out.

4.1 Motivation

the main trigger of interest and engagement for the audience, the song achieves its full potential of attention by people now receiving the video *and* the song in conjunction. Other examples for using music videos' potential of political expression are artists like the British rapper M.I.A. with roots from Sri Lanka, who has always picked up political topics in her music. In *Born Free* (2010) and *Borders* (2016) she addressed systematic prosecution of minorities and immigration politics. These songs gained great attention and encouragement mainly due to their visually powerful videos. This phenomenon is also to be found with big popstars: Taylor Swift's *You Need to Calm Down* (2019), for example raises attention against discrimination of LGBTQ people and even mentions an online petition started by Taylor Swift herself in support of an American Equality Act. Pop-musicians using their reach to convey political issues is always a balancing act between public relation and appreciation and allegations of ingratiation. Examples of that are ambivalent reactions to *You Need to Calm Down*[11] and to other videos like Miley Cyrus' *Mother's Daughter*[12].

Another example is the first single to be released after ten years by the German rock band Rammstein, *Deutschland* (2019). The video is a nine-and-a-half-minute epos with the band members reliving certain times and places in German history, like wars against the ancient Romans, the German revolution of 1918–1919, the holocaust, and riots in the GDR. The band made very sensational and effective use of teasing the video with a short scene of the band dressed as prison inmates in a concentration camp and with ropes around their necks. Within hours, the whole German press was engaged, discussing whether Rammstein had the right to depict such scenes and why this video can only be the new low point or highpoint in the band's history. When the full video was released, it obviously received great attention right from the start. In an interview with the Rolling Stone, Rammstein's keyboarder Flake explains their motivation and how a music video can expand or even complete a song's meaning: *'The song is about the ambivalent relationship we have with Germany. And the video shows where this relationship might come from. [...] We're not about shocking people [...] We want to provoke, get people moving.'*[13] Again, this is an excellent example for a mixture of expressing personal issues and economical procedure.

---

[11] https://www.nytimes.com/2019/06/18/arts/music/taylor-swift-you-need-to-calm-down-video.html (acc. July 12th, 2020) https://www.theatlantic.com/entertainment/archive/2019/06/taylor-swift-you-need-calm-down-hijacks-queerness/591829/ (acc. July 12th, 2020).

[12] https://www.jetzt.de/musik/mothers-daughter-von-miley-cyrus (acc. July 13th, 2020).

[13] Christian "Flake" Lorenz in: Rolling Stone (06/2019).

The findings of this category illustrate at least three of Jenkins' et al. characteristics of participatory culture very well, namely: 1.) Relatively low barriers to artistic expression and civic engagement, 2.) strong support for creating and sharing one's projects, and 4.) a belief that contributions matter.

3. Making use of the 'language'

The first two motivations are obviously not new in the late 2010s (although still valid), because they describe the process of making 'conventional' music videos as they have existed for decades.

This last one requires a certain evolvement of the music video medium itself and also its cultural context. That means the position or role it has taken on in its superordinate system, the internet, and the viewership that is willing to accept and consume music videos in new forms, shapes, styles, and contexts. These conditions are given today, especially in the milieu of younger generations with a high affinity to popular (or at least internet-) culture and digitality. All those factors make plausible an interpretation of the music video medium being a **language of pop and internet culture**. A language that was established over decades by the music industry and that the audience has grown accustomed to. Just like other language, it is a **tool to express content and a code with specific characteristics**. Especially prosumerism justifies this interpretation—now the circumstances for a conversation are given, since the medium is not one-directional anymore but in constant movement between transmitter and receiver. The characteristics of this language and first and foremost the possibilities it offers brings forth examples outside the pure music business that make use of music videos as a 'language' in order to convey and formulate specific contents in the aesthetics and infrastructural space of music videos.

We already encountered some of those in this work. There are the obvious videos that clearly were made with another objective than to accompany a song, for example, advertisements like *KENZO World* (2016). Then there are the song/video hybrids, in that song and video are written parallel and that are designed to function primarily in that combination. I already talked about older examples like 'The Lonely Island', but this format has also become particularly popular in entertainment or satire TV-Shows, like the Norwegian 'Ylvis' (*What Does the Fox say?* (2013), *Stonehenge* (2016)), or German 'Neo Magazin Royale' (*V for Varoufakis* (2015), *BE DEUTSCH!* (2015)). One final example shall be institutions like the National Parent-Teacher Association that believe music videos to be an adequate medium to express actions against bullying. For their purposes, they covered the song 'Perfect' by P!nk, re-wrote the lyrics, and produced a video[14] that addresses the topic.

4.2 Technical Conditions

The technical and financial conditions and efforts of filmmaking and, thus, in music video production nowadays cannot be compared to those before the age of YouTube. I do not want to go too deep into the matter, for it has been discussed many times before in scholarly literature. **Cameras and equipment have become significantly smaller and affordable to almost anybody,** and this process has been going on for decades. Today, there is a decent kit of equipment available for around 5,000 $, including a camera, lenses, gear for camera movements like tripods, gimbals etc., and a computer for editing. With a setup like that, prosumers can implement videos in the style of classics. One example of this would be *Smooth* (1999) by Santana feat. Rob Thomas that is shot on location and works primarily with natural light[15] and no complicated camera work. The industry is well aware of the prosumer market. It keeps introducing lighter, cheaper, and more innovative camera gear like flying drones, 360° cameras, action cameras, and of course, smartphones with more and more impressive and capable cameras. **The latter caused the extreme decay of entry-level equipment** sales like cheap DSLRs or similar cameras that would have been used for amateur filmmaking ten years ago.[16] So the market shifts to the mid-range and professional segment, in that prosumers are incited to invest some few thousand Euros in their equipment that again lets them take their work more seriously.

An ongoing development that is becoming more popular every day and worth mentioning is the next step towards popularizing and making technology available, which are **tutorials on YouTube.** They are a crucial part of the filmmaking world today and cover all stages of the production from planning to postproduction and make conventional film schools obsolete. I want to focus especially on the evolution of visual effects: Computers are becoming more powerful, and software is becoming more user-friendly and, and this is the most interesting part of it, there is a vivid community of VFX artists. There are high-level and

---

[14] Pink—Perfect (AHMIR cover)—Anti-Bullying video: https://www.youtube.com/watch?v=gliHyklHr6c

[15] Natural light means no additional lights other than daylight were added.

[16] https://petapixel.com/2017/03/03/latest-camera-sales-chart-reveals-death-compact-camera/ (acc. August 9th, 2019).

easy-to-understand tutorials even for complicated techniques and effects that are explained step by step, so that even amateurs with the appropriate software can follow. Let us take the most expensive music video of all time, Michael Jacksons *Scream* (1995), break down the most relevant visual effects and compare it to the quality of current YouTube tutorials: we will find various videos **explaining the techniques used in *Scream*** and even been done with a higher level of sophistication. Someone with a little experience, dedication, the right software, and the help of those videos **will be able to recreate them at home**. The most apparent visual effects in the original music video are the 3D-modeling of a spaceship and its interior, shattering of CGI glass and vases, and morphing objects, texts, and people. The first two of those in the prosumer-world are typically done in 3D software programs like Blender (which even is freeware) or Cinema 4D. In contrast, the latter most often is done with the most popular program for visual effects and compositing, Adobe After Effects. If one searches for 'Blender spaceship tutorial', one will find tons of videos explaining how to model spaceships, corridors, space nebulas etc., basically everything *Scream* offers, uploaded by such channels as called 'Blender Guru' or 'BlenderForNoobs[17]'. Despite being typically very long and detailed, these 3D tutorials can reach hundreds of thousands of views, like 'How to Create a Spaceship in Blender—Part 1 of 2'[18]. The same counts for shattering or exploding objects. After Effects tutorials are even more popular and a vital component of the (music) video community. In section 3.4, I noted that on the one hand, the field of music video production is (one of) the most important and fruitful spaces for filmmakers to develop and implement their ideas and on the other hand that music videos offer a space of unbridled creativity and experimentation.

This reflects in the landscape of YouTube tutorials that contribute significantly to this situation. Channels like the very popular 'Cinecom.net' release tutorials with hundreds of thousands of views every week in that effects from internet videos or movies, with the biggest part being music videos, get broken down and recreated (like for example 'Taylor Swift—'ME!' Flying Effect', 'Billie Eilish— Bad Guy HEAD in WATERBAG Effect' or 'FACE DISTORSION (Eminem— VENOM)')[19]. This is a fitting example of what Jenkins et al. meant by 'informal mentoring' as a characteristic of participatory culture.

But what do these findings mean for the analysis of contemporary music videos, their production and their role in internet culture? I want to take a look

---

[17] Slang for 'amateur, greenhorn'.

[18] https://www.youtube.com/watch?v=yaPd4ieTmng.

[19] https://www.youtube.com/playlist?list=PLV0ZcSTi6tB7O8Jkv1ifp3cIuNLeG6tGq.

4.2 Technical Conditions

at the most substantial observations in this relation of music videos and online tutorials and discuss their consequences:

1. **Music videos and tutorials share the same platform of distribution**

The platform's lack of exclusivity compared to channels like the early MTV and cinema or, to put it the other way around, its all-encompassing repertoire entails a unique and characteristic context of reception. Among prosumers, a music video with special or individual effects seldom will just be consumed and adored for its uniqueness, but rather be a reason to look up the making of the particular effects and have another element in one's horizon of imagination when thinking about own projects. From this follows the next important observation, namely:

2. Together, music videos and tutorials build a **system of supply and demand for aesthetic norms, techniques, and expectations**

Is it really beneficial for the creative evolution of music videos and their cultural appreciation, if any kind of mystery or the joy of being entertained gets deconstructed immediately by tutorials, one might ask. The answer obviously is yes. This very popularity of deconstructing tutorials and also official making-of videos is an **accelerator and replicator for the creative output** in the music video world. These tutorials are part of the democratization of creativity, as they give access to techniques and ideas that were very expensive and reserved for very few people some thirty years ago.

And is it really beneficial for the creative evolution of music videos and their cultural appreciation if prosumerism only revolves around the question of 'how?' and not 'why?', another one might ask. Here it gets more interesting. But to clarify, this work and the recent revival of scholarly interest in music videos wouldn't exist, should this really be the case. The knowledge of 'how' only allows more complex premises for the question of 'why'. But what role does the 'why?' in music video production play in current times anyways? On one side, the mentioned democratization of creativity, meaning simply 'because one *can*', is certainly one part of the answer to this question. The psychological and possibly economic reward of implementing an idea with one's favorite aesthetics and techniques is rather tempting.

The limits of what can be done within the multimedia world are thus becoming increasingly accessible. This inevitably leads to constant experimentation and research beyond these limits, too. Because music videos, as already explained, are always at the technical pulse of time, pioneering examples of video art appear here time and again. In the following subchapter, I would like to take a closer look at one of them and then leave the area of technical conditions for the time being.

4.2.1 Björk—losss \\ Pushing the Limits Back to the Roots

As an example for this, I chose Björk's _losss_ from 2019 from the album 'Utopia' (2017), which is her 59th music video. Björk's persona and music have been subject of academic discourse since the 1990s, and also many of her videos were analyzed in various contexts before.[20] Besides the fact that the video is technically very complex and progressive, it is also an interesting borderline case regarding a clear definition of music videos. That is, because it was created as a visualization for big screens at live concerts for Björk's 'Cornucopia' tour 2020, but it was previously released as a YouTube video and has just under one million views at the time of writing. The audio track differs from the album version. It is over two minutes shorter and also produced slightly differently, melodies are different here and there, and the mix is more intimate than in the album version, as for example there is no reverb on the main vocals.

The song is in an F# minor scale. In the first verse, the chordal scheme F# minor—E major—B major—F# minor is still clearly recognizable, after that, the harmonic structure dissolves more and more, but continues to hover around the tonal center of F# minor. The whole song is in 4/4 time, but the very glitchy and almost industrial-sounding percussion often blur the pulse. The flute, which plays in many layers, is the essential instrument in 'losss'. In addition, a harp plays a prominent role and also provides the harmonic structure. The busy percussions can almost be described as an acoustic jumble that does not leave the song in peace and seems to keep fighting against the persistent and calming sounds of the flutes and Björk's distinctive, vulnerable voice. The lyrics deal with the handling of loss, they are a constant weighing up of heaviness and desperation on the one

---

[20] E.g. Brozzoni (2017), *Completing the Mystery of Her Flesh: Love, Eroticism, and Identity in Björk's Videos*, in: Arnold et al. (eds.): Music/Video: Histories, Aesthetics, Media, 109–119; Dibben, (2006), *Subjectivity and the Construction of Emotion in the Music of Björk*. In: Music Analysis, 25 171–197; Korsgaard (2011), *Emotional Landscapes: The Construction of Place in Björk's Music and Music Videos*, in Thomsen, Ørjasæter (eds.), Globalizing Art: Negotiating Place, Identity and Nation in Contemporary Nordic Art; Marsh, West (2003), *The Nature/Technology Binary Opposition Dismantled in the Music of Madonna and Björk*, in: Lysloff, Gay (eds.), Music and Technoculture, Wesleyan University Press, pp. 182–196 (Fig 4.3).

4.2 Technical Conditions

hand and the optimism that lets one look ahead and see the good and the chance in loss on the other:

> *We all are struggling*
> *Just doing our best*
> *We've gone through the grinder*
> *[...]*
> *I opened my heart to you*
> *Your lower lip so heavy on you*
> *My spine curved erotically*
> *Finally vulnerable*
> *[...]*
> *I opened my heart for you*
> *Tied ribbons on my ankles for you*
> *Drew orchids on my thighs for you*
> *Your lower lip so heavy on you*
> *My spine curved erotically*
> *Finally vulnerable...*[21]

The video for 'losss' is directed and made by Tobias Gremmler, a German designer, author, and associate professor on new media. The video is one single, continuous metamorphosis of two insect-esque human faces in constant communication and negotiation. In the video description box under the YouTube video, Björk wrote:

> *it is time to show you another song visualised by the overwhelmingly talented Tobias Gremmler ..... noone captures digital sensuality like him, elegant and expressive !!!! this is made for the multiple screens of cornucopia and we share it all here on 1 for your laptop screen ... we based the visuals on the conversations between our inner optimist and pessimist, when i recorded this i tried to sing in a deeper tone for one of them in the left speaker and a higher optimist in the right. and if you listen on headphones it will match the imagery .....*[22]

Firstly, this is quite unconventional to write such an informal message under an official video, as there are no promotional links to other platforms, and not even the orthography is correct. Nevertheless, as viewers, we learn a lot about the background of the video. For example, that it was originally intended for screens

---

[21] Björk, One Little Indian Records 2017.

[22] https://www.youtube.com/watch?v=tIWhpI_unCo.

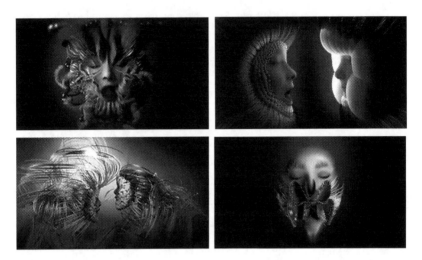

Fig. 4.3 Stills taken from Björk—*losss*. This time I deliberately say stills (even though all the figures from music videos are stills), because they cannot represent the concept of visualizing music as a continuous movement, as it is implemented in the video and which makes it so intense

at live concerts, what the content of the video is about, namely the conversation between the inner optimist and the pessimist, and how they adapted the audio track to the video by panning the vocals to make it fit together especially well. In addition, the last sentence *'and if you listen on headphones it will match the imagery'* is an invitation to the audience to experience the video with its full impact by wearing headphones. All this involves the viewer in the project, and Björk makes it accessible and experienceable to them.

The images in the video are simultaneously minimalist in their simple structure (the two faces against a mostly dark background) and yet highly complex in their shapes, surfaces, movements, and patterns with nature as a key influence. The faces without heads and necks constantly mutate into shapes reminiscent of the plant and animal world. Sometimes the faces seem to have hair that floats in the water like jellyfish or algae, sometimes a mouth turns into something that looks like a peacock butterfly. At other times, the faces inflate like a frog's vocals sac or look like birds of paradise during courtship display. Everything pulsates, everything is in motion. A cycle in which everything changes its form and yet is one.

4.2 Technical Conditions

Gremmler has already addressed the topic of the digital visualization of music and movement in several projects (including one for the London Symphony Orchestra, in which his approach is shown comprehensibly) and has also applied this technique in *losss*. He uses motion-capture or performance-capture procedures, in which he does not, as is customary, simply convert the recorded information into an analog movement for a virtual figure. The visual work Gremmler creates is time-based[23], which means he also makes the process of movement visible and applies it to specific structures. He also uses certain algorithms in order to create visuals that actually also appear in nature. In these works, certain formulas trigger growth or expansion, or movements we see in nature.[24] This makes the movements of the algae-like hair or the butterfly-like mouth appear particularly organic and natural, even though they are anything but, and grow and transform as if they were part of the natural world. In an interview, Gremmler said:

> *Nothing is static. Transformation is essential to distinguish and frame what we perceive. I am not interested in the static, nor in traditions or standards other than transforming them.*[25]

This statement is not only interesting as a background fact on the artist's motivation, it also fits well into the idea of the music video medium being a culturally and in this case technically pioneering 'melting-pot', as I called it in the introduction.

Taking up motifs from nature is also found in the music. It is very pulsating, too, like waves or gusts of wind or a heart that pumps the blood through the circulation, which is especially noticeable in the intro. The flute is very often a carrier of a rural, near-to-nature ambiance, and in the intro, you can even hear samples of birds or frogs as well as crickets. But in the outro it is quiet. No environment can be heard anymore, only the aggressive percussion sounds are left. So the back and forth between two sides, like optimism and pessimism, or nature and machines, is also reflected in the music. Both 'partners', as Vernallis suggest to understand music and images in a music video, enter into a true symbiosis here (and I consciously choose the word symbiosis with its biological origin). The music is so well complemented in its aesthetics and narration by the visual layer (and vice versa) that movement and sound, song, and textures, ultimately

---

[23] https://openlab.fm/news/artists-interview-tobias-gremmier#! (acc. August 4th, 2020).
[24] Ibid.
[25] Ibid.

image and music, merge into a breathing newness. In achieving this, the technical conditions and the artistic implementation play an essential role.

Losss can look back on a long tradition in Björk's work in many ways. The treatment of the subject of nature (and techno-culture) goes back to a large extent to Björk's native Iceland, and at the same time, she is a pioneer in breaking the belief that technology is cold and soulless.[26] Björk has always been known for her extravagant music videos in which she has worked with some of the most famous directors of the 1990s, such as Spike Jonze (*It's Oh so Quiet*, 1995) or Michel Gondry (*Army of Me*, 1995). *Losss* is very aware of its historical context, fits well into the creative outlet of audiovisual synthesis of the arts and even alludes to its predecessors in part with intertextual references. The sensual approximations of the faces are strongly reminiscent of the two robots that also wear Björk's faces, from one of her most famous music videos, *All is Full of Love* (1999), directed by Chris Cunningham. So while technical innovation continues to drive forward, a distinct aesthetic and content-related identity is maintained. Furthermore, the concept of the mask as something that can show but also hide internal reality has continuously played a role in Björk's art and was therefore chosen as a focus for *losss* (Fig 4.4).[27]

This observation finally leads over to the next question, which I will explore in the following and last subchapter on prosumerism, that is 'what is the influence of other material and how is it treated in new videos?'.

4.3 Context, Canons, and Inspiration

Now I will examine the **textual context** in which music videos are produced and published in today. Apart from the actual systems of distribution such as YouTube or other platforms such as vimeo, I want to cover the artist's treatment of existing material in the music video world with special focus on prosumerism. As we saw in the last subchapter and will see in sections 5.4 and 5.5, nowadays YouTube itself formally constitutes the main corpus of music video inspiration and thus a **self-propelling machinery**. Hence, it is no surprise that the matter of a production's literary context, that is intertextuality, is a critical one that shall be discussed here. Although the focus of this work until now hasn't been on literary studies, and I don't want to open up a whole new discipline here, intertextuality

---

[26] Marsh/West (2003), *The Nature/Technology Binary Opposition Dismantled in the Music of Madonna and Björk*, 183, 185.
[27] https://openlab.fm/news/artists-interview-tobias-gremmier#!

4.3 Context, Canons, and Inspiration

Fig. 4.4 From top left to bottom right: *Losss* (2019) and *All is Full of Love* (1999), Album cover from 'Utopia'[28], Björk wearing face piece by James Merry (2017)[29]

is a literary phenomenon, and I shall at least seek for indications from that field of studies in order to understand this term in our given context of music videos. I interpret the term 'text' broadly to include music, images, or any form of media. A focus on the understanding of 'text as music' is also proposed by Jan Hemming in his methodological framework for researching popular music.[30] Two important reasons for this are because music does not exist per se but always in a *context*, and in order for academia to be able to apply literary theory, such as the study of intertextuality, on music.

I want to demonstrate one example to get a feeling of how a prosumer's music video can take on referencing its medium and context of distribution. That is, how context itself is enough inspiration for a whole video. <u>Material</u> (2018) by the US-Indie-band Flasher is one single compilation of hypertextual references. The

---

[28] https://twitter.com/bjork/status/925346387780362240/photo/1.

[29] https://proxymusic.club/2018/07/08/james-merry-bjork-utopia/ (acc. August 4th, 2020).

[30] Hemming (2015), *Methoden zur Erforschung populärer Musik*, 28.

video starts as a more or less conventional performance video but then stops as if the YouTube player had lost internet connection. Then the screen changes into a YouTube surface, and a cursor begins to navigate through a tour of various videos within the video itself, from lyric videos to karaoke videos and even commercials (Fig 4.5).

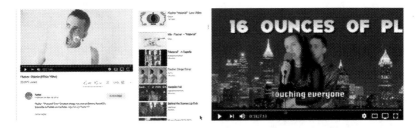

Fig. 4.5 Flasher—*Material*, 00:30 min. and Flasher—*Material*, 01:07 min

Why is this video remarkable as an example for this subchapter? Certainly, referencing and parodying the own genre is no new phenomenon, as for example Pulp's *Babies* (1992) that I addressed in section 2.1, illustrates and where the conventional and monotonous form of music videos got satirized. However, what new dimensions are there in today's videos, represented here by *Material*? Firstly, without YouTube, it would not exist in the form it does. It reflects the platform and especially the user's experience on it and focuses on YouTube's nerve-wracking and procrastinating parts like connection issues, ads, and the triviality of the mass that one clicks him-/herself through while spending time on it. While *Babies* would have worked in every context of presentation, *Material* would not make sense on any other platform than YouTube. By stepping outside its conventional limits of music and images into the distribution platform, it inevitably links them both together. Having demonstrated this example as an initial impulse, in the following I want to go deeper into the matter of intertextuality to explore further the possibilities for music videos and modes of analyzing them in that context.

Let's take a look at Harold Bloom's classic 'The Anxiety of Influence' from 1973. We learn that he understands literary products, in his case poetry, always as the result of preceding influence, that is, a **crossing point of intertextual effects**[31]. Translated to music videos, this can already be read as a confirmation of our

---

[31] Bloom (1973), *The Anxiety of Influence*, 5.

4.3 Context, Canons, and Inspiration

findings of section 4.1 that prosumers in most times and to different degrees, rely on existing codes when creating new works.

But going further into the matter, we learn that intertextuality is much more than just one writer or producer influencing or quoting another. In the late 1970s and in order to analyze relation of texts and their contexts, French literary theorist Gérard Genette proposed the term of the superordinate 'transtextuality' which consist of as much as five subtypes, 'intertextuality' and the mentioned 'hypertextuality' as in *Material* only being two of them.[32] With that in mind, we notice that first of all we may need to reformulate 'intertextuality', because it does not cover all the facets we might want to analyze, as 'transtextuality', following Genette's model. Secondly, that it is a dynamic matter that is interpretable and thereby definable by both authors and audience.

Daniel Chandler, in his book on semiotics, discusses various forms of transtextuality in a different approach. He explains one such form that alludes directly to other texts as being particularly self-conscious:

> *It credits its **audience with the necessary experience** to make sense of such allusions and offers them the **pleasure of recognition**. By alluding to other texts and other media this practice reminds us that we are in a mediated reality, so it can also be seen as an alienatory mode which runs counter to the dominant realist tradition which focuses on persuading the audience to believe in the ongoing reality of the narrative. It appeals to the pleasures of critical detachment rather than of emotional involvement.*[33]

According to Chandler, the notion of intertextuality also problematizes the idea of texts having boundaries and questions the dichotomy of 'inside' and 'outside'. What is 'text' and what is 'context'[34]?

These two theorems, the rewarding for recognition and subsequent **inclusion of the audience** on the one hand and the **ambiguity of music videos' textual boundaries** on the other, seem critical and interesting to me, now more than ever before in the current times and the culture of consumption we are in. Two findings of other chapters of this work are central to this consideration: 1.) a platform of distribution (preferably YouTube) with practically unlimited content and 2.) an

---

[32] Genette (1982), *Palimpsests: Literature in the Second Degree*. The complete model consists of intertextuality, paratextuality, architextuality, metatextuality and hypo-/hypertextuality.

[33] Chandler (2002), *Semiotics—The Basics*, 202.

[34] Ibid., 203, for further reading on this question see e.g.: Obert, Simon (2011): *Komplexitäten und Reduktionen. Zu einigen Prämissen der Popmusikanalyse*, in: Helms, Dietrich & Phleps, Thomas (eds.): *Black Box Pop—Analysen populärer Musik* (vol. 37, pp. 9–22). Bielefeld: transcript.

audience that is highly incited to interact with this platform and through daily use of the internet (unconsciously) is very affine to transtextual comprehension up to the point that it appropriates the internet's textual or cultural 'heritage' to build its own identity (see section 5.4.2).

In my opinion, Chandler's two theorems can be seen linked together in our modern circumstances of music videos in the current zeitgeist: *Because* music videos are **no longer isolated texts**—at least in the way they were during the MTV era and with regard to their mode of consumption[35]—**but integral part (supertext)** of the internet and thereby the internet's users, they automatically appear as something inclusive, not exclusive. I mean exclusive in how the audience needs to be persuaded by an unordinary text of any sort to involve itself emotionally and in contrast to inclusive, in which case the text is already embedded in and part of one's medial concept of the surrounding world.

Chandler's earlier point, the 'crediting the audience with the necessary experience to make sense of such allusions and offering them the pleasure of recognition', is worth taking a closer look at. Because at first sight, it assumes the concept of the 'ideal reader', who understands the work in a way that optimally matches its structure and adopts the interpretive position and aesthetic standpoint put forward by the work[36]. As an example for this, let us take Lady Gaga's *Telephone* (2010) again that clearly adapts a variety of elements from Quentin Tarantino's 'Kill Bill' (Fig 4.6):

Fig. 4.6 Quentin Tarantino—Kill Bill Vol. 1[37] and Lady Gaga feat. Beyoncé—*Telephone*

Here, the ideal reader has seen the movie 'Kill Bill' or at least knows its key elements, is aware of the movie's pop-cultural scope and value, and *also* knows

---

[35] I do not say there haven't been intertextual moments in music videos during the MTV-era, but I mean the isolated single-channel distribution with limited functionalities.

[36] Schmid (2013), *Implied Reader*, Paragraph 11.

[37] Kill Bill: Volume 1, DVD, A Band Apart, Miramax Films, 2003.

4.3 Context, Canons, and Inspiration

Lady Gaga and her preference for and influence on pop culture. He/she links all together in a sensible way, and only then by 'the pleasure of recognition' gets rewarded for getting it right.

While most viewers will probably be able to tell those rather obvious allusions in *Telephone* and thus are indeed 'ideal readers', I think that another concept of reading position might be more critical and interesting in today's music video world and that is Stuart Hall's concept of the **negotiated reading**[38]. I will later discuss this term as one of the central pillars of Cultural Studies' understanding of cultural reception in section 5.1. Here the reader partly shares the text's code and broadly accepts the preferred (ideal) reading, but sometimes resists and modifies it in a way that reflects its own position, experiences, and interests—and this position may involve contradictions. Pop culture, in contrast to other cultures such as the culture of the people of a certain geographic region, is not a fixed matter with rules and one single canon of traditional, cultural elements but represents a complex of mutually interdependent perspectives and values that influence society and its institutions in various ways. Given that, we must accept that there is always a slight variance in individual reception concerning specific codes. This stresses the importance of the reflection of one's own perspective with regard to the music video. A great number of videos offer content that is to be interpreted—matters for negotiated reading, that is. Some allude to pop-cultural elements or techniques, others build their own worlds of meanings and symbols. As a viewer, I have no choice but to confront it with my taste, my pop-cultural knowledge and my transtextual abilities to make individual sense of the video. However, I find it helpful to analyze this matter of negotiated reading **not only in the context of consumption**, as done by Cultural Studies but also in that of **transtextual production**. Music video production on YouTube and similar platforms like vimeo are spaces for prosumers where consumption and reception directly influence production. The concept of potential polysemy resulting in meanings that only appear as a consequence of the recipient's interaction with the texts, makes up for a significant portion of the creative process, too. We can take 'the weirdness' as an aesthetical trend that I discussed in section 3.3 as one example among many others for this:

> *Audiences in fact consist of numerous awkward individuals, whose interpretations and pleasures are complicated, informed and often downright weird.*[39]

---

[38] Hall (1973): *Encoding and Decoding in the Television Discourse*, 17.
[39] In: Cartmell (ed.) (1997): Trash Aesthetics—Popular Culture and its Audience, 1.

I.Q. Hunter and Heidi Kaye write this in their introduction to a work on trash aesthetics, which also uses 'weirdness' from 1997. This diagnosis of mechanisms of receptions just being 'weird' to some degree is rather sober but still acceptable. Since the consumers that interpret existing material in a certain way produce new material themselves, the cycle of meanings getting processed and ending up as 'weird', for example continues. Prosumerism does not stop at the mere interpretation, it constantly gives something back to the discourse. A second observation is that many videos that might get labelled as 'weird' subvert logical reasoning or at least are encrypted to a degree that there cannot be an ideal reader at all and therefore are designed to require negotiated reading.

As a final aspect that leads over to the next subchapter, I want to introduce one last term by Gérard Genette. He also established the 'architextuality'[40] as another one of the five subtypes of transtextuality, meaning a designation of a text as part of a genre or genres. This term in our scenario has multiple dimensions: On the one hand, it is a nod to the motivation of following conventions (section 4.1). If an artist chooses to **designate his or her video to a 'genre'**[41], be it for commercial or other reasons that shall ensure the video's fitting into an existing system, he or she will **make use of certain codes** that preferably have proven to be working in former videos with similar music, target group etc. Genette refers to designation by the text itself, but it could also be applied by the readers.[42] That means that the audience might adjudge a video to have enough impact of some sort to end up in a corpus of music videos with sufficient significance to represent certain qualities. With the architextuality, we have a second (after Bloom's thesis of influence) literary fundament to approach a topic that seems central to me in the prosumer-world: the **importance of canons in the music video world**.

A canon is a collection of official, authentic literary or artistic works that are accepted more or less formally as axiomatic and important. The term dates back to the biblical canon, meaning the selection of books that would constitute the bible before the concept was transferred to literature.[43] Today, the term is much less formal and is used to describe a variety of phenomena. There have been canons, strictly defined or less formal, for various periods of time for international literature, music, and movies (as for example the 'Top 50 movies of all time'

---

[40] Genette (1979, 1992), *The architext: an introduction*, 83–84.

[41] Again, I want to use the term with caution and only in the context of Genette's theory, since we already noticed that conventional genres cannot really be distinguished anymore.

[42] Chandler (2002), *Semiotics—The Basics*, 206.

[43] Pope (2002), *The English studies book: an introduction to language, literature and culture*, 186.

4.3 Context, Canons, and Inspiration

on imbd.com). And so there are for music videos, like 'The best/weirdest/most shocking/funniest/etc. music videos of all time' as they get popularly ranked in blogs and online magazines.[44] These are examples for strictly defined canons, although they serve mainly for entertainment purposes and are not compellingly put together for the target group of prosumers. Another example for a music video canon is the one that I used to study music videos of the late 2010s and that is provided at the end of this work, containing all videos referenced throughout the book. This again contributes to the idea of making the document a research tool itself, as proposed by Thoma et al[45]. And surely, a lot of the videos in 'my canon' will appear on lists by other scholars but also in certain canons. As discussed in the previous subchapter, canons can also be influenced or even defined by the YouTube tutorial community, which basically marks which videos are worth being deconstructed and thereby appreciated. And certainly, every filmmaker has its own collection of music videos, he or she will have (un)consciously in mind when starting a new project. In the next subchapter, I will illustrate this issue in an example.

Concluding this transfer, I want to note that I find treating music videos as a literary or linguistic discipline, like a language in my case, and applying their common analysis tools to be very fruitful. Another relatively modern way of looking at language, which also allows us to see more of the way language works, is Corpus Linguistics. This is a quantitative method and thereby not fitting for my work. However, there are very interesting fields of research within it, like the understanding of creative processes that I find promising for the application on music videos, too.[46]

In the following subchapter, I will look at one particular video that illustrates this last chapter's theoretical discussion with an example and hopefully clarifies some of the appealed thoughts on the contextual side of music video production in the late 2010s.

---

[44] E.g. https://www.rollingstone.com/music/music-lists/the-30-sexiest-music-videos-of-all-time-202547/ (acc. September 4th, 2019) or https://thebiglead.com/2018/04/11/best-music-videos-of-all-time-ranking-top-50/ (acc. September 4th, 2019).

[45] Thoma et al. (2010), *Interactive Publication: The document as a research tool.*

[46] See e.g. Jordanous & Keller (2016), *Modelling Creativity: Identifying Key Components through a Corpus-Based Approach*, https://doi.org/10.1371/journal.pone.0162959, O'Keeffe & McCarthy (2010), *The Routledge Handbook for Corpus Linguistics.*

4.3.1 Deichkind—Wer Sagt Denn Das? \\ Everything is a Remix

I want to introduce a specific video in order to illustrate some of the addressed topics of prosumerism and transtextual working. The electro-Hip-Hop group Deichkind, who are very successful in Germany, and their music video directors, the collective 'Auge Altona', took a progressive and interesting step in their 2019 video *Wer Sagt Denn Das?* (ger. 'But who says that?').

To begin with, the song is, musically speaking, fairly aggressive with a heavy halftime-drumbeat and layered synthesizers around a C minor chord. The lyrics question supposed realities and truths repetitively, almost always initiated with: 'But who says that…?' and thematizes filter bubbles and the difficulties of building an opinion in social media age:

> But who says that I'll be hungover tomorrow, if I drink that? [...] But who says that many clicks mean quality and that we don't just waste time while optimizing ourselves? But who says that this graffiti is really a Banksy? [...]: The signs, the rules, the press, the blog. The popes, the jedi, the haters, the bot. [...]
> [...] The facts from the filter bubble provide proof, experts say they know the score, they discussed a lot and thought for a long time, finally they had the question to all answers.[47]

Musically and lyrically, the song fits very well into Deichkind's former work, and what makes the video particularly interesting for this analysis is that it is a practical example of some of the theses put forward in this book, which I will go into in a second. *Wer Sagt Denn Das?* actually built all their visual outcome on existing material and included eight **links to sources of inspiration in the videos description box**.[48] These lead to four other music videos (Eminem—*The Real Slim Shady* (2000), Tyler, The Creator feat. Kali Uchis—*See You Again* (2018), Jamie xx—*Gosh* (2016) and Gesaffelstein—*Pursuit* (2013)), a scene from 'Matrix Reloaded' and two journalistic visual sources: One video of North Korea's leader Kim Jong Un's car accompanied by running bodyguards and a link to a collection of Chinese crowd formations. Some of these sources' visual content was reenacted almost one-to-one, like a shot from the Matrix-scene. Others were modified slightly and presented in a new garment, like the footage of the bodyguards running along the moving car or the idea of the Crowd Art, which got picked up with duplicating people both analogously and digitally. Here we have a joined form

---

[47] Bogojevic, Hartmann, Klug, Degner, Moser, Duerre, Gruetering, Sultan Günther Music 2019, Translation by the author.

[48] https://www.youtube.com/watch?v=w7KA2LSvsfM.

4.3 Context, Canons, and Inspiration

of **inter- and hypertextuality**, once in the text itself and also backed by actual, technical hyperlinks to the original sources in the description box (Fig 4.7).

The Matrix Reloaded[49]

Wer Sagt Denn Das?

Tyler, The Creator – *See You Again*

Wer Sagt Denn Das?

Daily Mail – Kim's Bodyguards [50]

Wer Sagt Denn Das?

Fig. 4.7 Comparisons between *Wer Sagt Denn Das?* and original references[49,50]

The result is an interesting potpourri whose different parts only the viewer may connect for him- or herself in an individual and sensible way. In an interview with

---

[49] The Matrix Reloaded, DVD, Village Roadshow Pictures, Warner Bros. Pictures, 2003.
[50] https://www.youtube.com/watch?v=Yqu0doiiP7k.

the author, Auge Altona said themselves that there was no real logline for the video, analogously to the lyrics that thematize the lack of liability with online information. Aesthetically and conceptually speaking, it illustrates prosumerism, negotiated reading, and the perception of music videos as a language of pop and internet culture that discusses the medial world by processing it and creating new meaning out of it. This is exactly the working process Salomé Berrocal described in her definition of prosumerism:

> In this conversation, the listener not only consumes this content but responds to and reproduces these messages and creates others almost simultaneously.

In the interview, Auge Altona speak further about their method of working:

> There are quite a lot of topics [in the song] like anonymity on the internet, authorship, filter bubbles and how algorithms shape our opinion and also the populism that arises from that, up to conspiracy theories and structures of power in the world. We worked associatively there and that's how you come to quotes like Kim Jong Un's bodyguards.[51]

They reveal their pool of inspiration for the video and parts of their personal canon by disclosing these exact associations. On the one hand, this is obviously highly interesting for both analysts and other prosumers. They get to understand the process of finding ideas, making aesthetic choices, and eventually finding new videos or directors, which they can include in their respective canon. On the other hand, this is also quite a generous act, as they willingly demystify the creative process and thereby sign the agenda of the prosumer. This is another level than only to release a making-of, as usually known from big and expensive productions and that always include some message of pride of the way the project has been done. Deichkind, by revealing their influences, are basically saying: 'We are just like you; we consume the internet and create our own vision upon the influence it has on us.' And also, they take the '**pleasure of recognition** for the audience', as Chandler says, **to another level**: Those, who actually know the original sources of inspiration, will still get this pleasure. On the other side, one does not necessarily need to recognize the referenced images to understand the video's meaning and context, as they are provided in the links. In the latter case, the pleasure of recognition gets turned around (that is, from the homage to the original), when the audience follows the links in the description box. Thus, Deichkind allows everybody to enjoy transtextual allusions and references, whether the audience is pop-culturally educated or not.

---

[51] Interview with Auge Altona.

4.3 Context, Canons, and Inspiration

Working with YouTube, being an essential source the most important archive of current and past phenomena and trends, as an initial starting point of inspiration is a central part of their creative process, Auge Altona continue: *'The circulation of content always has played a significant role with Deichkind. We quote things and bring them together in new contexts.'* Another technique that they and Deichkind use is to cut so-called mood-films from existing material on YouTube. That means they collect clips that in their opinion reflect the pursued aesthetic, mood or atmosphere and produce a music video 'dummy' for demonstrational purposes.[52] And in the case of *Wer Sagt Denn Das?*, the reenactment and combination of such extremely diverse stand-in footage as action movies from the 1990s, current rap-stars, and bizarre journalistic content culminate in a multilayered, transtextual audiovisual experiment. And it all happens with consciousness about the environment it takes place in:

> *We revealed the references offensively, because we did not want to steal anything from anybody, but rather repeat something in the sense of an homage.*[53]

Deichkind continued to name video references in their following videos <u>Keine Party</u> (2019) and <u>Dinge</u> (2019).

I think this video and the insights in Auge Altona's working process demonstrate adequately how mechanisms in today's prosumer landscape function and how YouTube, transtextuality, inspiration and the treatment of existing material shape the process of music video making in the late 2010s.

---

[52] Ibid.
[53] Ibid.

What is Music Videos' Cultural Impact ?

Cultural

Adjective

/ˈkʌl.tʃər.əl/

1. (WAY OF LIFE)
relating to the habits, traditions, and beliefs of a society

2. (ART)
relating to music, art, theatre, literature, etc.

Impact

Noun

/ˈɪm.pækt/

1. the force or action of one object hit- ting another

2. a powerful effect that something, especially something new, has on a situation or person.[1]

I now want to dedicate a few lines to this term, why I chose it and what dimensions I want to cover with it, before going into the further actual analyses of individual videos in the following chapters. The definitions of the Cambridge dictionary above are a first and general approach to the term and show the term's basic ambiguity in meaning one has to keep in mind when talking about culture. To begin with, I want to approach it by looking at the three matters music, video, and impact.

> *There were times and places – in the Europe of the Middle Ages, as an example – where music might remain largely the same for hundreds of years [...] And it is no coincidence that in medieval times something else also remained quite constant: culture. It is clear to me that changes in music hew closely to changes in society's consensus worldview.*[2]

---

[1] https://dictionary.cambridge.org

[2] https://www.thenewamerican.com/culture/item/17311-influential-beats-the-cultural-impact-of-music (acc. August 8th, 2019).

If we add the internet's and especially YouTube's function as a **cultural accelerator**[3] that is always ahead of its time, we end up with **music videos being an index** of exactly this society's consensus worldview, not only content-related but also aesthetically. Hence, they really are an expression of a Zeitgeist. This is why the linking of music videos to cultural impact suggests itself already. Music videos as space for expression and disseminator of critical reflection have gained subversive potential through their embedding in social media and the algorithm distribution: the ideas and visions depicted in the individual videos are received by more people and from a variety of perspectives, interests, and personal and situational backgrounds. This subversive potential is used to question political conventions of identity, gender, and geopolitics and shape the audience in their aesthetic preferences.

> *[...] Thanks to the insistence of [...] musical and moving image pioneers on honoring the legacies of artists who have come before them, the most evocative and challenging images of black life today can be found in another medium that's being consumed by mass audiences: the music video.*[4]

Danielle Scruggs writes this on artsy.net and takes up the idea of the Renaissance again. Especially in the segment of black music, music videos may even be seen as a new form of audiovisual online activism. But how did that happen?

With the rise of pop culture in the 1950s, one can claim that music at the latest has become the foremost medium to articulate ideas in a mass scale (and is maybe losing that status in younger years due to the pluralization). Thomas Turino explains music's special role of being especially effective at forming ideas and identities with semiotics. He explains music's particular power to create affect, social unity, and purpose (that is identity) with its great multiplicity of potentially meaningful parameters sounding simultaneously and its status as a potential collective.[5]

> *Music has the potential of comprising many signs simultaneously which, like other art forms, makes it a particularly rich semiotic mode. The multicomponent nature of music functions in the same way and can be a multiplication of 'semantic snowballing' in relation to the interpretant: the ambiguity or density of the sign complex*

---

[3] I chose this term according to Lord (2007), *Introduction. In Lord, B. (Eds.), The Manual of Museum Learning.* There he claims that museums can become cultural accelerators by being at the center of the ongoing endeavor to create civil society. This interpretation may very well fit (maybe even better) with the infrastructural spaces of the internet and YouTube.

[4] https://www.artsy.net/article/artsy-editorial-golden-age-black-music-video.

[5] Turino (1999), *Signs of Imagination, Identity, and Experience*, 236.

[...] encourages unanalyzed feeling. It is this multi-componential, and yet non-linear character of musical 'sign bundles' that allow for a [...] creation of complex, densely meaningful musical signs that compound the condensation of meaning, the polysemy, and the affective potential.[6]

Since the early 2000s, digitalization, social media and not only the accompanying visualization that had already been there decades before, but also the '**videolization**', made possible through faster data transfer and cheaper access to the web, arose. Moving images quickly became the most attractive channel to not articulate ideas but to convey and present them. Music videos, once more, built the bridge between the two media and facilitated a potentially highly impactful own medium. Furthermore, they expand Turino's idea with yet another semiotic layer, the images, that allow for a multiplication of the described processes and result in an even higher affective potential.

On a formal and technical layer, music videos' impact on other audiovisual media has been recognized and analyzed in many publications—terms like 'MTV-Aesthetics' (that I mentioned in sections 2.2 and 3.3) are around (and meanwhile even outdated) for some time. Peter Weibel noted already in 1987 that '*music video belongs to the most influential of all media [...] since an important contribution of music video to culture is [...] that **it transforms culture**.*'[7] This statement is part of the fundament of a chapter in 'Music Video After MTV' by Mathias Bonde Korsgaard, in which he explores the influences and relationships music videos have on other media. But how about the research that goes beyond the media-immanent interplay and that interprets culture not as 'relating to music, art, theatre and literature' but to 'the habits, traditions, and beliefs of a society'?

Back in the early days of scholarly research on music videos (then in the context of music television) and their possible effects on society other than being enjoyable, something that could be described as a 'cultural impact' has already been analyzed. I mentioned this field of research that Müller & Behne called 'the critical mass-medial analysis of the medium'. Again, many publications of the late 20th century were culture pessimistic and worrying for the youth regarding music videos. However, fearing the loss of intelligence or emotional numbness, triggered by a new medium with new images has been around for tens or even hundreds of years, covering presumed phenomena like 'reading mania' and possible dangers of using media like radio, television, and movies. I see no evidence of why music videos (especially after almost 40 years since MTV launched) need

---

[6] Ibid., 242.

[7] Weibel (1987), *Was ist ein Videoclip?*, in eds. Bódy/Weibel (1987), Von der visuellen Musik zum Musikvideo, 275.

to be treated differently than other media, concerning their potential to negatively influence young people, which is why I don't want to dive deeper into that matter. Apart from that, scholars dedicated themselves to a different sort of cultural impact as E. Ann Kaplan did in 1987:

> Music television has become a force which influences popular culture in ways that are important for consumer researchers to understand.[8]

Or as Basil Englis did in 1991:

> Thus, the recent development and enormous popularity of music television has the potential to influence consumers via its power to shape consumer culture and also through its influence on commercial structure and positioning.[9]

Both were researching in the field of consumer culture, as the titles of their publications suggest. However, it is noticeable that a very large part of the academia of that time stops at the mere conclusion that music videos *did* influence the viewers and thereby society and does no more than investigating the psychological background of the videos and respective effects on the audience:

> They create a state of sustained tension and attention to what is likely to come next. [...] The visual imagery of music television is often dreamlike and highly ambiguous which should also serve to heighten arousal and attention [...] videos were identified which evoked happiness, poignancy, disgust-anger-scorn, confusion, anxiety and disgust.[10]

That method of research surely is to a certain degree due to the stage of development music videos were at that time. In most cases, they were experimenting with purely artistic or promotional intentions and were not aware of the medium's potential it would have in the future, which is why research also was limited. But the dimensions have changed. An artist, who is uploading a music video today is familiar with the scope the video might take on, even outside the musical world. Every newspaper, every private person on social media or every algorithm can provoke that any video intentionally or unintentionally ends up in public or private discourse and has some sort of cultural or social impact on it. Participatory culture, that we discussed in the last chapter, itself causes cultural impact in both production and consumption, as Henry Jenkins noted: *'Participation [...] refers*

---

[8] Kaplan (1987), *Rocking around the clock. Music Television, Postmodernism and Consumer Culture*.

[9] Englis (1991), *Music Television and Its Influences on Consumer Culture and the Transmission of Consumption Messages*, 111.

[10] Ibid. 112.

5 What is Music Videos' Cultural Impact ?

to properties of the culture, where groups collectively and individually make decisions that have an impact on their shared experiences'. And Eggo Müller claimed already back in 2009: *'YouTube is first and foremost a cultural space of community building and shared experience'*[11]. And again, with music videos being the most popular genre on YouTube, their contribution to those collective decisions and shared experiences is to be considered enormous.

Will Straw stated in an article of 2018, delivering a concrete but pessimistic contribution to our topic: *'Through the videoclip, YouTube has become the largest disseminator of music in the world, but this has diminished rather than magnified the clip's status as cultural form.'*[12] He refers to the already referenced findings of Sunil Manghani (2017), the fact that music videos basically have done their deed, can't hold up with social media, and have become *'little more than the sheathing in which a song is enclosed'*. Still, he grants it to be *'**a highly revealing index of our contemporary cultural condition.**'* Despite being a small side note that is not further discussed, this latter claim is critical to me and coincides with my earlier thesis that music videos are an index of society's textual and aesthetical consensus. From my point of view, several arguments are speaking against Straw's opinions on music videos' diminished cultural status or, more precisely, perspectives that he did not consider: First up, as I already laid out, the discussion around the presumable 'death of the music video' and its many causalities has been debated for decades, and until now it was proven wrong every time. But I admit, this is a rather dull defense of the medium.

Going beyond that in this chapter, I will demonstrate the very impact on different levels current music videos can have on our socio-medial world and vice versa and how an audiovisual product can shape a socio-cultural process in the first place. I will work exemplarily with particular music videos that illustrate the respective levels. Therefore, my analysis is mainly of contextual nature and only exegetical when necessary and fruitful for the chapter's topic. This is also why I only partly follow the classical methodological three-step-process of Description, Analysis, and Interpretation, proposed among others by Christofer Jost[13] or other methods of video-immanent analysis by Carol Vernallis[14]. I selected the videos either because they stand exemplary for certain phenomena to be analyzed, such as participatory culture in a music video or reflection of socio-political conditions,

---

[11] Müller, E. (2009), *Where quality matters: Discourses on the art of making a YouTube video*, 126.

[12] Straw (2018), *Music Video in its Contexts: 30 Years Later.*

[13] Jost et al. (2013), *Computergestützte Analyse von audiovisuellen Medienprodukten*, 58.

[14] Vernallis (2004), *Experiencing Music Video*, 199.

or they illustrate a certain contemporary condition of the music video medium that yet facilitates the respective outcome.

The following chapter is subdivided into different subchapters: First, providing a theoretical background and then looking into actual music videos respecting the following three chapters, in order to be able to demonstrate and cover the forms I find worth analyzing in which music videos are impacting culture. These are:

1. Observing culture
2. Generating culture
3. Appropriating culture

This construction is inspired by reflections by sociologists like Jürgen Straub and his handbook on intercultural communication[15] and media academics findings about participatory culture, for example the already mentioned five characteristics of participatory culture by Jenkins et al. Furthermore this model correlates with my experiences from the prosumer-perspective of what make music videos culturally relevant.

The first subchapter 'observing culture' represents a rather widely interpretable form of confrontation with culture, meaning I want to cover videos that reflect their surrounding culture in any form, whether it be through criticizing and just portraying it. This concept of discussing culture is always of an intentional nature on the artists or the director's side. What these possible intentions could be and how they manifest in music videos shall be subject to this subchapter. The next one, 'generating culture', could colloquially be translated with 'trend-setting', suggesting that this chapter covers videos that in some form, intentional or unintentional, trigger a cultural or social imitation of the videos visual and/or lyrical appearance. The belief that individual contributions matter[16] to a public discussion or even cultural actions is key to the assumption that music videos may 'generate culture'. Finally, the third subchapter that seems worth analyzing to me is 'appropriating culture', in which I will explore the handling and the use of elements of one culture adopted by another culture in music videos. I chose this parameter also because it is subject to a current and vivid scholarly discourse, especially in the context of art and media, and I want to contribute to it.

The transitions between those chapters or rather the different approaches to culture in the videos can be somewhat overlapping, nevertheless, focuses are

---

[15] Straub, Jürgen et al. (2007), *Handbuch interkultureller Kommunikation und Kompetenz: Grundbegriffe—Theorien—Anwendungsfelder*, 429.

[16] Jenkins et al (2006), *Fans, bloggers, and gamers: Exploring participatory culture*, xi.

5 What is Music Videos' Cultural Impact ?

set in each following analysis. These parameters are by no means a universally applicable categorization that every music video can be fitted in, it is a proposal for the analytical debate on music videos' treatment of culture. And although all these phenomena aren't new or particularly representing our current time, they have to be reconsidered under the current technological and medial circumstances differently than they would have been twenty years ago. In the analyses of this chapter I will combine the two categories of research of music videos as defined by Müller & Behne—On the one hand the analysis of the product itself and on the other hand the one of its effect and reception and how one affects the other.

Firstly, we have to consider the mere dimensions in that music videos are consumed/prosumed in recent years: in 2008, when music videos due to commercialization and self-copying seemingly were facing their ruin[17], Markus Altmeyer describes the symbiosis of song and video with the words:

> 'A clip popularizes the song and the song popularizes the clip. The popular music video thus must be fitting for mainstream.[18]'.

This quite narrowing and homogenizing condition claims on one hand that it is exclusively reserved for the 'mainstream', to produce music videos and on the other hand it demonstrates that the term of 'mass suitability', at the latest with the democratization of technology and resources, has been relativized. A music video can be an absolute niche product, aloof from traditional 'mass-culture', but still can have over a million views in YouTube (for example *Spirit Quest Journey* (2011) by Professor Soap[19]). It won't constitute any competition to a video with a view number 100 times higher, but nevertheless, one has to speak about a 'mass' concerning the reached audience, which would have been remarkable in the early days of YouTube. Hence, the terminology of 'mass and mainstream suitability' is to be handled with care, also in their meaning of possible cultural impact. Videos with comparably small audiences, like 50,000—100,000 clicks, objectively speak to a significant number of people that, through YouTube's multiple functionalities, debate, share and process them.

---

[17] *'The thoroughly justified impression emerges that now even the music video as the last resort of innovation within pop culture, got devoured by the culture industry.'* (Altmeyer, 2003, 45).

[18] Altmeyer (2003), *Die Filme und Musikvideos von Michel Gondry—Zwischen Surrealismus, Pop und Psychoanalyse*, 42.

[19] https://www.youtube.com/watch?v=NNJureMTeZA Professor Soap—*Spirit Quest Journey*.

In 'Understanding New Media—Extending Marshall McLuhan', Robert Logan asserts that digital media have obsolesced mass media[20]. Taking YouTube and its former slogan 'Broadcast Yourself' as an example, there is no need for centralized TV stations or other big media houses anymore because production and consumption have pluralized significantly. This, by the way, it did before according to quote McLuhan's famous claim: *'the photocopier made every man a publisher'*.[21] Sticking with McLuhan and his arguably most famous line 'the medium is the message', we have to assume that there is no music video that is not mass suitable. Because every video in its audiovisual concept being the message being the medium being (in most occasions) YouTube, is part already part of a singular mass, in this case the biggest video-platform[22] on the current internet. In 1997, Cultural Studies researcher Lawrence Grossberg formulated similar thoughts and defined the 'mainstream' not by certain texts or audiences but by the relation of cultural practices and their relative social contexts. Hence, there cannot be one homogenous mainstream, but only a variety of overlapping styles that compete for public attention[23].

Until here I now have discussed some existing scholarly work on the topic 'Impact and Music Videos' and formulated an array of ideas and problems that shall be the point of departure for the chapters to follow.

5.1 A Short Theoretical Context

To be able to give that background, I must start with the phenomenon of culture itself, which, especially in the research field of media, has been covered a lot with rather differing results and facets. I want to critically review existing theories on culture and its relationship with social reactions and finally apply them to our modern world and, more precisely, on the topic of music videos. I want to find out how a theory on music videos and their possible cultural impact can be built on that foundation.

Of course, all observations and theories on culture heavily depend on the definition of culture at all. The 'classical perception of culture' emerged in the late 18th and early 19th century and has been used especially by German historians

---

[20] Logan (2010), *Understanding New Media—Extending Marshall McLuhan*, 40.
[21] Ibid., 182.
[22] And media host in general, including e.g. YouTube Music and YouTube Originals.
[23] Winter (1999), *Spielräume des Vergnügens und der Interpretation*, in: Engelmann (1999), Die kleinen Unterschiede—Der Cultural Studies Reader, 45.

5.1 A Short Theoretical Context

and philosophers to differentiate from the term of civilization.[24] Here, culture is understood as the refinement of one's abilities by adopting humanist works and art and is clearly privileging certain values over others, implying a hierarchy of symbolic forms and cultural practices. This concept is, of course, widely criticized for its exclusivity and inflexibility; John B. Thompson explains its origin as follows: '*This privilege accorded to certain works and values was linked to the self-affirmation and self-image of the German intelligentsia and, more generally, to the confident belief in progress associated with the European Enlightment.*'[25] Andreas Reckwitz in the year 2000, called this idea the 'normative concept of culture', dissociating it from the 'totality-oriented concept', which refuses any hierarchy between individual works and even cultures and focuses on the entirety of ways of thinking and acting.[26] He concludes:

> '*Cultural phenomena, on this account, may be seen as symbolic forms in structured contexts; and cultural analysis may be regarded as the study of the meaningful constitution and social contextualization of symbolic forms.*'

Moving on, I want to briefly summarize some more concrete and influential theses on culture, starting in the first half of the 20th century and continuing chronologically. In 1940, **Ernst Cassirer** perceived the human being as an 'animal symbolicum' (symbolic creature) that, through his ability to work with symbols, has raised from other animals, but for the price of being bound to those self-made symbols:

> *[Man] has surrounded himself with linguistic forms, artistic images, mystical symbols and religious rites in a measure that he cannot see or recognize anything, without having this artificial medium shoving itself between him and reality.*[27]

Four years later, **Max Horkheimer and Theodor W. Adorno** developed the concept of the **Culture Industry**, saying that this conditioned bond between mankind and symbols is imperatively to be claimed and shaped by capitalist systems, resulting in the perception of culture as goods and thus a significant shift in the culture's content and meaning. Whereas earlier, according to Horkheimer and Adorno, culture has been autonomous, critical, and emancipative, in the age of

---

[24] Elias (1986), Bd. 1, 14.

[25] Thompson (1990), *Ideology and Modern Culture: Critical Social Theory in the Era of Mass Communication*, 125.

[26] Reckwitz (2000), *Die Transformation der Kulturtheorien. Zur Entwicklung eines Theorieprogramms*, 64.

[27] Cassirer (1940), 50.

late capitalism, culture devotes itself to a means of an end, which is generating capital. Artists must find buyers of their works and thereby adapt to him/her and lose the critical moment of their art. And finally, the communication between artist and costumer is not given, since the costumer (spoken from Culture Industry's perspective) does not demand but just lets the artist deliver. Two central findings of Horkheimer and Adorno thus are: a) The Culture Industry reduces the individual person to his/her function as costumer/consumer and b) The Culture Industry feeds the costumers trivial and shallow content. What does not conform with the Culture Industry gets struck by economic powerlessness and is easily surrendered to insufficiency. Horkheimer illustrates the relation of audience and industry very drastically as an inevitable dependency[28]. Up to the affirmation that even a person's most intimate reactions are reified to him-/herself to that extent that the actual idea of their peculiarity only persists in extreme abstraction[29]. This is because he cannot differentiate between his own personality and desires and the image imposed by the 'triumph of advertising'. Hence, the Frankfurt School supposes a directing and decisive top-down culture industry, which leads to believe the recipients to have autonomy and freedom: *'The costumer is not king, as the culture industry wants to make him believe, he is not its subject, but its object'*[30], says Adorno.

The Cultural Studies relativize this unambiguous encoded and dictating message under consideration of the reception aesthetic[31]. Here, culture is understood as *'a process of communication, in which new common senses emerge permanently between historically given and individually created meanings'*[32]. Pop-cultural products are to be read as texts with a potential polysemy, with the consequence that their meaning cannot be understood as something fix and inherent but only result in the recipient's interaction with the texts, making them a **matter of negotiation**. A central statement of the British Cultural Studies regarding qualitative research of media is that medial texts do not exist just by themselves but always in variably structured social contexts, which in turn participate in forming a text's meaning[33]. John B. Thompson, therefore, defines media analysis *'as the study of symbolic forms [...] in relation to the historically specific and socially structured contexts*

---

[28] Horkheimer (1944/2008): *Dialektik der Aufklärung: Philosophische Fragmente*, 134.

[29] Ibid., 176.

[30] Adorno (1967), *Resumé über die Kulturindustrie*, 60.

[31] Altmeyer (2008), Die Filme und Musikvideos von Michel Gondry, 36.

[32] Ibid., 38.

[33] Winter (1995), *Der produktive Zuschauer—Medienaneignung als kultureller und ästhetischer Prozess*, 108.

5.1 A Short Theoretical Context

and processes within which [...] these symbolic forms are produced, transmitted and received.'[34]

These definitions in the context of music videos and the growing participance of the fans suggest that the audience more and more not only is part of the reception, but part of the concept, the 'message' as well, to quote Marshall McLuhan once again. This link between the Cultural Studies and McLuhan's 'the medium is the message' is very well illustrated by the case of music videos.

In Lawrence Grossberg's 'Re-placing Popular Culture' one can find a definition of culture being almost a biological necessity, a similar interpretation to Cassirer's 'animal symbolicum'. Following Grossberg, culture fills *'in for the lack of an adequate instinctual apparatus in human beings [... It] is that which mediates between people and reality, turning chaos into order.'*[35] Following that idea, scholars of the Cultural Studies presume that media has power at least in that measure as to provide categories and frames in which members of a society perceive and interpret reality. Because they provide the most differentiated and realistic perspective on complex matters of media practice.

> *[One of culture's most relevant functions is] the provision and the selective construction of social knowledge, of social imagery, through which we perceive the 'worlds', the 'lived realities' of others, and imaginarily reconstruct their lives and ours into some intelligible 'world-of-the-whole', some 'lived-totality'.*[36]

Hence, Horkheimer's and Adorno's theory of the Culture Industry and the Cultural Studies do not necessarily rule each other out, as also Friedrich Krotz points out:

> *The underlying concept of culture consisting of cultural objects, produced under industrial and capitalist aspects, finds itself in the Cultural Studies in the popular triad of culture, media and power, thought in a different direction, but still basically the same.*[37]

Summing up so far, I briefly outlined some general concepts of culture that shall be consulted again later in the different examinations of specific analyses and observations. What we have, is **culture as a human necessity**, manifested in either text or way of life, as something on the one hand socially generated and equally deconstructed on the other. **Culture mediates our perception of reality**.

---

[34] Thompson (1990), *Ideology and Modern Culture—Critical Social Theory in the Era of Mass Communication.*, 136.

[35] Redhead et al. (1997), *The Clubcultures Reader*, 221.

[36] Hall (1977), *Culture, the Media, and the Ideological Effect*, 340.

[37] Krotz (2006), *Gesellschaftliches Subjekt und kommunikative Identität*, 117.

I also noted the tension between **power and cultural texts** and their effects on ways of life as a strongly debated matter, making it one considerable component of what accounts for cultural impact. Of course, all the theories must be read in their historical context and may not be transferred analogously to current times. For example, the theses of the Frankfurt School are some 80 years old as one has to keep in mind. While they are understandable and certainly applicable to some parts of the medial world of production and consumption we can observe today, they clearly do neither represent all of the producers' intentions and nor all the consumers' attitude of reception, as the results from previous chapters, especially the participatory culture, show. As the Frankfurt School calls them, the costumers today are neither subject nor object, but an integral part of production. I will discuss the viability of the mentioned theories more concretely in the following chapters. Moving closer to the cultural texts of choice in this work that are music videos, I want to address one last, more concrete aspect to this work by Simon Frith: *'What makes music special as a cultural practice, is its sociability'*[38]. Given our findings of chapter 3, especially the enormous number of social feedback channels and functionalities Paula Hearsum pointed out, contemporary music videos might provide an even more dynamic field of research as cultural practice.

In the following, I want to present examples of music videos concerning the three parameters *Observing, Generating* and *Appropriating* culture. I will especially focus on music video's sociability and aim to analyze it in the context of the Cultural Studies' triad of culture, media, and power. By doing so, I hopefully can work out new perspectives on music videos and their social and cultural impact. I must point out that the following processes and phenomena described are not necessarily reserved exclusively for music videos, but can also take place in other media, offers and expressions of popular culture such as music itself. However, in this work, music videos are not explicitly compared with other media offerings[39], which is why I will take the liberty of looking at music videos in isolated form at first.

---

[38] Frith (1999), *Unscharfe Grenzmarkierungen*, in: Die kleinen Unterschiede: Der Cultural Studies Reader, 171.

[39] Jacke (2003), *Kontextuelle Kontingenz—Musikclips im wissenschaftlichen Umgang*, 33–34, Schmidt (2002), *Medienwissenschaft im Verhältnis zu Nachbardisziplinen*, 56–57.

5.2 Observing Culture

'Observing' is a term that must be clarified because no product results yet from pure observation. In this chapter, I understand the observation of certain parts of one's surrounding culture as the point of departure for certain music videos. This observation, or say, the perspective from where artists see and reflect their environment, can be very diverse. However, in their entirety of doing so they form a mirror of society which makes them very powerful as a medium and important for scholarly research and society itself. Again, music videos (culture) mediate our reception of reality. The audience can identify with the contents, can share, or refuse the videos' comments or at least can feel somehow connected to them because they speak of something from their everyday lives. In the next subchapters I want to demonstrate two examples of observations that result in extremely different music videos, *#SELFIE* (2014) by The Chainsmokers and *I'm Not Racist* (2017) by Joyner Lucas, but in my opinion root from a comparable starting point.

5.2.1 The Chainsmokers—#SELFIE \\ The Mirror in the Mirror

The first video I want to take a closer look at is the 2014 breakthrough hit by the US-American future-bass duo 'The Chainsmokers'. *#SELFIE* is a straightforward EDM (Electronic Dance Music) song that in its video features a clubbing scene with a protagonist and many, many selfies submitted by celebrities and fans. For the submission, The Chainsmokers uploaded a separate video[40] with instructions and a link to a 15-second piece of the song that the fans could use to lip-sync etc., making the project genuinely interactive and crowd sourced. It was directed and produced by Taylor Stevens and Ike Love Jones, who, other than that until now, have not directed music videos, and at the time of writing, it counts over half a billion views on YouTube. *#SELFIE* is an exact commentary about the youth and media culture of 2014. Visually, the verses consist of the protagonist in a club's bathroom speaking rhetorically to her friends while they fix their makeup and wardrobe, cut together extremely fast, and rushed with shots on dance floors. The hook's (or chorus, as one would say in other musical genres) visuals are mainly rapidly changing selfies, both stills, and videos, layered on top of clubbing scenes (Fig 5.1).

---

[40]. https://www.youtube.com/watch?v=54ILwmcLuZY.

Fig. 5.1 *#SELFIE* is a colorful and ecstatic collage of club scenes, selfies, and the protagonist in the bathroom. Only here and there can one spot a selfie by a celebrity such as David Hasselhoff, the rest of the visuals is cut so fast that single images simply blend into a single rush of visual impressions

There is no singer in this song nor a sung melody, the lyrics are basically a monologue by the protagonist, played by Lindsey Diane, a model and blogger from the US, in which she rants about herself and other people and their appearance and their on- and offline behavior:

> *When Jason was at the table*
> *I kept on seeing him look at me while he was with that other girl*
> *Do you think he was just doing that to make me jealous?*
> *[...]*
> *Did you think that girl was pretty?*
> *How did that girl even get in here?*
> *Do you see her?*
> *She's so short and that dress is so tacky*
> *Who wears Cheetah?*
> *[...]*
> *After we go to the bathroom, can we go smoke a cigarette?*
> *I really need one*
> *But first,*
> *Let me take a selfie*
> *[...]*
> *Wait, pause, Jason just liked my selfie*

> *What a creep*
> *[...]*
> *That girl is such a fake model*
> *She definitely bought all her Instagram followers*
> *Who goes out on Mondays?*
> *[...]*
> *Oh my God, Jason just texted me*
> *Should I go home with him?*
> *I guess I took a good selfie*[41]

It is obvious that the protagonist is portrayed as a cliché persona who is judging and condemning other people by things and behaviors she very obviously does herself as well, which is the point and the humor of the whole video. Now, one could think until here that the video is criticizing or making fun of the depicted people. However, by showing tons of fan-selfies and thereby rewarding them for having sent in their pictures, it simultaneously embraces the selfie-culture and the triviality. #SELFIE really is a mirror in the mirror. It does not hold up the mirror to society to make them reflect or criticize it, but just to be another part of it and keep the momentum going. At the end, it even says: *'Didn't see your SELFIE? Watch the video again'*, which, granted, is a very clever way to generate even more views but follows only the psychologic rewarding principle of getting satisfaction from (maybe) spotting one's own picture in a mass of others. This is comparable to getting pleasure from getting likes on uploaded photos that actually don't necessarily stand out from the mass but just contribute to a whole medial system we pay attention to and not the individual posts. This again applies well to McLuhan's famous line: 'the medium is the message'.

Another considerable component is the music. As I mentioned, it is very much straightforward, with the verses repeatedly building a rise-up, ending in a four-on-the-floor hook. The hook-line, played by a nasal square-waved synthesizer over a simple bass and drums, resembles to a great extend the well-known hook-line from 'We no speak americano' (2010) by Yolanda Be Cool & DCUP (Fig. 5.2) (Fig. 5.3).

The Chainsmokers apparently approach their music equally as their visuals (or maybe directors Taylor Stephens and Ike Love Jones did the other way around): They make use of existing song structures, sounds, and even melodies to create

---

[41] Taggart, Dim Mak Inc. 2014.

Fig. 5.2 Hook-line (excerpt) from "#SELFIE"

Fig. 5.3 Hook-line (excerpt) from 'We no speak americano'

something like a musical selfie of EDM. Additionally, the reference to Sir-Mix-A-Lot's 'Baby Got Back' (1992), in that white women talk in a remarkably similar intonation about another woman's appearance, is not to be overseen:

> *It is so big, she looks like*
> *One of those rap guys girlfriends.*
> *But, ya know, who understands those rap guys?*
> *They only talk to her, because,*
> *She looks like a total prostitute, kay?*
> *I mean, her butt, is just so big*
> *I cant believe its just so round, it'"s like out there*
> *I mean gross, look*
> *She's just so, black*[42]

Together with the video, it forms the perfect homage to the mass culture of 2014, and pseudo-criticizes/reflects and embraces it at the same time. Now, this tension between reflecting and (re)producing reminds Simon Frith and his question of how art comes to make its own claims under varied circumstances. He himself writes in 'Music and Identity': '*The issue is not how a particular piece of music or performance reflects the people, but how it produces them, how it creates and constructs an experience [...] that we can only make sense of by taking on both a subjective and collective identity.*'[43] First up, one already can see how close to each other and sometimes linked *Observing* and *Generating* culture really are. What are the consequences of either imitating existing artistic elements or

---

[42] Ray, Universal Music Publishing, 1992.
[43] Frith (2011), *Music and Identity*, in: Hall, du Gay (2011), Question of Cultural Identity, 109.

'producing' them in order to give people the opportunity to make sense of it? And do these questions actually rule out each other?

#SELFIE indeed creates an experience that is easy to relate to, that is, taking on a subjective identity due to a simple and familiar audiovisual style. The collective identity for me manifests in different layers: First, there is the decision to include literally hundreds of fans in the actual video and thus creating a low-threshold fan relation. Therefore, we come across another facet of participatory culture again. The other part is the enormous number of views the video has. With over 500 million views, the viewer knows that what he/she is watching, and possibly engaging to, already has got a community around the world that again already built a subjective identity on the video and that he/she can now be a part of.

The Chainsmokers made it their concept to reproduce existing audiovisual and cultural (both in the meaning of text and way of life) elements, which earned them great successes like <u>Closer</u> (2016) and <u>Paris</u> (2017). These are oriented heavily to Instagram-travel-trends that again have among others been established by social media stars like Jay Alvarrez, who made <u>travel-videos</u> that formally are hard to distinguish from The Chainsmokers' music videos or also, <u>The Ocean</u> (2016) by Mike Perry. These, just as the KENZO World ad by Spike Jonze, are further cases of needing to overthink the limits and definitions of music videos (Fig. 5.4).

5.2.2 Joyner Lucas—I'm Not Racist \\ Sit Down, Be Humble!

I continue with another example that is drastically different in aesthetics and content. Before I start, I must remind the reader again that I mentioned at the beginning of this chapter that the transitions between the parameters Observing, Generating, and Appropriating might be blurry, and <u>I'm not Racist</u> (2017) by US-American rapper Joyner Lucas is a perfect example for that. It provides a very detailed observation of the current American society regarding problematics of race relations while at the same time reflecting it constructively and even offering a solution. This example ranges right on edge between observing and generating culture. Still, here I want to focus on the ways and methods the video uses to deal with existing political grievances and what makes it so special at it, so the subchapter of Observing Culture seems adequate to me.

'I'm not Racist' definitely is not a 'conventional' Hip-Hop-track, with its most apparent characteristics being its length with 6:55 minutes and its extremely minimalistic and mantra-like half-time-beat that really isn't a beat: It's in the key of B

Fig. 5.4 The Chainsmokers—*Closer*, Paris, Mike Perry—*The Ocean*, Jay Alvarrez & Alexis Ren—*Summer (2015)*[44]. All feature a couple with a young guy and a female model that are having a great time at some holiday destination. All are very popular, meaning they count from 30 million to 2,5 billion views each

minor and for most parts features a motif of G, A# and B, played by a warm and clean synthesizer with rich overtones, sometimes doubled by a synth bass. Very occasionally on lyrical climaxes, only once in the first verse, at 02:34 minutes into the song, and more often in the second verse, a very reduced drumbeat comes in, but only for three to eight bars each. Between the verses and in the outro a Fender Rhodes is playing jazzy, almost cheesy chords with a soft synth melody on top. Scarce atmospheric sounds, a brief, recurring piano riff, and percussions on count three are the only other musical elements apart from Lucas's rapping. This rather unusual minimalism in Hip-Hop already is a sign for the lyrics' significance and downright urges the listener to pay great attention to them. The song is divided in two verses, forming a dialogue, or rather, two monologues of two men (both lip syncing to Joyner Lucas' rapping), having very oppositional perspectives and opinions about black culture in the USA. The first one is portrayed as a white and corpulent male, wearing a plain shirt and red cap with the slogan 'Make America Great Again', an apparent intertextual reference to Donald Trump's electoral campaign 2016. The man delivering the second verse is a black

---

[44] https://www.youtube.com/watch?v=P22gcb4YHso.

male wearing a Wildcats sports sweater and braids. They both tell their stories and explain their standpoints:

> *With all due respect*
> *I dont have pity for you black niggas, that"s the way I feel*
> *Screami'' "Black Lives Matter"*
> *All the black guys rather be deadbeats than pay your bills*
> *Yellin' "Nigga this" and "Nigga that"*
> *Call everybody "Nigga" and get a nigga mad*
> *As soon as I say "Nigga" then everyone react*
> *And wanna swing at me and call me racist 'cause I ain't black*
> *[...]*
> *Talkin' about slavery like you was around back then*
> *Like you was pickin' cotton off the fuckin' ground back then*
> *Like you was on the plantation gettin' down back then, Aight, look*
> *I see a black man aimin' his gun*
> *But I'd rather see a black man claimin' his son*
> *[...]*
> *I'm not racist, my sister's boyfriend's black'm not racist, my sister-in-law'*
> *Is baby cousin Tracy*
> *Got a brother and his girlfriend's black*
> *[...]*
> *I worship the Einsteins, study the Steve Jobs*
> *But you ride 2Pac's dick like he was a fuckins dick like he was a fuckin' god, oh my god!*
> *And all you care about is rappin'*
> *And stuntin' and bein ratchet, and that's the nigga within you*
> *Music rotting your brain and slowly start to convince you*
> *Then you let your kids listen and then the cycle continues*
> *Blame it all on the menu, blame it on those drinks*
> *Blame it on everybody except for your own race*
> *Blame it on white privileges, blame it on white kids*
> *[...]*
> *It's like we livin' in the same buildin' but split into two floors*
> *I'm not racist*
> *But there's two sides to every story, I wish that I knew yours...*
> *I wish that I knew yours*
> *I'm not racist, I swear*

> *With all disrespect*
> *I don't really like you white motherfuckers, that's just where I'm at*
> *Screaming "All Lives Matter"*
> *Is a protest to my protest, what kind of shit is that?*
> *And that's one war you'll never win*
> *The power in the word "Nigga" is a different sin*
> *We shouldn't say it but we do, and that just what it is*
> *But that don't mean that you can say it just 'cause you got nigga friends*
> *[…]*
> *You wanna copy our slang and everything that we know*
> *Tryna steal black culture and then make it your own, whoa*
> *[…]*
> *Yeah, I praise 2Pac like he was a fuckin' god*
> *He was fighting for his life right before he fuckin' died nigga, die nigga!*
> *And all you care about is money and power*
> *And being ugly and that's the cracker within you*
> *Hatred all in your brain, it slowly start to convince you*
> *And then you teach it to your children until the cycle continue*
> *Blame it on Puerto Rico, blame it on OJ*
> *Blame it on everybody, except for your own race*
> *[…]*
> *I love you but I fuckin' hate you at the same time*
> *I wish we could trade shoes or we could change lives*
> *So we could understand each other more but that'd take time*
> *I'm not racist*
> *It's like we livin' in the same buildin' but splittin' the both sides*
> *I'm not racist*
> *But there's two sides to every story and now you know mine*
> *[…]*[45]

Joyner Lucas and Ben Proulx directed the music video from 2017 and, at the time of writing, counts over 121 million views on YouTube[46]. It is playing a similarly minimalistic role as the beat: they both leave very much space and attention for the lyrics and the actors' performances. The whole video is set in one location, a kind of empty warehouse with nothing more than two chairs and a table in it. And all the two men do, is talk to each other, both first calmly and then, as the

---

[45] Lucas, WEA International Inc. 2017.
[46] https://www.youtube.com/watch?v=43gm3CJePn0.

5.2 Observing Culture

verses progress, with more and more rage, ending up in one of them eventually knocking the table over. At the end of each verse, though, they calm down again physically and also lyrically: *'But there's two sides to every story, I wish that I knew yours...'*. Over the span of each verse, the listening actor's reactions evolve, too: Each first lines they listen with defiance, neglection, and even disgust. However, as the arguments become more detailed and personal, they both show signs of understanding and contemplation. At the very end of the video (*'But there's two sides to every story and now you know mine'*), they even manage to hug each other. Maybe Lucas and Proulx were indeed inspired by Kendrick Lamar's line from *Humble*: *'Bitch, sit down, be humble!'*... In fact, the visual approach of two people sitting at a table in the video is essential to it and also to the song. Without this concentrated and minimalist setting, the viewer or listener would not be so absorbed in the events, the argumentation, and the reactions of both sides (Fig. 5.5).

Fig. 5.5 Joyner Lucas—*I'm not Racist*. Two stereotypical men are staged in an empty hall and argue out the lyrics, rapped by Lucas. Although the content and body language is rough, they never attack their opposite physically and sit through the others' thoughts. Separated by opinion, attitude and camerawork at first, they come closer to each other over the video's timespan and finally even come to an understanding

Knocking over the table is on the one side, destroying their basis for discussion, as it is the place on which they sit down to talk to each other. But on the other side, by eliminating the thing that stands between them, the man only makes possible the physical closeness for the final hug.

The way this video observes and reflects its surrounding cultural issues and how it seems to hit a nerve in society deserves special attention. The directness with which music and video speak, the unencrypted and pure language, the sparse set and simple but tense plot has as effect that everybody *must* build an opinion on the video. It leaves no excuses whatsoever. No effects, no groovy beat, nor anything else one could satisfy him-/herself with, while ignoring the video's real message. This also is a great example of how a music video *'produces the people, how it creates and constructs an experience [...] that we can only make sense of by taking on both a subjective and collective identity'*, as Simon Frith put it.

Of course, there are countless other and drastically different examples for music videos that take the observation of certain parts of one's surrounding culture as their point of departure. What they all have in common, though, and what makes 'Observing Culture' a viable approach of analysis and production to me is their contribution to forming a mirror of society. A visual mirror that reflects habits, issues, and topics to be processed in a certain time—**it reflects the Zeitgeist.** This is another strong component of music videos being a 'cultural melting-pot' that I mentioned in the introduction. In the following, I want to discuss two more.

5.3 Generating Culture

As I marked in the introduction to this chapter, I define *generating* culture as everything that **entails some form of imitational or triggered reaction**. For example, this can be the mere influence music videos have on fashion and style trends. In 2017 Vevo published a white paper on that topic. This study certainly is biased because of its lack of independence. Nevertheless, it demonstrates that especially the generation Z and millennials have a strong affinity towards musicians and their sense of style:

> *The apparel worn in music videos can create the latest trends, from Beyoncé's kale sweatshirt (from 'Flawless') to Drake's Moncler puffer jacket ('Hotline Bling'). [...] Beauty also plays a role in an artist's signature look, from Adele's winged eyeliner to Taylor Swift's vintage red lipstick. These videos make a mark on pop culture, and in turn, create an opportunity for brands to connect with key consumers.*[47]

---

[47] http://hq.vevo.com/white-paper-influential-music-videos-beauty-style/?lang=gb (acc. September 12th, 2019).

5.3 Generating Culture

Some artists even wear and promote their own clothing labels in their videos, such as Jay Z's 'Rocawear' or Tyler, the Creator's 'Golf'.

Generating culture can also be the simple joy of imitating specific dance moves of a certain music video as it was the case with *The Ketchup Song (Aserejé)* (2002) by Las Ketchup, or more recent, Psy's *Gangnam Style* (2012), or even more recent, *SKIBIDI* (2018) by Little Big. All these cases generated a virality of thousands of videos with parodies and imitations of the respective dances, uploaded by users from all over the world. Applying a theory by Gina Arnold, their 'cultural impact' is based on a rather transparent formula that is 1.) a straightforward dance routine, 2.) an incitement to audience participation (e.g. in the case of Little Big, creating the #skibidichallenge) and 3.) humor.[48] Hence, cultural impact is, to some extent and given the right marketing, calculable. The app TikTok launched in 2018 and already in 2019 was the most downloaded app in the app-stores[49], takes this concept to the next level. It is based on the concept of people making videos with lip sync and specific dance choreographies to short clips of music that are up to 60 seconds long. They then can apply all sorts of filters to make their clips as attractive as possible. Especially among teenagers, the app often is a multiplicator for streams, as was the case with Billy Ray Cyrus' feat. Lil Nas X *Old Town Road*. It was the trigger for the hashtag #yeehaw on TikTok in that users imitated dance moves from the music video and other western-related scenes while every time sampling the song. A compilation of some of those videos can be found here. The videos under this hashtag reached over 67 million views and significantly impacted the streams on other platforms such as Spotify.[50]

Apart from that, music videos can have cultural impact on their own medium, like the mentioned auteurs of the 1990's like Chris Cunningham, Spike Jonze or Hype Williams did with establishing new standards and styles in their genres that still are noticeable today. Infrastructural innovations may impact the medium, too: The launch of YouTube in 2005 massively changed the concept of the music video (chapter 3). The example of Thom Yorke's *Anima* being released not on YouTube but on Netflix (section 3.5) might trigger a new era of appreciation for music videos going so far as for the consumers to actually pay for them, which shall be interesting to observe in the future.

---

[48] Arnold (2017), *Music/Video—Histories, Aesthetics, Media*, 248.

[49] https://www.businessinsider.de/tech/tiktok-wird-inzwischen-oefter-heruntergeladen-als-whatsapp-2019-9/ (acc. June 19th, 2020).

[50] https://time.com/5561466/lil-nas-x-old-town-road-billboard/ (acc. June 19th, 2020).

Since music videos are pop-cultural products and process existing material, it is no surprise that they have become a matter for other pop-cultural processing themselves. For instance, this is where we enter the wide field of parodies in their multiple forms and styles. One noteworthy example is the phenomenon of so-called 'musicless' music videos: Here, users remove the audio track from 'real' music videos and replace it with self-made foley and atmosphere sounds, so that a singer performs awkwardly on a silent stage or dances in a quiet street and the only things audible are for example footsteps, breaths and a barking dog in the background. Their appeal is due to the new and absurd contextualization of the original with that the viewer is familiar. This format is extremely popular on YouTube with hundreds of such parodies by different users and is even subject to scholarly research.[51]

Original music videos also might imply some sort of imperative, for instance, an encouragement to engage in acts of greater social responsibility, which is something Carol Vernallis dedicated a few lines to in 'Experiencing Music Video' and in the context of Whitney Houston's *Step by Step* (1997). She notes, the video might be capable of raising consciousness and engagement in volunteerism by showing people doing generous things, such as saving a child from a burning house or people helping each other out on the streets, intercut with dancing people having a good time. Through the formal linking of the two visual segments, consequential, psychological reactions are triggered, which is basically what the so-called classic 'Kuleshov-effect' describes: the shots of the dancing crowd make me, as a viewer, feel like I am part of them and that being generous is easy and fun. However, in the next sentences, Vernallis writes: '*I realize that this is not very likely. I am sitting on the couch—not going anywhere. In the video's moment, however, I feel I have done the necessary social work.*'[52] Simon Frith says something similar in the context of music and political movements: '*If listening to an album* [or in this case watching a music video] *without any condition is understood as resistance, resistance means purely nothing.*'[53] So, the question has to be asked: Are music videos as triggers of social engagement or movement therefore just an illusion? To shed more light on this question, I have to elaborate a bit further and will consult current examples in this next paragraph.

---

[51] Sánchez Olmos & Viñuela (2017), *The Musicless Music Video as a Spreadable Meme Video: Format, User Interaction, and Meaning on YouTube*.
[52] Vernallis (2004), *Experiencing Music Video—Aesthetics, and Cultural Context*, 115.
[53] Frith (1999), *Unscharfe Grenzmarkierungen*, in: Die kleinen Unterschiede: Der Cultural Studies Reader, 171.

5.3 Generating Culture 131

Excursus: Social Engagement in High Selling pop-music-videos Or Textual Authenticity

At this point, before going into the next analysis, I must disclaim that of course pop-music, like any other business, is subordinated to certain rules of the market. Ergo, we cannot deny that the incitement for social awareness sometimes may be the result of calculated market analyses and not always comes from the artists' pure heart. Taylor Swift's *You Need to Come Down* (2019) that I already wrote about, is as example that generates culture by thematizing equal rights of queer people and links her music with an act of social responsibility that she tries to pass on to the viewers. Hence, generating culture can be a reference back to the motivation of expressing oneself politically from section 4.1, meaning that an artist chooses to expand their music video's functions in order to convey personal concerns to a greater audience. And here, authenticity comes back into play. If we take a brief look at *Mother's Daughter* (2019) by Miley Cyrus, we see a more drastic example of social engagement, wrapped in a music video. The video was announced by Cyrus as a 'feminist anthem'[54] with lyrics that are indeed empowering women: '*Don't fuck with my freedom, I came up to get me some, I'm nasty, I'm evil, Must be something in the water or that I'm my mother's daughter*'. The video itself contains Cyrus dancing in a red latex suit, just like Britney Spears wore in *Oops!... I Did it Again* (2000), portraits of non-binary people and flashing texts like 'Every woman is a riot', 'Virginity is a social construct' or 'Feminist AF [as fuck]' (Fig. 5.6).

While I do not want to judge the actual authenticity of this video or its messages' veracity regarding gender and feminism, I do note it for its impactful and self-conscious appearance. The context in which this video is produced and released clearly is different to Whitney Houston's *Step by Step*. This is why the analysis regarding social engagement needs to be reviewed as well. Again, the communication enabled by music videos' multiple functionalities makes the difference: In the release post on Twitter, Cyrus wrote: '*MOTHER'S DAUGHTER VIDEO OUT NOW! Music makes Movements! We got the power! #MothersDaughter*'[55]. With this post only, she established two things: The ability of music (videos) to generate culture in the form of social movements on the one hand and with the hashtag #MothersDaughter she provided the platform for the discussion on the video to be held on the other hand. Shortly after, the hashtag was trending on Twitter, collected over 43,000 posts on Instagram, and the video was received widely positively by the media. Again, one must not disregard the

---

[54] https://twitter.com/MileyCyrus/status/1145818700114792449.

[55] https://twitter.com/MileyCyrus/status/1146041040928944128.

Fig. 5.6 *Mother's Daughter* evokes mixed feelings. Granted, it is a really catchy song that stayed in my head for days as did the video with the glossy depiction of Cyrus and a diversity of other women. Nevertheless, the texts, the announcement and the fact that Cyrus occupies over 50% of the video's lenght showing off dance moves in a Britney Spears suit make the video feel awkwardly commercial and targeted for both fans of the 'sexy' and the 'progressive' Miley Cyrus

economic dimension in productions like this, especially with such a well-planned and offensive campaign to announce it. However, *Mother's Daughter* shows that the way social engagement and a strongly proposed authenticity are treated in current music videos indeed is different from older examples as discussed by Carol Vernallis.

Back to the main text. Keeping in mind that *Step by Step* is more than 20 years old and I am not content with Vernallis' conclusion, I want to analyze this matter with contemporary examples. Harriet Gibsone, music editor of the Guardian, said in 2016:

> Something is about to happen. With the likes of Beyoncé, sister, Solange, and Kendrick Lamar taking their major budgets to spend on meaningful pieces, many other artists will most likely follow suit.[56]

---

[56] https://www.theguardian.com/music/2016/sep/28/solange-new-album-q-tip-lil-wayne-kelly-rowland-a-seat-at-the-table (acc. September 15th, 2019).

5.3 Generating Culture

Therefore, singular videos might not implicitly be the impulse for social impact but rather contribute to a shifting mindset on what music videos' functions and opportunities are. 2Pac Shakur's famous quote: *'I'm not saying I'm gonna change the world, but I guarantee that I will spark the brain that will change the world.*[57]' thus seems to be viable in the evolution of the music video world, too.

5.3.1 Childish Gambino—This Is America \\ Dance the Riot Away

This is America (2018) by the US-American musician and actor Childish Gambino aka. Donald Glover and directed by Hiro Murai is a textbook example for a music video that had an enormous cultural, or at least, social impact. Hours after its release in May 2018, it already counted millions of views and went through international press and various online magazines, blogs, and social-media pages. This is mainly due to two graphic executions shown in the video and its evocative and ambiguous visual nature. These immediate reactions and those to follow are what I want to discuss here.

The song itself can be divided into three parts—chorus/intro, verse, and outro. The choruses feature choir-type, melodically uplifting vocals and an equally light-hearted guitar pattern in F major. In both instruments and vocals, a heritage of African music is noticeable (just as in the dance choreography, which features the South African Gwara dance[58]). The verses are rhythmically very dense with busy percussion and vocal ad-libs in the background, while the only tonal information is a continuous and almost threatening bass sound on E♭, sometimes adding higher octaves. The outro is formally as well as musically separated from the rest of the song, making it sound like an epilogue or even an obituary.

The lyrics are encrypted in a way, at least compared to, for example, *I'm not Racist* and are not understandable without certain background knowledge about the actual situation in the USA that Glover is talking about from a critical perspective, and the willingness to interpret them:

> *We just wanna party, Party just for you*
> *We just want the money, Money just for you*
> *I know you wanna party, Party just for me*

---

[57] https://www.youtube.com/watch?v=uijBebYpoto Min. 01:07.

[58] https://i-d.vice.com/en_us/article/qvn4qw/this-choreographer-brought-the-african-diaspora-to-childish-gambinos-this-is-america (September 15th, 2019).

> *Girl, you got me dancin' (yeah, girl, you got me dancin'), Dance and shake the frame*
> *This is America*
> *Don't catch you slippin' up*
> *Look what I'm whippin' up*
> *[...]*
> *This is America (skrrt, skrrt, woo), Don't catch you slippin' up (ayy)*
> *Look at how I'm livin' now, Police be trippin' now (woo)*
> *Yeah, this is America (woo, ayy), Guns in my area (word, my area)*
> *I got the strap (ayy, ayy), I gotta carry 'em*
> *[...]*
> *Ooh-ooh-ooh-ooh-ooh, tell somebody*
> *You go tell somebody*
> *Grandma told me*
> *Get your money, Black man (get your money)*
> *Look how I'm geekin' out (hey), I'm so fitted (I'm so fitted, woo)*
> *I'm on Gucci (I'm on Gucci), I'm so pretty (yeah, yeah)*
> *I'm gon' get it (ayy, I'm gon' get it), Watch me move (blaow)*
> *This a celly (ha), That's a tool (yeah)*
> *On my Kodak (woo, Black), Ooh, know that (yeah, know that, hold on)*
> *[...]*
> *(Refrain)*
> *You just a Black man in this world, You just a barcode, ayy*
> *You just a Black man in this world, Drivin' expensive foreigns, ayy*
> *You just a big dawg, yeah, I kenneled him in the backyard*
> *No probably ain't life to a dog, For a big dog.*[59]

The lyrics are about distraction, about always having to feel to be under observation (Don't catch you slippin' up), about the exhausting dominance of stereotypes and the ongoing oppression of people of color in the United States (You just a Black man in this world, You just a barcode, ayy). They also allude to the problem of gun violence in America and can be read as to link to specific incidents of police violence against people of color: the line *'This a celly (ha), That's a tool (yeah)'* may refer to a police killing in 2018 of a black person, who was alleged to hold a gun which turned out to be a phone (Fig. 5.7).[60]

---

[59] Goransson, Glover, Williams, RCA Records, 2018.
[60] https://edition.cnn.com/2018/03/22/us/sacramento-police-shooting/index.html (acc. September 15th, 2019).

5.3 Generating Culture

Fig. 5.7 Childish Gambino—*This is America*. The chaotic action is staged in the abstract space of an industry hall with a strict color scheme of grey and greenish tones. It is defined by rapidly changing scenarios and emotions, jumping between horror, joy, and frenzy

This whole musical discrepancy and tension between the parts and the intricacy of the lyrics are very well adapted in the video. It is shot in some sort of industrial hall and consists of only six takes. Glover himself is the protagonist and embodies various characters at once; the musician Childish Gambino, an assassin, victim, spectator and commentator of the scene, and possibly even America itself. This makes him a very ambiguous and complex persona. Frank Guan of vulture.com writes:

> It's not a white policeman pulling the trigger, but Glover himself, and after each killing he resumes his dancing with the same livewire energy and his rapping with the same assured flow, as if nothing had happened. If black culture affirms itself, accurately, as a testament to its makers' capacity for grace, invention, and vigor in the face of an

inhuman social reality, Glover's own affirmation contains a shadowy admission that such makers cultivate their own agony in the act of representation.[61]

While the choruses consist of seemingly harmless dancing scenes, they always get disrupted by unpredictable violence in form of graphic executions and transform to confusing and confused verses with crowded and chaotic actions going on: riots, burning cars, police cars and horses always with a group of teenagers dancing behind Glover to distract from all of what is happening in the background. The video contains countless symbols and hidden allusions, from references to Civil War, specific historic assassinations to African heritage, but I do not want to go too deep into exegetical analysis at this point for this has been done numerably and can be read easily on the internet's various sources[62]. I can go back to the findings of Thomas Turino on semiotic music theory and apply them here: The juxtaposition of the many indices in novel ways that play off of the original meanings of the signs and its various micro-components are again compounded in multileveled and conflicting ways ('snowballing' effect). These, once more, allow a flexibility in the creation of complex, densely meaningful signs that compound the condensation of meaning and the affective potential.

This is America in all its poetry and ruthlessness can be interpreted as a nod to 'This is not America' (1985) by Pat Metheny and David Bowie, soundtrack for the feature film 'The Falcon and the Snowman' and at the same time attacking the euphemistic image of the land of the free, stemming from America's 'Cowboy Poetry' and remarkable self-consciousness. One might even interpret Childish Gambino himself with his multiple personalities as the country America (USA), which would allege the country to have some sort of mental illness. So, the title alone, with its engaging commitment, stresses the importance and the urgency Glover conveys with the song and the visuals. Doreen St. Felix of the New Yorker sums it up as follows:

This is what it's like, Glover's video seems to say, to be black in America – at any given time, vulnerable to joy or to destruction.[63]

---

[61] https://www.vulture.com/2018/05/what-it-means-when-childish-gambino-says-this-is-america.html (acc. September 16th, 2019).

[62] A detailed breakdown of the video's symbols and references can be found for example here: https://www.washingtonpost.com/news/arts-and-entertainment/wp/2018/05/07/this-is-america-breaking-down-childish-gambinos-powerful-new-music-video/ (acc. September 16th, 2019).

[63] https://www.newyorker.com/culture/culture-desk/the-carnage-and-chaos-of-childish-gambinos-this-is-america (acc. September 16th, 2019).

5.3 Generating Culture

What I call 'cultural impact' in this video has multiple manifestations. For one part, the general medial discussion it has triggered makes it one of, if not the most discussed music video of 2018. Online magazines, blogs, newspapers from the Washington Post to The Sun, major TV shows—there probably was no news source that did not somehow react to *This is America*. Most of them with pure appreciation: '*A painful yet perfectly timed masterpiece*'[64], '*One of the most important pieces of music and visual art of our time*'[65], but also on a meta-level; Talking Heads singer-songwriter David Byrne shared the video on Twitter with the quote by Nina Simone: '*An artist's duty, as far as I am concerned, is to reflect the times.*'[66]. That quote fits perfectly in this chapter, stressing that, as I noted earlier, the borders of observing and generating culture might be blurry, or that through observing, or say, reflecting the times, progressive culture can be generated.

Another outlet of generated culture through *This is America* is an impressive number of imitations and parodies it provoked by prosumers worldwide. At least 20 covers like *'This is Iraq'*, *'This is Sierra Leone'*, *'This is Nigeria'* etc. can be found on YouTube at the time of writing this. All of them use either the instrumental version of the original song or created an own version of it and rewrote the lyrics, fitting to their respective country and made videos similar to Childish Gambino's. While some of them only pursue comical intentions, many others use their music videos to actually draw attention to political and social issues their countries have, like violence, corruption, and the lack of prospects, and that the world around them possibly is widely neglecting. All these artists really do use music videos as a promotional tool, though neither for a single song nor a product as we have seen in *KENZO World*. It is promoting an artist's or a whole country's concerns and is trying to convey them to the internet while at the same time showing appreciation for the original song and its way of addressing problems. Thereby, the cover-versions use and are part of the generated culture at the same time, posing a very interesting facet in this topic. Formulating and responding to certain (cultural) issues is the basic concept of communication, supporting, again, the idea of music videos being a language of pop and internet culture.

As the last form of generated culture, I want to include a rather new form of social impact online videos can have that are so-called **reaction videos**. Their concept is simple: A user films him or herself while watching an existing clip for

---

[64] https://www.washingtonpost.com/news/arts-and-entertainment/wp/2018/05/07/this-is-america-breaking-down-childish-gambinos-powerful-new-music-video/

[65] https://www.instagram.com/p/Bkc_rJJg27q/

[66] https://twitter.com/DBtodomundo/status/993965662941925376.

the first time. Usually this clip is copied into the image, so that the viewer can see to what the person is reacting to (Fig. 5.8).

Fig. 5.8 Dad Reacts to Childish Gambino—This Is America (Official Video)

While some users basically just film and upload their facial expressions and some comments on the video, others repeatedly stop the video and tell their thoughts and impressions on what they have seen so far. In that case, the reaction video can be much longer than the original video. The interesting thing is that this genre evolved in a rather short period of time and became a very popular thing to do and watch on YouTube. For *This is America* alone, there are literally hundreds of such videos from all over the world, many of them reaching from a few ten thousand to over five million views, showing that it has become an established category.

One of the most famous reaction videos to *This is America* is 'Dad Reacts to Childish Gambino—This is America (Official Video)' (10:58 min.) on the YouTube channel 'BucketHeadNation', reaching 8.6 million views at the time of writing[67]. In this video (like many other 'Dad reacts to…'-videos), a young American of color shows the clip to his father, and they have a conversation about the different topics the clip offers. The format indeed has some interesting potential because of the different generations coming together and sharing their thoughts on certain issues in an intimate manner, which is what presumably makes the channel so popular. The father at the end of the video very adequately concludes:

> This is a **conversation starter**, this conversation is about guns, this conversation is about how we see America going forward […]. So we have an opportunity right now to have a conversation about guns, about issues we have in our communities. All this

---

[67] https://www.youtube.com/watch?v=ZVhg3FJrSDE.

5.3 Generating Culture

is, is a thought-provoking conversation starter, and that's what we need to do, we need to have conversations.

A similar diagnosis is made by the New York Times in 2019:

These videos are designed as provocations of a sort, thinkpiece-bait event releases designed to cut through online clutter. [...] In this crowded climate, creating a vivid video is a survival strategy, especially with no tastemaker outlet (à la MTV) directly promoting/privileging the format. That is how the most effective music videos function today: as time-stopping conversation pieces.[68]

Firstly, this can be understood as a reference to the reception aesthetics and the concept of pop-cultural texts of the Cultural Studies, I wrote of earlier this chapter. There is no singular static meaning in the video; we have to fill it with meaning and sense and message by interacting, negotiating, and conversing about it. Secondly, mere information for example, on the news about certain issues might be a conversation starter as well, but an artistic engagement in a social or political matter always and through all genres has offered new perspectives, new ideas or simply made the topic somewhat entertainable. From visual propaganda like poster art during times of revolution and war, most prominently the Spanish Civil War, to music and visual arts and performances. And today, the music video medium is one of the most-consumed art forms and extremely versatile in both its appearance and its intentions. So, what I encounter here is the dimension of responsibility in music videos. Certainly, every art form can obtain and claim this responsibility but given the circumstances, we have to consider the music video an especially powerful tool. That is because it has the potential to reach and influence people all around the world with comparably very little effort, exposing it as probably one of the most convenient art forms regarding its economic aspects. Economic is to be understood not just in a financial and representational manner but also in the meaning of drawing attention. If an artist has a clear message to convey that has the potential to rouse people, even if he or she is not a musician, a music video (at least in the broad sense of a *'relation of sounds and image that we recognize as such'*) might just be the best shot to get the attention the message deserves.

---

[68] https://www.nytimes.com/2019/01/30/arts/music/grammy-awards-music-video.html?fbclid=IwAR3xk6zCzIIJ8j1jwpR0_ssPswEgnuF19mmVXY5gLWap51SWqB4Jj_i5F24 (acc. September 15th, 2020).

5.3.2 BTS—Fake Love \\—Real Industry

I now briefly want to explore a manifestation of Generating Culture that is much more calculated and clearly has commercial intentions. Since the early 1990 s, initiated by a group called Seo Taiji and Boys, the audiovisual phenomenon known today as 'K-Pop' (K is for Korea) arose from South Korea. K-Pop compounds a great variety of musical styles, from R'n'B to EDM and Rock to Hip-Hop all of which are mixed together in single songs very often. After Seo Taiji and Boys laid the foundation in 1992 for many artists and groups to follow, K-Pop dominated the East-Asian market and had its international breakthrough with Psy's Gangnam Style (2012), which was still an exotic singularity in the international market. Around the year 2018, the K-Pop group BTS had great successes and established the genre in the US market, becoming #1 on the Billboard 200.[69] In other words, K-Pop's popularity grew exponentially over the last decade and has gained a wider audience throughout the globe, and music videos play a significant role in this as Michael Unger argues:

> The proliferation and popularity of Korean [...] music videos in recent years, both in South Korea and internationally, epitomizes the Korean music industry's embrace of Western music video paradigms, while also creating its own specific formula to give K-pop a seemingly unique brand identity.[70]

Scholars and journalists widely agree on the fact that K-Pop is an industry[71]. This is in the sense of big agencies recruiting teenagers (which are the main target group for K-Pop) and training them between two and four years before they assemble in so-called 'idol-groups' of around four to twenty singers to make their debut. Estimations vary from 50,000 USD to 500,000 USD spent on the making of just one idol.[72] They then make extensive use of social media in order to integrate the channels under their business strategy and maximize the potential.[73] Clearly, parallels to Horkheimer and Adorno's concept of the top-down Culture Industry, which leaves little room for own interpretations, niches and development of individual currents are to be noted.

---

[69] https://www.rollingstone.com/music/music-news/on-the-charts-bts-become-first-k-pop-act-to-reach-number-one-629174/ (acc. June 27th, 2020).

[70] Unger (2015), *The Aporia of Presentation: Deconstructing the Genre of K-pop Girl Group Music Videos in South Korea*, 25.

[71] See for example Fuhr (2015), Ahn (2013), and Giuffre & Keith (2014).

[72] Fuhr (2015), *Globalization and Popular Music in South Korea—Sounding out K-Pop*, 76.

[73] Ahn (2013), *Korean pop takes off! Social media strategy of Korean entertainment industry*,775–776.

5.3 Generating Culture

K-Pop's most apparent characteristics are the lyrics that, for the most part, are in Korean and also the general style of their music videos, which I will go into in a second. At first sight, remarkably, the international market does not seem to have a problem with foreign languages. That is, even more foreign than Spanish, which is also very common in pop music, but a considerable part of the vocabulary of which has now become part of everyday life in the western world (chica, amor, me gusta, amigo, beso, etc.) and can therefore no longer be considered a major hurdle for listeners. However, Liz Giuffre and Sarah Keith suggest that the lyrics' language is not critical in terms of their communication and discuss this phenomenon in an article on K-Pop as follows: *'Pop music, throughout its history, has often attracted audiences using means other than direct lyrical engagement and literal meanings.'*[74] They name Psy's *Gangnam Style* as an obvious example but also The Beatles' iconic 'Ob-La-Di, Ob-La-Da' and the documentation of such instances as part of the appeal of music for audiences.[75] They further argue that:

> *Therefore, the literal notion of a 'preferred language' does not necessarily relate to the context of music and video [...but] can instead be defined as music and music video itself.*[76]

This statement is very interesting in various ways: On the one hand, it once again adds another facet to my perception of music videos being a language of pop and internet culture itself that my generation grew up with. On the other hand, it sensibly combines the two most apparent characteristics of K-Pop in the effect they have on the young, international, and digitally affine audience. At this point, it is time for a closer look at one example.

I chose the video *Fake Love* (2018) by the group BTS, consisting of seven people and still one of the most popular K-Pop idol groups there are, because either the song and the video represent many of the characteristic facets of K-Pop very well. At the time of writing, *Fake Love* counts over 700,000 million views on YouTube.

The song itself harmonically consists of only three chords that are repeated in all parts, B♭ major, C major, and F minor. Although with apparent borrowings from Hip-Hop such as the half-time drumbeat with its sounds similar to a Roland TR-808 drum machine and the rapping in the verses, it is a straightforward pop

---

[74] Giuffre & Keith (2014), *SBS PopAsia: non-stop K-pop in Australia*, 95.

[75] E.g. West & Martindale (1996), *Creative trends in the content of Beatles lyrics*, Popular Music and Society, 20:4, 103–125.

[76] Giuffre & Keith (2014), *SBS PopAsia: non-stop K-pop in Australia*, 95.

song. The pre-choruses and choruses have the potential for staying in the listener's head because of their many repetitions, their simple melodies, and the fact that they are sung in English, which according to Hemming is an important factor for memorizing the music[77] (Fig. 5.9).

> *[Pre-Chorus:] Love you so bad, love you so bad*
> 널 위해 예쁜 거짓을 빚어내 [For you, I'm enacting a pretty lie]
> *Love it's so mad, love it's so mad*
> 날 지워 너의 인형이 되려 해 [I'm erasing myself to become your doll][78]
> *[Chorus:] I'm so sick of this*
> *Fake love, fake love, fake love*
> *I'm sorry but its*
> *Fake love, fake love, fake love*[79]

Fig. 5.9 Memorable melodies from pre-chorus and chorus. The motif of the chorus a' c" c" a' appears 18 times throughout the song, the 'love you so bad'-motif 16 times

After having briefly laid out the musical layer of the video, I will now go deeper into the imagery and its content (Fig. 5.10).

With the short intro and the interlude without music, the video is 01:17 minutes longer than the audio single. It does not follow a stringent plot; it basically is an excellent example for Michael Shore's definition of a hybrid-clip that 'mixes the performance with a conceptualized plot or with flashes of associative imagery'. There are various sets in which the group, individually and as an ensemble, act, dance, and lip-sync to the music. All the sets have in common that they look like dreams, lonely, sometimes paranoid dreams. Persecution, forces of

---

[77] Hemming, Jan (2009), *Zur Phänomenologie des ‚Ohrwurms'*.

[78] https://colorcodedlyrics.com/2018/05/bts-bangtansonyeondan-fake-love (acc. July 18th, 2020).

[79] Bang, Kang, Rap, Big Hit Music 2018.

5.3 Generating Culture

Fig. 5.10 BTS—*Fake Love* is a mixture of highly sophisticated dance choreographies on extravagant sets, cinematic action-moviesque scenes and usage of symbols, such as one of the singers, J-Hope, lying in a room full of Snickers chocolate bars that are strongly connotated with the western world. For me, the depicted themes in the video are loneliness, finding hold and coping with loss

nature, and being locked up are themes in the individual scenes, the urge to break out of something can be recognized as a topic in the dance choreographies.

A recurring motif is a smartphone as a sign of the (in itself fake) relationship to the (ex-)partner and the failed communication. One time (02:02 min.) it melts away like sand in the hand of a singer, another time (04:44 min.) one of the singers stands dejectedly in a room whose walls are full of flickering smartphones.

The colors are poppy and contrast and the cutting frequency is very high. For example, in the first pre-chorus from 01:46 minutes to 02:11 minutes, there are 24 cuts. *Fake Love* basically is a reminiscence to the old-fashioned, so-called MTV aesthetics and their 'hyperedited shot fragment editing' as Wheeler Winston Dixon called it.[80] Generally, memories of boybands that were popular in the 1990s and 2000s are coming back while watching BTS's music videos. In fact, aesthetically and content-wise, the video does not deliver anything we haven't seen in videos over 20 years ago.

So, why are K-Pop videos such as *Fake Love* so successful? On the one hand, this video surprisingly is as sleek and edgeless as a music video can be. There are no provocations neither in content nor aesthetics, no violence, no erotica, no humor. Nothing that has not been done earlier and that would surprise me as a viewer. The music does not provide any innovations in this respect either. Yet still, the director YongSeok Choi and the producers found a perfect recipe for a video that, paired with heavy marketing, hit the global market massively. In the context of Generating Culture, I want to take a look at some formulas the producers use in order to have that impact on the market.

On the video side, there is obviously the extreme technical sophistication that defines the product. All the sets, the lighting, the coloring, the VFX, and the cinematography were done at a very high level. All the performers are deeply engaged to deliver an intimate and powerful scenario that the viewer can sink into. While the whole concept of this video and K-Pop in general strongly recalls the phenomenon of the 90s and 00s boy-bands such as the Backstreet Boys and others, it takes the idea to a next level[81]: The dance choreographies are much more elaborated, the appearance of the performance is much more dramatic and the videos above all are much more complex. All of this is only logical since today's youth grew up and still is surrounded by different medial standards as they had been twenty years ago. When comparing *Fake Love* to something like the Backstreet Boys' *I Want it That Way* (1999), the latter seems profoundly outdated in its whole appearance for today's youth. This phenomenon of the boy-band comeback in a new and contemporary garment is also worth a sidenote regarding the idea of a Renaissance of music videos (see section 2.2.1).

Some of the concepts the producers use to generate an impact on the market are not video-related but still worth mentioning: Most of the popular K-Pop idol groups have very short and non-Korean names, many times even only acronyms, such as BTS, CLC, DIA, or EXID. Most times, the song names are also in

---

[80] Dixon (2001), *Twenty-five Reasons Why It's All Over—The End of Cinema as We Know It*, 360.

[81] This is a good, practical example of Michael Unger's claim that *'the Korean music industry's embrace of Western music video paradigms, while also creating its own specific formula to give K-pop a seemingly unique brand identity.'*

5.3 Generating Culture

English, making it easy for international fans to relate to the group and share it with friends, for there is no pronunciation barrier whatsoever. As I said, the lyrics still are 90 percent Korean, but often there are just enough English phrases woven in so that the listener has a rough idea of what the song is about. For example, here are the English bits of 'Fake Love' that correlate with the presumed themes in the video that are loneliness, finding hold, and coping with loss:

> *I'm so sick of this*
> *Fake Love*
> *I'm so sorry but it's*
> *Fake Love*
> *I wanna be a good man just for you [...]*
> *Now I dunno me, who are you? [...]*
> *Love you so bad Love you so bad [...]*
> *Love it's so mad Love it's so mad [...]*
> *Why you sad? I don't know...*

Thus, one can notice that K-Pop is careful to ensure to keep the content of the songs very accessible for everybody.

It is interesting to note that before every video by BTS, the logo of their music label Big Hit Entertainment appears. This stresses that the following video is made under very clear circumstances and is not the work of the singers themselves or that of a specific director for which I showed examples earlier (Fig. 5.11).

Fig. 5.11 BTS—Fake Love, 00:02 min

The effort that the industry is undertaking to produce these videos is enormous. K-Pop videos with budgets ranging from 200,000 USD to almost a million USD are not uncommon.[82] Thus, the dimension of Generating Culture in the case of K-Pop music videos, on the one hand, lies in the economic effort that labels and production companies undertake in order to keep creating products for a massive fan culture. Here, music videos indeed serve as a visual promotional tool, but not for specific songs but for the whole K-Pop industry itself. At 0.3% of South Korea's 2018 GDP, BTS's share alone was comparable to that of Korean Air.[83] So K-Pop is an important industry for the whole country. They emphasize the visual appearance of its performers that often ranks over musical talent; that is, they deliver a 'complete package' of an idol, how Unger calls it.[84] And on the other hand, closing this brief exploration of how K-Pop generates culture, they create the 'genre' (in the sense as used before in this work) and the K-Pop culture itself as they do have strict rules to follow:

> If genre in music videos is a fluid concept, the term K-pop is useful as it implies a narrow definition of visual properties and practices while allowing endless ancillary variations so that one K-pop music video ultimately looks like another.
> [...]
> K-pop emulates [...] aesthetics from Western pop music videos, but then adds its own Korean cultural [masculinity] to the representations it embraces creating what I call a 'K-pop pastiche.' Thus, these videos are also a site of the 'transnational cultural exchange' of hybridity, whereby they may be consumed in transnational or trans-Asian markets, but their production is nationally branded.[85]

This last statement directly leads over to the last of my three proposed perspectives on how to analyze music videos in their cultural context.

5.4 Appropriating Culture

This aspect of treating culture seems especially interesting to me because of the many facets it implies, particularly in the field of music videos, which I want to explore in this subchapter. We have to be very careful with interpreting the term 'appropriation' since there are various contexts and fields of research in that it

---

[82] https://theculturetrip.com/asia/south-korea/articles/the-biggest-budget-k-pop-videos-from-korea/ (acc. July 4th, 2020).

[83] https://www.statista.com/chart/19854/companies-bts-share-of-south-korea-gdp/ (acc. August 9th, 2020).

[84] Unger (2015), *The Aporia of Presentation: Deconstructing the Genre of K-pop Girl Group Music Videos in South Korea*, 25, 26.

[85] Ibid, 25, 27.

5.4 Appropriating Culture

is discussed, so I will try to approach its critical meanings for this work step by step. One widely discussed understanding of appropriating cultural elements that is by far not a new one covers the culture of sampling in Hip-Hop music, where so-called samples (bits of existing music or other audio sources) are copied and sometimes modified to create a new musical piece. Here 'appropriation' is understood as 'quotation' or 'deliberately re-using' and can be described with the words of Paul Gilroy as following:

> The aesthetic rules that govern [sampling] are premised on a dialect of rescuing appropriation and recombination that creates special pleasures, in which aesthetic stress is laid upon the sheer social and cultural distance that formerly separated the diverse elements now dislocated into novel meanings by their provocative aural juxtaposition.[86]

This reading has its right, also in the analysis of music videos, as we saw in Deichkind's *Wer Sagt Denn Das?*, where sampling and processing of material brought up a product with provocative visual juxtaposition. However, the most common use of the term 'Cultural Appropriation' one will find looking for it online in these times is in the context of people adopting elements of foreign, chiefly indigenous, cultures. These most commonly are icons, clothing and rituals that are then used in order to profit from the presumably exotic nature or just to expand a visual appearance, one could say. Usually, there is a power gap involved, namely that elements are taken from a subordinated or in some way oppressed culture by a dominant culture[87]. To remain in the musical context, two examples for this are Pharrell Williams, wearing a Native American war bonnet for an advertising photo for the fashion company Elle and Katy Perry, who performed as a Geisha at the American Music Awards 2013. Since neither Williams nor Elle have no Native American roots whatsoever, this is a classic case of (inappropriate) appropriating of culture because the heritage of the Indigenous People of the Great Plains and Canadian Prairies is taken out of its historical and traditional context, only for the purpose of commerce. The case of Perry is similar. If published via the internet, those incidents usually are followed by a reaction of protest on social-media-platforms, for example, along with the hashtag #NotHappy (referencing Williams' hit 'Happy' from 2013).

---

[86] Gilroy (1990), *Sounds authentic: black music, ethnicity, and the challenge of a changing same*, Black Music Research Journal, 10, 2, pp. 128–131.

[87] See e.g. Matthes (2019), *Cultural appropriation and oppression*, in: Philosophical Studies, 176 (4): 1003–1013., Rogers (2006), *From Cultural Exchange to Transculturation: A Review and Reconceptualization of Cultural Appropriation*, in: Communication Theory, 16, 474–503.

A common point of criticism of cultural appropriation is that it is converting culturally significant artifacts, practices, and beliefs into 'meaningless' pop culture or giving them a completely different or less nuanced significance than they would have had originally. Just as Joyner Lucas put it in *I'm Not Racist*: *'You wanna copy our slang and everything that we know, Tryna steal black culture and then make it your own, whoa'*. The commercialization of culture has the disturbing effect that what was once an element of a cultural way of life has become a profitable product, rather than something unique which a culture made to suit their specific needs and circumstances[88].

But why would anybody claim foreign cultural elements to use in his or her visual appearance in the first place? Certainly, the profitability of cultural appropriation is reasonable. The dominant culture sees objects and traditions of marginalized cultures as exotic, edgy, and desirable, which translates to profits. However, Justin Charity, staff writer of Complex magazine, says:

> *[Cultural appropriation] is what pop culture does. You know, you can look to the fact that in the late '90s and beyond, like, hip-hop went from being a very New York-local genre of music to being a multimillion dollar [...]. That's sort of the M.O. [modus operandi/method of operation] of pop music. That's the M.O. of record labels. That's the M.O. of artists once they engage with pop culture on a certain level, is to find ways to commodify imagery that's interesting to people, even if that imagery is interesting to consumers at a great distance.*[89]

Before I go into other meanings the term of cultural appropriating can have in the context of music videos, I want to discuss one example that illustrates this common concept and the problematics of cultural appropriation very well.

5.4.1 Coldplay—Hymn for the Weekend \\ An Interesting Cocktail

Hymn for the Weekend is the second single off Coldplay's Album 'A Head Full of Dreams' and was released on January 29th of 2016. The video was directed by Ben Mor and produced by Black Dog Films and River Studios and, at the

---

[88] Nwegbu et al. (2011), *Globalization of Cultural Heritage: Issues, Impacts, and Inevitable Challenges for Nigeria*, 5. Available from: https://www.researchgate.net/publication/265241 456_Globalization_of_Cultural_Heritage_Issues_Impacts_and_Inevitable_Challenges_for_ Nigeria (acc. April 4th, 2019).

[89] https://www.npr.org/2016/02/07/465901864/cultural-appropriation-in-pop-music-when-are-artists-are-in-the-wrong (acc. June 12th, 2019).

5.4 Appropriating Culture

time of this analysis, counts over 1,1 billion views on YouTube. It was shot on location in India and features Beyoncé as some sort of Bollywood actress, many local people, and places as well as the band performing in the streets.

As the title suggests, the song itself is a very straightforward pop-hymn and fits well into the album's style of uplifting and transfiguring devotions to peace of mind, such as 'Adventure of a Lifetime Up&Up', 'Amazing Day' or 'Fun'. It follows a simple song structure of: Intro—Verse—Pre-Chorus—Chorus—Verse—Pre-Chorus—Chorus and a very long outro and uses the same three chords (A♭ major, B♭ major and C minor) in all the parts, except for adding an F minor in the pre-choruses. The instrumentation is typical for Coldplay, featuring a prominent piano, drums, bass, and electric guitar, thickened up by synth sections in the pre-choruses and choruses. The lyrics almost undoubtedly use a language of Christian salvation and speak of an unknown angel that 'comes from above' to 'light up' the singer's world and makes him 'feel high and drunk of love and life':

> *Oh, angel sent from up above*
> *You know you make my world light up*
> *When I was down, when I was hurt*
> *You came to lift me up*
> *[…]*
> *When I was a river, dried up*
> *You came to rain a flood*
> *You said drink from me, drink from me*
> *When I was so thirsty*
> *Poured on a symphony*
> *Now I just can't get enough*
> *Put your wings on me, wings on me*
> *When I was so heavy*
> *Poured on a symphony*
> *When I'm low, low, low, low*
> *I, oh, I, oh, I*
> *Got me feeling drunk and high*
> *So high, so high*
> *[…]*[90]

The resemblance to biblical verses like the following is unmistakably apparent, as examples from the Psalms, the Book of Revelation and Jeremiah show:

---

[90] Hermansen, Eriksen, Martin et al, Parlophone Records Limited 2015.

- *He makes me lie down in green pastures. He leads me beside still waters. [...] Your rod and your staff, they comfort me. [...] anoint my head with oil; my cup overflows.*[91]
- *They feast on the abundance of your house, and you give them drink from the river of your delights. For with you is the fountain of life; in your light do we see light.*[92]
- *And he will guide them to springs of living water, and God will wipe away every tear from their eyes.*[93]
- *For I will satisfy the weary soul, and every languishing soul I will replenish.*[94]

Given this strongly connoted lyrical content and the ideal of light, western pop music, the video actually is quite a surprise: Its basic concept namely is to show the singer, Chris Martin, exploring urban parts of what the viewer may recognize as India, and playing in-sync with the audio track with his band in the streets. They are accompanied by inserts of supposed elements of Indian culture, such as monks and frolicking people celebrating a Holi-festival. In addition to that, Beyoncé appears throughout the video, dressed up as kind of a Bollywood actress that never physically interacts with the other protagonists but appears in a movie shown in very old or vintage-looking cinemas. Everything is very colorful and shot in the hours of sunset, many shots are in slow motion, and the color grade has a very warm touch. All of that gives the video a very comforting and exotic (some might say those were predestined ingredients for kitsch) feel (Fig. 5.12).

So, one might ask, why would a western pop band with a song, lyrically set between Christianity and Friday-night-party-atmosphere, use a video with strong symbolism of Hinduism, Indian culture, and analog-daytime-partying? One of the VFX artists, Yaron Yashinski explains it as follows:

> *The video came out of respect and appreciation. Ben isn't only about the visual but the subtext, and the subtext here is full of respect. To Ben, India is an amazing, visual, mystical atmosphere worth recreating for history.*

That is, in fact, almost cynical, talking about the country with the world's second-largest population, 23 official national languages, a tradition reaching back over 30,000 years and at the same time having a booming technology industry. So seeing the need to make a pop-music video to recreate the culture of India for

---

[91] Ps. 23, 1.
[92] Ps. 36, 9.
[93] Rv, 7, 17.
[94] Jr. 31, 25.

5.4 Appropriating Culture

Fig. 5.12 Coldplay—*Hymn for the Weekend*. The singer Chris Martin is featured by traditional elements like monks and dancers in folkloristic costumes while embracing a colorful and warm color palette and mood. Beyoncé (middle left) dressed up and henna-painted like a Bollywood actress

history seems highly presumptuous. Even more so concerning the actual elements of culture Mor and the crew illustrated in the video. The clip's whole concept is a true romanticizing of Indian poverty and past times, meaning that there is not one modern building shown and the most advanced technical device in the images is probably Johnny Buckland's electric guitar.

In an interview, the director Ben Mor says he '*was deeply inspired by the colors and people. The resulting visuals are a love letter of sorts—one that exalts the country's culture, vivid hues, and extravagant style.*[95]' and he continues: '*If you work in a visual medium you have to be moved by India. It's hard to take a bad picture there.*[96]'. That again is cynical, concerning India's actual wealth and social context; in 2012, 270,000,000 people were living below the poverty line,

---

[95] http://www.blackdogfilms.com/15396/interview-director-ben-mor-talks-coldplay-beyonce-and-the-making-of-hymn-for-the-weekend/ (acc. June 16th, 2019).
[96] Ibid.

making up one out of five citizens that had to cope with max. 1,90$ per day[97]. So, as a matter of fact, it would be fairly easy and obvious to take a bad picture there. Yet this is exactly proving the thesis I posed in section 5.4 that objects and traditions of marginalized cultures seen by the dominant culture as exotic, edgy, and desirable, get taken out of their original context in order to gain not only financial but also entertaining profits.

Furthermore, in this case it is interesting that the video does not only make use of certain elements of Indian culture but pretends to depict a whole country and society through a highly romanticized and narrow lens. Hence, this is not only appropriating of cultural icons but even arrogating to understand and the need to seriously illustrate a whole culture that does not even exist in the depicted form. Moreover, the video also makes quite heavy use of CGI (Computer Generated Images) and visual effects, but in relatively subtle ways—that is, making major adjustments to the images that the viewer might not necessarily notice, because the final image looks real but in reality, for example, has CGI-moving tree roots, fireworks or even entire buildings, flags and backgrounds placed in the images afterward:

> *I tried to use the special effects in a way that just heightened what was already there. Almost trying to make the surreal real. […] Almost every shot of the video has something in it. There are a lot of techniques you might not necessarily see.*[98]

says the VFX artist, Yaron Yashinski.. This detail makes the depicted vision of India even more abstract, as it does not even come from what is there on location and in the actual country and culture, but what is in the producers' visions. In the end, what we are left with in this video is an interesting and actually not so easily digestible cocktail of motives, religions, world views and electric-guitar-pop. Probably the best medicine against the hangover is just to keep drinking.

This film is obviously no singularity in the field of cultural appropriating music videos. Especially black culture was always a target to adopt for white media industry with figures like Madonna or, more recently, Miley Cyrus with her dancing style, first and foremost the twerking, basically a certain style of shaking one's behind she made prominent in white culture. US-Singer Katy Perry is known for seemingly poorly reflected music videos like *Dark Horse* (2014), in

---

[97] http://www.worldbank.org/en/news/infographic/2016/05/27/india-s-poverty-profile (acc. June 16th, 2019).

[98] https://www.billboard.com/articles/news/6867252/vfx-artist-yaron-yeshinski-coldplay-beyonces-hymn-for-the-weekend-video (acc. June 16th, 2019).

5.4 Appropriating Culture

which all of the costumes and sets are dressed up in ancient Egyptian style, seemingly for no lyrical or other reason than embracing the look. The South African duo 'Die Antwoord' has repeatedly been in the press for incidents of appropriating culture, most prominent, their video *Fatty Boom Boom* (2012), where they make use of black facing. This is one of the practices of cultural appropriation with the longest history, going back to so-called minstrel shows during the 18th and 19th century, in that white US-Americans painted their faces black, usually to make fun of the slaves. While Die Antwoord's visual style is highly provocative and sometimes not unproblematic, they are aware of the topic and address it for example in videos and interviews and use certain elements with a reason to somehow stress their message and not purely arbitrarily, as it is seemingly the case with *Hymn for the Weekend*. In 2017 black US-rapper Aminé released his video REDMERCEDES, in that he and his posse used 'white facing' to switch racial roles and in Benzo's *Blood Orange* (2019) typical white culture of the 19th century is satirized as well, so it can be observed that this topic continues to be a matter of interest (Fig. 5.13).

Fig. 5.13 Anime, *REDMERCEDES* and Benzo, *Blood Orange*

But let us step back a little bit and look at one of the initial statements by Justin Charity[99] about cultural appropriation: '**This is what pop culture does**.' And he is completely right about it. While the debate on the topic about the perception of an imbalance of power between a dominant and a minor/oppressed culture certainly on most occasions is important to be held, the appropriation itself simply *is* and has always been part of culture. As long as it is alive, culture is a dynamic matter, and music videos are one medium that illustrates that very well.

---

[99] https://www.npr.org/2016/02/07/465901864/cultural-appropriation-in-pop-music-when-are-artists-are-in-the-wrong.

5.4.2 Appropriating the Internet Universe Due to Lack of Own Cultural Heritage

What if we understand Cultural Appropriation not only as a commercially driven, respectless act of self-enrichment by an artist, but as a **logical consequence** that 'creators', as producers of audiovisual content often call themselves, and prosumers, inhabit while browsing the web for new inspirations?

Cultural identity is either passed on laterally or inherited from one generation to another (cultural heritage), or, in the case I want to explore, horizontally passed on from one society to another through such agent as globalization[100]. Nowadays, in the times of a globalizing and shrinking world, hardly anybody is shaped by only one culture. Here, I want to demonstrate this phenomenon via the music video medium and once more point out the viability of music videos as an exemplum for such cultural mechanisms and processes.

As the title of this subchapter suggests, the internet itself may be understood as a manifestation of what James Lull in 2000 introduced as the 'super-culture', the field of tension between 'the local and the global, between the collective and the individual, and between mediated and unmediated forms of experience'.[101] And because the internet offers more or less everything the world ever brought up and everybody potentially could be an equal internet-user, the chances are high that one identifies him- or herself with the global content he or she sees and is part of every day. To put it more drastically and in the wake of a question about context losing relevance, especially on newer platforms like TikTok: once diverse cultural identities are stripped away, **the only culture left to identify with is digital culture**. This is one aspect of assimilation, in which marginalized communities lose their cultural markers and are folded into the dominant culture. Even Horkheimer and Adorno noted this phenomenon in the 'Dialektik der Aufklärung', not in an ethnical, but artistic dimension:

> *What Expressionists and Dadaists meant polemically, the untruth of the style itself, today triumphs in the singing jargon of the Crooner*[102]*, in the perfectly staged grace of a movie star, even in the competition for the photographic shot of a peasant's poor hut.*[103]

---

[100] Nwegbu et al. (2011), *Globalization of Cultural Heritage: Issues, Impacts, and Inevitable Challenges for Nigeria*, 2.

[101] Lull (2000), *Media, Communication, Culture: A Global Approach*, 267.

[102] Crooning is an intimate and warm vocal technique or style that is linked to singers like Frank Sinatra or Bing Crosby.

[103] Horkheimer (1944/2008): *Dialektik der Aufklärung: Philosophische Fragmente*, 138.

5.4 Appropriating Culture

This still sounds pessimistic, but I want to try to look at the topic as rational as possible, continuing with *Hymn for the Weekend*. After a brief research, one will find at least two music videos by comparably famous artists that use very similar aesthetics and content, namely Major Lazer & DJ Snake—*Lean On* (2015) and Iggy Azalea—*Bounce* (2013). Both are also set in (what the viewer will identify as) India, use traditional costumes for the singers and feature Bollywood-like dancers and scenes in the streets. Even a Holi-scene as in *Hymn for the Weekend* is to be found in *Bounce* (Fig. 5.14).

Fig. 5.14 Major Lazer—*Lean On* and Iggy Azalea—*Bounce*

Considering that these videos together count over 2,5 billion views on YouTube and were released relatively short before *Hymn for the Weekend*, I have to assume that director Ben Mor had watched them as well and somehow got (unconsciously) influenced by them. In that case, what exactly is he appropriating? Objectively judging and in terms of political correctness and, granted, taste, he still adopted a foreign culture, which he has nothing to do with, staged questionable stereotypes and very likely didn't do India and its people a favor with it. On the other hand, it is in fact a **meta-appropriation, inspired by already inspired media, a transtextual appropriation of meta-culture,** one could say.[104] This is another manifestation of the 'cultural melting pot' that I have already mentioned. Here cultural phenomena and characteristics from all social and geographical areas mutate into new interpretations of culture in general.

The choice of these visuals for the specific song with its strong Christian language, however, still is interesting and objectively not understandable; in the already quoted interview, Mor says, he 'was deeply inspired by the colors and people.'. So, either I must assume that the director did not pay attention to the

---

[104] For further general research see Minsu park et al. (2017), *Cultural values and cross-cultural video consumption on YouTube*. PLoS ONE 12(5): e0177865 https://doi.org/10.1371/journal.pone.0177865

lyrics and just implemented his dream of making a film about 'India', or, more likely, he interpreted the lyrics as universal and diffuse spirituality and found his adopted construct of India, being a mystical and cheerful place to him, to be fitting for them.

Looking back to the initial question of 'What is a music video's cultural impact?', the parameter of cultural appropriation becomes central, at least in this last reading of it. Music videos pose a heavy and, most importantly, **ubiquitous visual influence**, not only formally for other producers of visual content as it is the case with the so-called 'MTV-aesthetics', but also content-wise and for everybody. As we see with the enormous response for *Hymn for the Weekend*, the visuals were not only unquestioned for the producers but for the audience as well. I think, it is fair to say we have come so far (speaking about observations made with music videos and thus for the first instance only applicable to them) that real and pure **cultural heritage is not existent on YouTube**, because, even if it is, at the moment it is consumed, it already gets diffused by the internet's context and the consumer's perspective. Vladimir Mironov takes up the term of the super-culture again in 2006 and states that this modern, integrative super-culture of global communication absorbs the variety of local cultures.[105] The reaction videos I wrote of earlier also play a significant role in the process of relativizing local cultures as Korean media scholar Kyong Yoon claims in the context of K-Pop music videos:

> [...] Reaction videos prove that YouTube and other social media significantly lower the barrier of audience's reworking of original cultural texts, as fans can easily upload and circulate their own video commentaries or reaction videos with having high level of digital media literacy. [...] By watching other watching K-Pop music videos, overseas K-Pop fans who do not understand the Korean language attempt to figure out the meanings and [sometimes complex] narratives of the videos.[106]

As Marx wrote, the sailors' pidgin language, blending elements from Europe and the colonized worlds of the Indies and Americas, was '*neither French, nor English, nor German, but the salty air of the Atlantic and oppressive heat below decks.*'[107]. One could compare that presumably authentic culture depicted on YouTube, especially in music videos, is also neither truly and substantially the one nor the other, but **the digital breath of movement and color**, inhaled in front of screens all over the world.

---

[105] Mironov (2006), *Modern Communication, Culture & Philosophy*, 18.
[106] Yoon (2019), *Digital Mediascapes of Transnational Korean Youth Culture*, 15,16.
[107] Marx (1845); Crane (2018), *Cultural Formation and Appropriation in the Era of Merchant Capitalism*, in: Historical Materialism.

Or, formulated pessimistically by Max Horkheimer again: '*Even a person's most intimate reactions are reified to him-/herself to that extent that the actual idea of their peculiarity only persists in extreme abstraction, because he is not able to differentiate between his/her own personality and desires and the image imposed by the 'triumph of advertising'.*'[108]

Having found these results, I want to offer another reading of the three parameters *Observing, Generating,* and *Appropriating* culture that is a chronological sequence of actions that has to forerun the production of contemporary music videos, which I want to discuss in a new chapter.

5.5 Observing/Appropriating/Generating YouTube

If we understand Culture not as a situational way of life, customs and beliefs of certain people at a certain time as it was the case in the previous chapters, but as human-made products of art in the widest sense, that is texts, a new meaning of the terms *Observing/Generating/Appropriating* culture emerges. Firstly, *Observing* now becomes basically the consumption of, in our case, music videos and other popular phenomena. I imply hereby that 'consuming' always has an aspect of activity, contrary to an act of passivity such as pure 'watching'. *Generating* becomes, very simply, the actual production of a cultural (in the reading of art-related) work. And finally, *Appropriating* becomes the crucial part in between, which I will go into in a second. Hence, what we get is a **chronological order** of these actions that illustrates a process **of artistic practice** on the internet:

1. Observing Culture—Consuming YouTube
2. Appropriating Culture—Identifying oneself *with* YouTube
3. Generating Culture—Producing own content *for* YouTube

The cultural appropriation in this case thus is building one's own cultural identity on the influential basis of more or less self-curated content, be it on the internet or other offline sources the consumer may choose. One will adapt his or her position to everything he or she consumes. Even if one is not searching for specific content but only browsing, the emotional, social, and situational circumstances of consumption will shape his or her aesthetic concept.

---

[108] Horkheimer (1944/2008), *Dialektik der Aufklärung: Philosophische Fragmente,* 176.

In this context, we come across the concept of appropriation being a common topic in scholarly media analysis—in their handbook for intercultural communication and competence from 2007[109], Straub et al. name examining appropriation as a key method of sociological film analysis:

> *Meanings unfold only in the confrontation and appropriation of the visual material by recipients. Here, not only the mere observation plays a significant role, but the embedding in a horizon of meaning as well as the effect that it evokes in a social context. Only the reception and appropriation of a visual material thus creates its objective meaning. Hence, the appropriation is a decisive component not only for understanding the analyzed pictures but also for understanding cultural peculiarities or differences.*[110]

So far, we have come a long way from a negative and condemnable definition of the term 'appropriation' and have found that the term has a multitude of dimensions, all of which are applicable to music videos. Let me introduce yet another approach that hopefully serves to explain the music video market mechanisms, and that is the relation of **appropriation and innovation**. Early scholars like Charles Keil brought up the topic in the 1960s by saying:

> *Each successive appropriation and commercialization of a Negro [sic] style by white America through its record industry and mass media has stimulated the Negro community and its musical spokesmen to generate a 'new' music that it can call its own. [...] This appropriation-revitalization process deserves careful study.*[111]

This theory is also to be found in Nelson George's 'The Death of Rhythm and Blues' twenty years later. There he shows that continual appropriation by white youth of black style is what necessitates black innovation[112]. In more recent years, Barbara Bradby instances the consequence of the birth of Hip-Hop to 'cultural watering-down through ever-growing crossover audiences of black American music'.[113] One can try to transfer this idea to music videos and to find parallels, or say, examples for the appropriation of music video styles or other visual media by current music videos and inspect the possible effects on each media this appropriation might have had. We will come across various cases and patterns, some

---

[109] Straub, Jürgen et al. (2007), *Handbuch interkultureller Kommunikation und Kompetenz: Grundbegriffe—Theorien—Anwendungsfelder*, 429.

[110] Ibid.

[111] Keil (1966), *Urban Blues*, 43.

[112] George (1988/2003), *The Death of Rhythm and Blues*, 56.

[113] Bradby (2016): Too Posh too Rock? *The Exposure of Social Class in Popular Music*, in: Marshall & Laing (2016), *Popular Music Matters*, 13.

of which I already laid out in chapter 3. For example, the 'cinematization', that is, the visually very sophisticated and movie-oriented approach to music videos (e.g. M.I.A.—*Born Free* (2016), Woodkid—*Iron* (2011)) is one, the adoption of trashy looks and amateurish techniques (e.g. Young Thug—*Wyclef Jean* (2017), Vulfpeck—*Dean Town* (2016)), another. These two may be summarized as 'borrowing from technical extremes', but there are other examples, as well. While the search for forced or further extrinsically motivated evolutions in the appropriated media, as it was the case with black American music and Hip-Hop, may be a difficult undertaking or even pointless, however one still can ask the question: how are appropriation and innovation related in the field of music videos?

The first thesis I would like to bring up is that appropriation of basically everything visual, aesthetic, and textual by music videos does not necessarily affect these original visuals, aesthetics, and texts but puts forth a **liberalization of taste in the mass culture**. To put it in an example: If a music video with straight pop-music adopts from videos with trashy acid house, it does not mean that acid house videos get affected by that, but that consumers of both 'genres' find themselves to become more liberal towards the 'other genre'. Hence, the innovation does not take place within the cultural products themselves but within their recipients. This also has to do with the changed behavior of reception and consumption I discussed in section 3.2, namely algorithms that recommend videos we would not have watched otherwise, new forms of advertising etc. While earlier literature often speaks about 'the rock-video' or 'the metal-video'[114], such categories and categorizations do not hold up any more, as we have seen. Every genre, if one dares to use that term, has numerous examples of any imaginable aesthetic that one would not have connoted with the respective style of music twenty or thirty years ago. And the pleasant part of this is that viewers of any genre today are more open to other videos due to their possible visual resemblance. We can witness that for example in YouTube's comment-section: under Salvatore Ganacci's *Horse* (2019), a humorous video celebrating non-sense and trash about random people hurting animals, somebody posted a comment, comparing it to Billie Eilish's *bad guy* (2019) (Fig. 5.15) (Fig. 5.16):

This comment and its popularity (measured by the 7512 likes at time of writing) is noticeable in two ways: First off, the form of such comments as 'A: Proposes a challenge, B: Hold my beer (as in 'I can do that, you'll see')' currently is very popular among YouTube videos. And secondly, we have to take into account that Billie Eilish and Salvatore Ganacci are very different musicians, namely an extremely successful, young emo-esque pop singer, known for

---

[114] See section 3.2.

Fig. 5.15 Salvatore Ganacci—*Horse*. The video opens with four apathic people punching or somehow hurting animals in other ways. Salvatore Ganacci then arrives at the scene in a driving shoe and revenges the animals by punching (etc.) the people back, equally unemotional

Fig. 5.16 Comments on Salvatore Ganacci—*Horse* (2019)[115] and Billie Eilish—*bad guy* (2019)[116]

her character and visual appearance both on stage and in music videos, and a way less famous EDM-DJ. This comment although shows that a considerable amount of people is consuming both artists, at least on YouTube where they are connected by their, or most significantly their videos', 'weirdness'. This does not inevitably mean that the video has gotten more important than the song. However, the fact that musical parameters seem to play an inferior role in the public perception and debate of music videos surely adds to the proposition that they can be understood as an own language that *can* be discussed without the linking to specific songs, genres, and aesthetics. Accepting the 'weirdness' as a common parameter to compare and even appreciate both *Horse* and *bad guy*, we already leave the music behind because neither of the songs could be objectively described as 'weird'. 'Horse' is a very straight forward ravy instrumental with no particular unexpected elements in it, 'bad guy' is a dark but upbeat pop-song that

---

[115] https://www.youtube.com/watch?v=DyDfgMOUjCI (accessed 05/18/2019).
[116] https://www.youtube.com/watch?v=NkRkuI0ZgX0 (accessed 05/17/2019).

5.5 Observing/Appropriating/Generating YouTube

is somewhat unconventional in its scarce arrangement and catchy in its sounds used, but nonetheless likable and pleasing.

So, the assessment by Ted Polhemus from 1997 *'Who is real? Who is a replicant? Who cares? Life is a fancy-dress party, enjoy.'*[117] is now evenly applicable to the music video world as to subcultures, in which context he wrote it in originally.

The second thesis I want to address refers to a topic brought up by Simon Frith in 'Performing Rites', quoting Karl Marx. It is fairly easy, Frith says, moving analytically from cultural to the material world, that is, interpret cultural products based on social circumstances. Whereas it is much more crucial, to turn around the direction of analysis and to find out why an idea takes on a specific artistic or aesthetic form and not some other and how art can pose demands to itself under varied conditions.[118] Or, as he formulates in 'Music and Identity':

> *After the cultural event, as a historian might agree, we can say why expression had to happen this way; before it there is no creative necessity at all. And if art is therefore, so to speak, originally accidental, then there is no particular reason to accept its makers' special claims on it. The interesting question, rather, is how art comes to make its own claims, in other circumstances, for itself*[119]

While I don't want to discuss this theory's claim to absoluteness concerning art in general, I still find it to be very fitting into this chapter, if read under the premise of innovation. That means, how are accidentality and innovative claims to be seen in our construct of Observing/Appropriating/Generating YouTube?

Considering the construction and functioning of the space of music video production and consumption (YouTube, if you like) itself, its vastness and extreme pace of guiding one through this audiovisual universe helps to approach this subject. I want to consult McLuhan's (having almost become placative) line 'The medium is the message' again. When interpreting 'message' as 'the essential' ('The medium is the essential'), I might be so bold and change the line to 'The medium is the answer'. In order to actually answer Frith's question for art's own innovative claims, one must, though, read 'medium' more widely than just the website www.YouTube.com. If we understand the medium YouTube as a holistic system of prosumerism and consider its monopolistic position in the visual world and at the same time its qualities of intense intimacy and experienced independency, all its technical processes, and the overwhelming resonance by the users,

---

[117] Polhemus (1997), *In the Supermarket of Style*, in: Redhead (ed.), The Clubcultures Reader, 151.

[118] Frith (1996), *Performing Rites*, 13.

[119] Frith, *Music and Identity*, in: Hall, du Gay (1996), Question of Cultural Identity, 109.

we end up having a space where **innovation is almost a deterministic necessity**, unattached to singular persons like the auteurs of the 1990s like Cunningham, Gondry, etc. Again, it is a self-propelling machinery. Authorship becomes more abstract in this world of steady innovation and creation. Every day one might find a new favorite video or a new favorite band. This is not necessarily a sign of lacking appreciation for individual artists or artistic products, but still, the relation between recipient and artist becomes more arbitrary. I do not mean this in a pessimistic sense; these are just the rules of consumption on this platform. The symptom of the growing appearance of the directors' names in the videos that I described in section 3.4, is a further indication to this thesis. Just *because* the directors/authors generally become less important for the system, it is more important to them to place themselves in the product and thereby in the market.

This last segment of this work explored further readings of and approaches to the three categories Observing, Appropriating and Generating Culture and focused on the matter of innovation in producing music videos. In my opinion and experience, the three proposed aspects offer a fruitful starting point to music videos' analysis in their cultural environment and could be used in future discussions, also with different focuses and scientific issues.

Conclusion 6

In this work, I have tried to theoretically grasp how music videos are situated in the late 2010s, what role they play in our media and cultural environment, and how the phenomenon of the prosumer affects their production and reception. The technological and legal development brought the ability to produce cultural goods, in our case, music videos, in whatever style and to whatever technical and textual extend we want and also, the possibility to consume whenever and whatever we want. There is no doubt that moving images (and music videos in particular) today have become an integral part of pop music. The extreme freedom, popularity, and basically infinite space to create led to my proposition of understanding of music videos as a language (just as music is often perceived as a universal language) in that every cultural phenomenon is formulated and somehow treated with specific codes and combinations of signs to create meaning. By doing so, the videos cover a variety of functions and intentions: from pure entertainment over advertising or promoting to raising awareness for specific issues. The in-depth analyses of the videos *Humble* and *Gosh* have shown how high they set their own standards and that they want to contribute to the public discourse on social issues as an established medium. Not only honors, such as the Pulitzer Prize for Kendrick Lamar, demonstrate that they were successful. Music videos keep leading the most popular category on YouTube by a margin, and the technology market continues to offer equipment more affordable and thereby make the implementation of ideas more plausible. This mixture of supply and demand has as consequence that every thinkable topic or motivation is getting put into practice, so what we end up with is a landscape of audio-visual products that is highly up to date, if not ahead of time. It is available to most people and encompasses the entire corpus of cultural issues and their treatment, making the music video a true supertext. Not just formally, as Carol Vernallis proposed, meaning its visual influence on other audiovisual media, nor just for its persistence as a stoical medium that time yet struggles to erase or push to insignificance—Also in the function it has on culture and society and on their viewers: I have demonstrated by using different examples how music videos function as an index of our current cultural and technical condition, as Will Straw put it. Or, as I formulated a thesis in the introduction to this work: Music videos are indeed interpretative methods that are used to make sense of the world of the social entity's members. YouTube's dense environment and high pace offer a compact and always pioneering space that reflects our treatment of cultural, political, and social issues. Beyond that, I showed that the music video medium is a prime example of participatory culture, as formulated by Henry Jenkins, and therefore contains a remarkable but often neglected dimension of interaction and participation. The medium's effect or impact on its cultural environment is no longer only noticeable in formal ways, such as movies borrowing aesthetics or editing methods from it, for example. It goes well beyond that: music videos are opinion leaders of the Zeitgeist. They pre-define and reflect how open and liberal we are as a society towards certain stylistics, topics, and the way they are treated, as for example, the depiction of women, camp, or violence. Consequentially, they represent particular collective judgments concerning society. And finally, they may dictate how or at least *that* we react to certain political issues as discussed in-depth with the example of *This is America* in this work.

Several aspects of music videos' relation to activism were discussed in chapter 5 and the question that was asked in section 5.3: 'Are music videos as triggers of social engagement or movement just an illusion?' is yet to be answered. I think that Vernallis' and Frith's ideas indeed are correct: '*I am sitting on the couch—not going anywhere. In the video's moment, however, I feel I have done the necessary social work.*' and '*If listening to an album [or in this case watching a music video] without any condition is understood as resistance, resistance means purely nothing.*'. From their perspective, only in very few instances, if any at all, music videos could be understood as impulses for social activism concerning political disbalances, gender, identity, or any other topic. What they both could not have known in their statements from 1999 and 2004, though, is the fact that we do not consume music (videos) merely sitting on our couch anymore. We comment, share and rate them, and most importantly: we have the ability to produce them ourselves. And in their design, we implement our ideas, concepts,

6 Conclusion

and urges we have towards the world we live in, because we believe that our contribution matters[1]. More individually speaking, music videos shape our taste and aestheticize our perception. Hence, the question: 'Are music videos as triggers of social engagement or movement just an illusion?' is to be answered with 'no'. Firstly, because they provoke us and speak to us in a native but exclusive language that we are willing to react to. And secondly, because they are social engagement themselves and may raise awareness of the potential of cultural impact music videos have. They might get sampled in other videos or processed differently as it was the case with *This is America* and the many reactions in various formats and shapes. Every week another number of videos is released that give reason to think and talk about: One might break loose a debate about a certain sociocultural topic, another one might either push the technical and conceptual limits of what is possible (like Björk—*losss* (2019), Aphex Twin—*T69 Collapse* (2018) or SOPHIE—*Faceshopping* (2018)) or question the value of technical limits at all (Ed Sheeran feat. Justin Bieber—*I Don't Care* (2019). Jörn Heitmann, who directed eight of Rammstein's iconic videos, said in a making-of video from 2019:

> **Nothing is convention anymore.** *Art changes convention and art changes the image of society.*[2]

And next to these already noteworthy characteristics, music videos constitute a constant commentary on a society's technology, values, problems, issues—its culture. I pointed out in section 4.5 that music videos act representatively and even play a vital role themselves in the handling of building medial profiles and images. Both actively for individuals that curate their program and also passively for abstract matters that get shaped and filled with certain meanings through their depiction and reception.

Coming back to Sunil Manghani's theory that the actual music video medium is slowly being replaced by a new form of video by YouTubers and other social media users: I have found, just by looking at the numbers (see page 19), that indeed an increasing saturation of the music video market is happening, but it certainly isn't replacing music video itself—it only adds to the medial spectrum orbiting around it. It demonstrates its great impact and that it has truly become much more than just a supplement, a promotion for a song, or even just a visual product. Through its omnipresence, it shapes its own evolution, compromising

---

[1] Jenkins, five characteristics that define participatory culture, see chapter 4.
[2] Rammstein—Radio (Official Making Of) https://www.youtube.com/watch?v=Erg0LU ViHL4.

more and more secondary products and becoming a powerful tool that has the potential to reach and influence people all around the world with comparably very little effort, exposing it, economically seen, as one of the most convenient art forms. This is why I am looking optimistically on the discussion if or when music videos' death has finally come: I see no evidence for a near end of the music video, but quite the contrary. The idea of a Renaissance of the music video is obvious: After a previous, glorious heyday and its decline, we experience the 'new emergence', as Giorgio Vasari writes, as a redefinition under new rules and conditions that have now become established, more than ten years after the founding of YouTube and the dissolution of MTV. From my perspective, the second golden age, or even a completely new age of music videos that needs no back reference to former times because it stands on its own feet and is leading a new form of media practice, has just begun. As I have laid out, there are many cases where music videos are not inspired by preceding cultural products but are the influence on other media and collective responses such as activism or multimedia production themselves.

We must, of course, distinguish between the music video medium and individual videos, since many of the major results this work has delivered are only applicable to **the entirety of the medium**, not to any random industry hall performance or beach party video. Nevertheless, a great number of music videos do not cease to provide original and progressive material for society, prosumers, and scholars to enjoy, inspire, and talk about, in whatever combination.

This work has been an attempt to show as many facets as possible in order to give a proposal on how to talk about music videos, captured in a moment in time. Or as I formulated it in the introduction: to contribute to a developing understanding of the medium. I hope to have delivered impulses that might be new to someone or to have formulated my ideas in ways and contexts that might spark others to dive deeper in certain topics and, first and foremost, realize music videos' importance and keep their analysis current. The findings of this book may not be applicable for music videos in some years' time, but still, they illustrate a status quo that may be valuable for further developments in both production and analysis. They also have shown how multifaceted the matter music video is and how many approaches there are to discuss it at which I tried my best to illustrate a sensible overview. This is why I appreciate transdisciplinary attempts to holistically analyze music videos in all their dimensions and consider them to be fruitful for a vivid scholarly discussion. A well-done and successful example for this way of working is Vernallis et al. with *Introduction: APES**T (APESHIT)*

6 Conclusion

Beyoncé and Jay-Z at the Louvre[3], in that specialists from different disciplines, from music over pop culture to sociology and history, analyze one single music video.

Open Research Questions:
In this work, I addressed film studies, cultural studies, literary studies, and linguistics in order to analyze our given research issues. Nevertheless, some more specific fields of research worth discussing could not be covered in this work. I chose not to go deep into the matter of gender and music videos for example, since the long tradition and relation this discipline has had with the medium in my opinion would require more than just one subchapter in a work like this. However, there is significant movement to all extremes on the market regarding that subject whose scholarly and social debate still is a vital part of music videos' identity. Furthermore, there is the connection between youth culture and music videos that I could not go into particularly in this work. Music consumption and the music market will always be heavily dependent on youth culture or at least on the youth as a target group. But how youth culture's role may have evolved or diminished in context of prosumerism shall be interesting to find out. The question if adolescents produce their music videos differently than older generations could be addressed empirically, with surveys or in case studies.

Another interesting topic is how the issue of the Renaissance of the music video could be analyzed empirically. The comparison of music videos from different periods of time, for example between 1985–1995, 2000–2010, and 2015–2020 concerning certain characteristics such as budget, originality, resonance from the audience should be profitable for the discussion of music video's history.

Other topics that would require empirical analysis are: It seems that the imagery is often the decisive factor if a music video is liked or not and that in these cases, the valuation of the music loses importance. This is a bold thesis that is plausible in the context of this work, but also gives reason to further research empirically and quantitively to analyze this question from other viewpoints. Other questions are: Which peer groups are affected mostly by music videos and with which consequences? What are the differences between MTV and YouTube concerning youth culture and target group? Since prosumerism clearly is not restricted to people of a certain age, this shall be an interesting topic.

---

[3] Vernallis et al. (2018), *Introduction: APES**T (APESHIT) Beyonce and Jay-Z at the Louvre*, in: Journal for Popular Music Studies.

This work was written with a background in media practice and making music videos myself and methodologically, I made this background the premise for my research. The next step in this direction that I want to encourage and that I may dedicate myself in the future is ethnomethodological work by music video makers on their particular artistic work. The interconnection of practice and theory can only help us understand the medium holistically and create an appropriate lobby in academia.

Another field of research that was discussed briefly here but holds great potential for the scholarly debate is that of the economic aspects of music videos for the music and internet market. While there have been positive and optimistic quotes in this work from players in the industry, such as Sarah Boardman, Head of Music at Pulse Films, there is much more to say and to research about the economic role music videos play and will play in the future. Several questions arise in a time when prosumerism has also caught up with music production and music videos are considered 'cultural events' that attract enormous attention and are distributed alongside movies and series: How will music production companies and labels calculate their budgets in the future and what do they expect financially from music videos compared to the actual music? Will there be (more) collaborations with major film studios like Warner Bros., 20th Century Fox, Netflix etc., now that the first experimental music videos are released on Netflix and the press says that some music videos are more exciting than any American feature film having come out that year? (see section 3.5)

Time will tell. Until then, we can only state that every music video is done in a specific context that incorporates particular conditions, perceptions, and concepts. Some will be aware of certain assumptions that I covered in this work, some may have completely different approaches that I could not address or even think of. However, what makes the music video market so interesting and grants it such a key role in both the medial and musical world is exactly that: Every video brings other facets of styles and motivations to mind and in the big picture, they assemble a **cumulated creative and transcultural outlet beyond comparison**. I want to encourage both scholars and prosumers to **explore the limits of the mechanisms of action** music videos offer. If they all keep understanding and making use of music videos' opportunities of cultural impact, I am very much looking forward to the medium's future.

Bibliography

List of Referenced Music Videos[1]

Aminé—REDMERCEDES (2017), dir. Adam "Aminé" Daniel
Aphex Twin—*T69 Collapse* (2018), dir. Weirdcore
Ariana Grande—*7 rings* (2019), dir. Hannah Lux Davis
Ariana Grande—*Monopoly* (2019), dir. Alfredo Flores & Ricky Alvarez
Backstreet Boys—*I Want it That Way* (1999), dir. Wayne Isham
Beastie Boys—*Sabotage* (1993), dir. Spike Jonze
Benzo—*Blood Orange* (2019), dir. Devonté Hynes
Beyoncé—*Lemonade* (2016), dir. Khalil Joseph et al.
Billie Eilish—*when the party's over* (2018), dir. Carlos Lopez Estrada
Billie Eilish—*bad guy* (2019), dir. Dave Meyers
Björk—*Army of Me* (1995), dir. Michel Gondry
Björk—*It's Oh So Quiet* (1995), dir. Spike Jonze
Björk—*All is Full of Love* (1999), dir, Chris Cunningham
Björk —*losss* (2019), dir. Tobias Gremmler
Blackstreet—*No Diggity* (1996), dir. Hype Williams
boy pablo—*Everytime* (2017), dir. cutefabio777
Bruno Mars feat. Cardi B.—*Finesse* (2017), dir. Bruno Mars
BTS (방탄소년단)—*Fake Love* (2018), dir. YongSeok Choi
The Buggles—*Video Killed the Radio Star* (1981), dir. Russell Mulcahy
Camila Cabello—*Havana* (2017), dir. Dave Meyers
The Cars—*You Might Think* (1984), dir. Charlie Levi
The Chainsmokers—*#SELFIE* (2014), dir. Taylor Stephens & Ike Love Jones
The Chainsmokers feat. Halsey—*Closer* (2018), dir. Rory Kramer

---

[1] All music video stills used were taken from the official YouTube channels of the respective artists.

The Chainsmokers—*Paris* (2018), dir. Rory Kramer
Childish Gambino—*This Is America* (2018), dir. Hiro Murai
Coldplay—*Adventure of A Lifetime* (2015), dir. Mat Whitecross
Coldplay—*Hymn for the Weekend* (2016), dir. Ben Mor
Deichkind—*Wer sagt denn das?* (2019), dir. Auge Altona
Deichkind—*Keine Party* (2019), dir. Auge Altona
Die Antwoord—*Fatty Boom Boom* (2012), dir. Die Antwoord
DJ Khaled feat. Justin Bieber—*I'm the One* (2017), dir. Eif Rivera
Drake—*Hotline Bling* (2015), dir. Director X
Drake—*God's Plan* (2018), dir. Karena Evans
Ed Sheeran feat. Justin Bieber—*I Don't Care* (2019), dir. Emil Nava
Eminem—*The Real Slim Shady* (2000),
Eminem—*River* (2018), dir. Emil Nava
Eminem—*Framed* (2018), dir. Emil Nava
Fatboy Slim—*Weapon of Choice* (2000), dir. Spike Jonze
Flasher—*Material* (2018), dir. Nick Roney
Gesaffelstein—*Pursuit* (2013), dir. Nicholas Loir
Iggy Azalea—*Bounce* (2013), dir. Jonas & François
Imagine Dragons—*Thunder* (2017), dir. Joseph Kahn
Jamie xx—*Gosh* (2016), dir. Romain Gavras
Joyner Lucas—*I'm Not Racist* (2017), dir. Joyner Lucas & Ben Proulx
Justice—*Stress* (2006), dir. Romain Gavras
Kanye West—*Famous* (2016), dir. Kanye West
Kate Bush—*Wuthering Heights* (Version 1 and 2)
Katy Perry—*Dark Horse* (2014), dir. Matthew Cullen
Katy Perry—*Swish Swish* (2017), dir. Dave Meyers
Kendrick Lamar—*Alright* (2015), dir. Colin Tilley & the little homies
Kendrick Lamar—*Loyalty* (2017), dir. Dave Meyers & the little homies
Kendrick Lamar—*Humble* (2017), dir. Dave Meyers & the little homies
Lady Gaga—*Poker Face* (2009), dir. Ray Kay
Lady Gaga—*Paparazzi* (2009), dir. Jonas Åkerlund
Lady Gaga feat. Beyoncé—*Telephone* (2010), dir. Jonas Åkerlund
Lady Gaga—*G.U.Y.* (2010), dir. Lady Gaga
Las Ketchup—*The Ketchup Song (Aserejé)* (2002), dir. Mark Kohr
Lil' Budget—*DEFLUENCER* (2018), dir. Pretty Ugly Motion Pictures
Lil Nas X — *Old Town Road* (2019) ft. Billy Ray Cyrus, dir. Calmatic
Little Big—*HATEFUL LOVE* (2016), dir. Alina Pasok, Iliya Prusikin
Little Big—*SKIBIDI* (2018), dir. Alina Pasok, Iliya Prusikin
Major Lazer & DJ Snake—*Lean On* (2015), dir. Tim Erem
Marshmello feat. Bastille—*Happier* (2018), dir. Mercedes Bryce Morgan
M.I.A.—*Born Free* (2010), dir. Romain Gavras
M.I.A.—*Borders* (2016), dir. M.I.A.
Michael Jackson—*Billie Jean* (1982), dir. Steve Barron
Michael Jackson—*Thriller* (1982), dir. John Landis

Michael Jackson—*Bad* (1987), dir. Martin Scorsese
Michael Jackson—*Black and White* (1991), dir. John Landis
Michael Jackson—*Scream* (1995), dir. Mark Romanek
Mike Perry feat. Shy Martin (2016)—*The Ocean*, dir. Jimi Drosinos
Miley Cyrus—*Wrecking Ball* (2013), dir. Terry Richardson
Miley Cyrus—*Mother's Daughter* (2019), dir. Alexandre Moors
Milky Chance—*Blossom* (2017), dir. Anthony Molina
OK Go—*Here It Goes Again* (2006), dir. Damian Kulash
OK Go—*WTF?* (2009), dir. Damian Kulash, Tim Nackashi
OK Go—*This Too Shall Pass* (2010), dir. Damian Kulash
OK Go—*Upside Down & Inside Out* (2016), dir. Damian Kulash, Trish Sie
OK Go—*Obsession* (2018), dir. Damian Kulash, Yusuke Tanaka
Professor Soap—*Spirit Quest Journey* (2011), dir. Professor Soap
Psy—*Gangnam Style* (2012), dir. Cho Soo-hyun
Pulp—*Babies* (1992), dir. Martin Wallace
Queen—*Bohemian Rhapsody* (1975), dir. Bruce Gowers
Rammstein—*Deutschland* (2019), dir. Specter Berlin
Reggie Watts—*Waves* (2017), dir. Benjamin Dickinson
Robin Thicke—*Blurred Lines* (2013), dir. Diane Martel
Romano—*Copyshop* (2016), dir. Jakob Grunert
Romano —*Mutti* (2017), dir. Justin Izumi
Run the Jewels—*Crown* (2014), dir. Peter Martin
Run the Jewels feat. DJ Shadow—*Nobody Speak* (2016), dir. Sam Pilling
Salvatore Ganacci—*Horse* (2019), dir. Vedran Rupic
Santana feat. Rob Thomas—*Smooth* (1999), dir. Marcus Raboy
Slipknot—*All Out Life* (2018), dir. M. Shawn Crahan
SOPHIE—*Faceshopping* (2018), dir. SOPHIE
Taylor Swift feat. Kendrick Lamar—*Bad Blood* (2015), dir. Joseph Kahn
Taylor Swift—*Delicate* (2018), dir. Joseph Kahn
Taylor Swift—*You Need to Calm Down* (2019), dir. Drew Kirsch & Taylor Swift
The Notorious B.I.G.—*Juicy* (1994), dir. Sean "Puffy" Combs
Thom Yorke—*Anima* (2019), dir. Paul Thomas Anderson
Tyler, The Creator—*IFHY* (2017), dir. Wolf Haley aka Tyler, The Creator
Tyler, The Creator feat. Kali Uchis—*See You Again* (2018), dir. Wolf Haley
Vulfpeck—*Dean Town* (2016), dir. Jack Stratton
Whitney Houston—*Step by Step* (1997), dir. Paul Hunter
Wir bringen kalten Kaffee mit—*Heiße Luft* (2016) dir. Leo Feisthauer & Tim Koglin
Woodkid—*Iron* (2011), dir. Yoanne Lemoine
Ylvis—*Language of Love* (2016), dir. Ole Martin Hafsmo
Young Thug—*Wyclef Jean* (2017), dir. Ryan Staake

References

ADORNO, Theodor W. (1967): *Resumé über die Kulturindustrie*, in: Ohne Leitbild, Parva Aesthetica, Frankfurt am Main.
AHN, Joong Ho et al. (2013): *Korean pop takes off! Social media strategy of Korean entertainment industry*, 2013 10th International Conference on Service Systems and Service Management: pp. 774–777.
ALTMEYER, Markus (2008): *Die Filme und Musikvideos von Michel Gondry – Zwischen Surrealismus, Pop und Psychoanalyse*, Tectum, Marburg.
ALTROGGE, Michael & AMANN, Rolf (1991): *Videoclips – Die geheimen Verführer der Jugend?*, VISTAS, Berlin.
ARNOLD, Gina et al. (2017): *Music/Video – Histories, Aesthetics, Media*, Bloomsbury Academic, New York.
BACKER, Gordon & HACKER, Peter (1980): *Understanding and Meaning. An Analytical Commentary on the Philosophical Investigations I*. Blackwell, Oxford.
BALAJI, Murali, & SIGLER, Thomas (2018): *Global riddim: cultural production and territorial identity in Caribbean music videos*. In: Visual Communication, 17(1), pp. 91–111.
BECK, Klaus (2006): *Computervermittelte Kommunikation im Internet*, Oldenbourg Verlag, Munich/Vienna.
BERROCAL, Salomé et al. (2014): *Prosumidores mediáticos en la comunicación política*: in: El «politainment» en YouTube Comunicar, vol. XXI, (43), pp. 65–72.
BLOOM, Harold (1973, 1997): *The Anxiety of Influence*, Oxford University Press.
BÓDY, Veruschka & BÓDY, Gabor (eds.) (1986): *Video in Kunst und Alltag - Vom kommerziellen zum kulturellen Videoclip*, DuMont, Cologne.
BRACKETT, David (2016): *Categorizing Sound: Genre and Twentieth-Century Popular Music*, University of California Press.
BRÄUTIGAM, Gregor (2006): *Kulturökonomie: Kulturgenerierung – Kulturanalyse – Kulturkontakt – Wie gesellschaftliche Verfahrensmuster die Ausprägung des Humankapitals beeinflussen*, Shaker, Aachen.
BROWN, J. D., & CAMPBELL, K. (1986). *Race and gender in music videos: The same beat but a different drummer*, In: Journal of Communication, Vol. 36, pp. 94–106.
BRUNS, Axel (2008): *Blogs, Wikipedia, Second Life, and Beyond: From Production to Produsage*. Digital Formations, 45, Peter Lang, New York.
BURKART, Roland (2002): *Was ist eigentlich ein ‹Medium›? Überlegungen zu einem kommuni-kationswissenschaftlichen Medienbegriff angesichts der Konvergenzdebatte*, in: Haas, Hannes/Jarren, Otfried (eds.): Mediensysteme im Wandel. Struktur, Organisation und Funktion der Massenmedien, Wien: Braumüller (Studienbücher zur Publizistik- und Kommunikationswissenschaft, vol. 3), pp. 15–23.
CASSIRER, Ernst (1940/1990): *Versuch über den Menschen. Einführung in eine Philosophie der Kultur*, Fischer, Frankfurt a.M.
CALAVITA, M. (2007): *"MTV Aesthetics" at the Movies: Interrogating a Film Criticism Fallacy*, in: Journal of Film and Video, 59 (3), pp. 15-31.
CARTMELL, Deborah (ed.) (1997): *Trash Aesthetics – Popular Culture and its Audience*, Pluto Press.

Bibliography

CHANDLER, Daniel (2002): *Semiotics – The Basics*, Routledge.
GIUFFRE, Liz & KEITH, Sarah (2014): *SBS PopAsia: non-stop K-pop in Australia*, in: CHOI, JungBong & MALIANGKAY (eds.): K-pop - The International Rise of the Korean Music Industry *Media, Culture and Social Change in Asia*, Routledge.
COOKE, Deryck (1959): The Language of Music, Oxford University Press.
COVINGTON, Paul et al. (2016): *Deep Neural Networks for YouTube Recommendations*, in: Proceedings of the 10th ACM Conference on Recommender Systems, New York.
CRANE, William (2018): *Cultural Formation and Appropriation in the Era of Merchant Capitalism*, in: Historical Materialism, 26 (2).
CSEKE, Iris (2018): Protest, Kunst und Theater auf YouTube, epodium.
DARLEY, Andrew (2000): *Visual Digital Culture: Surface play and Spectacle in New Media Genres*, Routledge, London.
DAVIDSON, James et al. (2010): *The YouTube video recommendation system*, RecSys.
DENISOFF, R. Serge (1988): *Inside MTV*, Transaction Publishers, New Jersey.
DIXON, Wheeler Winston (2001): *Twenty-five reasons why it's all over. The End of Cinema as We Know It: American Film in the Nineties.* Ed. Jon Lewis, NYU Press, New York, pp. 356–366.
DOLATA, Ulrich & SCHRAPE, Jan-Felix (eds.) (2018): *Kollektivität im Internet – Soziale Bewegungen, Open Source, Communities, Internetkonzerne*, Springer VS, Wiesbaden.
EDMOND, Maura (2014): *Here We Go Again: Music Videos After YouTube*, in: Television and New Media, 15.4, pp. 305–320.
ENGELMANN, Jan (ed.) (1999): *Die kleinen Unterschiede – Der Cultural Studies Reader*, Campus, Frankfurt am Main.
ENGLIS, Basil G. (1991): *Music Television and Its Influences on Consumer Culture, and the Transmission of Consumption Messages*, in: NA - Advances in Consumer Research Volume 18, eds. Rebecca H. Holman and Michael R. Solomon, Provo, UT: Association for Consumer Research, pp. 111–114.
FAULSTICH, Werner (2002): Einführung in die Medienwissenschaft. Probleme – Methoden – Domänen, Fink, Munich.
FISKE, John (1986) *MTV: Post Structural Post Modern*, Journal of Communication Inquiry 10 (1), pp. 74–79.
FRITH, Simon (1996): *Performing Rites – On the Value of Popular Music*, Oxford University Press, Oxford.
FRITH, Simon (2011): *Music and Identity*, in: Hall, Stuart & du Gay, Paul (2011): Question of Cultural Identity, SAGE Publications Ltd, pp. 108–150.
FUHR, Michael (2015): *Globalization and Popular Music in South Korea – Sounding out K-Pop*, Routledge.
GENETTE, Gérard (1982): *Palimpsests: Literature in the Second Degree*, University of Nebraska Press.
GENETTE, Gérard (1992): *The architext: An introduction*, Berkeley, University of California Press.
GEORGE, Nelson (1988, 2003): *The Death of Rhythm and Blues*, Penguin Books.
GERHARDS, Jürgen/NEIDHARDT, Friedhelm (1990): *Strukturen und Funktionen moderner Öffent-lichkeit. Fragestellungen und Ansätze*,

Berlin, WZB, available on:http://www.polsoz.fu-berlin. de/ soziologie/arbeitsbereiche/makrosoziologie/mitarbeiter/lehrstuhlinhaber/dateien/Gerhards Neidhardt-1990.pdf (07.11.2020).

GILROY, Paul (1990): *Sounds authentic: black music, ethnicity, and the challenge of a changing same*, Black Music Research Journal, 10, 2, pp. 128–131.

GOODWIN, Andrew (1992): *Dancing in the Distraction Factory. Music Television and Popular Culture*, Minneapolis.

HALL, Stuart (1973): *Encoding and Decoding in the Television Discourse*, Birmingham University Press.

HALL, S. (1977): *Culture, the Media and the Ideological Effect*, in Curran, Gurevitch & Woolcott (eds), Mass Communication and Society, London, Edward Arnold, pp. 315–348.

HALLIGAN, Benjamin (2016), *A promo video is simply an advertisement for a song?*, in: Heinze, Carsten & Niebling, Laura (eds.) (2016): Populäre Musikkulturen im Film: Inter- und transdisziplinäre Perspektiven, pp. 399–428.

HANSEN, C. H., & HANSEN, R. D. (1988). *How rock music videos can change what is seen when boy meets girl: Priming stereotypic appraisal of social interactions*, in: Sex Roles, vol. 19, pp. 287–316.

HAUSHEER, Cecilia & SCHÖNHOLZER, Annette (eds.) (1994): *Visueller Sound – Musikvideos zwischen Avantgarde und Populärkultur*, Zyklop, Luzern.

HEARSUM, Paula (2013), *The Emancipation of Music Video*, in: Richardson, John et al. (eds.) (2013): *The Oxford Handbook of New Audiovisual Aesthetics*, Oxford University Press, pp. 483–500.

HECKEN, Thomas (ed.) (2017): *Handbuch Popkultur*, Metzler, Stuttgart.

HEGEL, G. W. F. (1986): *Vorlesungen über die Ästhetik I*. Suhrkamp Verlag, Frankfurt am Main 1986.

HEIDENREICH, Stefan (2019): *Demokratisiert die Kunst!*, https://www.deutschlandfunk.de/bildende-kunst-die-kunst-demokratisieren.1184.de.html?dram:article_id=445968

HEMPFER, Klaus W. (ed.) (1993): *Renaissance – Diskursstrukturen und epistemologische Voraussetzungen*, Franz Steiner, Stuttgart.

HEMMING, Jan (2009): *Zur Phänomenologie des ‚Ohrwurms'*, in: Musikpsychologie (20), Hogrefe Verlag, Göttingen, pp. 184–207.

HEMMING, Jan (2016): *Methoden der Erforschung populärer Musik*, Springer VS.

HELMS, Dietrich & PHLEPS, Thomas (eds.) (2013): *Ware Inszenierungen – Performance, Vermarktung und Authentizität in der populären Musik*, transcript, Bielefeld.

HESMONDHALGH, David (2013): *Why music matters*, Wiley Blackwell, Chichester.

HIGGINS, Kathleen Marie (2012): *The Music Between Us: Is Music a Universal Language?*, University of Chicago Press.

HINRICHSEN, Hans-Joachim (2012): *Was ist „das Werk selbst"?* in: Rössner/Uhl (2012), *Renaissance der Authentizität – Über die neue Sehnsucht nach dem Ursprünglichen*, transcript, Bielefeld, pp. 159–175.

HOLT, Fabian (2007): *Genre in Popular Music*, University of Chicago Press.

HORKHEIMER, Max (1944/2008): *Dialektik der Aufklärung: Philosophische Fragmente*, Frankfurt am Main, Fischer-Taschenbuch-Verl., Frankfurt am Main.

JACKE, Christoph (2003): *Kontextuelle Kontigenz: Musikclips im wissenschaftlichen Umgang*, in: Helms, Dietrich & Phleps, Thomas (eds.) (2003): Clipped Differences – Geschlechterrepräsentationen im Musikvideo, transcript, Bielefeld, pp. 27–40.

JENKINS, Henry et al. (2006): *Fans, bloggers, and gamers: Exploring participatory culture*. New York: New York University Press.

JENKINS, Henry et al. (2015): *Participatory Culture in a Networked Era: A Conversation about Youth, Commerce, and Politics*, polity.

JOST, Christofer et al. (2013): *Computergestützte Analyse von audiovisuellen Medienprodukten*, Springer VS, Wiesbaden.

KAPLAN, E. Ann (1987): *Rocking around the clock. Music Television, Postmodernism and Consumer Culture*, Routledge, London.

KEAZOR, Henry & WÜBBENA, Thorsten (2007): *Video Thrills the Radio Star*, transcript, Bielefeld.

KEAZOR, Henry et al. (2011): *Imageb(u)ilder – Vergangenheit, Gegenwart und Zukunft des Videoclips*, Telos, Münster.

KEAZOR, Henry (2018) *Portable music videos? Music video aesthetics for handheld devices*, in: Volume! : la revue des musiques populaires, 14:2 (2018), Nr. 1. pp. 201–210

KEEN, Andrew (2007), *The Cult of the Amateur - How Today's Internet is Killing Our Culture and Assaulting Our Economy*, Nicholas Brealey, London.

KEIL, Charles (1966, 2014): *Urban Blues*, University of Chicago Press.

Keller, Reiner (2012): *Das Interaktive Paradigma – Eine Einführung*, Springer VS, Wiesbaden.

KORSGAARD, Mathias B. (2017): *Music Video After MTV: Audiovisual Studies, New Media, and Popular Music*, Routledge.

KROTZ, Friedrich (2006): *Gesellschaftliches Subjekt und kommunikative Identität – Zum Menschenbild von Cultural Studies und Symbolischen Interaktionismus*, in Hepp (ed.) (2006): Kultur – Medien – Macht: Cultural Studies und Medienanalyse, Westdt. Verlag, Opladen.

KURTIŞOĞLU, Belma (2014), *Ethnomethodology in the use of Ethnomusicology and Ethnochoreology*, in: Fourth Symposium of the ICTM Study Group on Music and Dance in Southeastern Europe (2014), Colografx, Belgrade, pp. 281–286.

LETTS, Richard (1997): *Music: Universal language between all nations?*, in: International Journal of Music Education. 1997 (1), pp. 22–31.

LILKENDEY, Martin (2017): *100 Jahre Musikvideo – Eine Genregeschichte vom frühen Kino bis YouTube*, transcript, Bielefeld.

LORD, Barry (ed.) (2007) Introduction. In Lord, B. (eds.), *The Manual of Museum Learning*. Lanham, AltaMira Press.

LULL, James (2000): *Media, Communication, Culture: A Global Approach*, John Wiley & Sons.

LYONS, John (1981): *Language and Linguistics*, Cambridge University Press.

MACHART, Oliver (2018): *Cultural Studies*, UVK Verlag, Munich.

MAGGIO, J. (2007): Comics and Cartoons: *A Democratic Art-Form* in: PS: Political Science & Politics, 40 (2), pp. 237–239.

MAREK, Roman (2013): *Understanding YouTube – Über die Faszination eines Mediums*, transcript, Bielefeld.

MARSH, Charity & WEST, Melissa (2003): *The Nature/Technology Binary Opposition Dismantled in the Music of Madonna and Björk*, in: Lysloff, Gay (eds.), Music and Technoculture, Wesleyan University Press, pp. 182–196.

MARSHALL, Lee & LAING, Dave (eds.) (2016): *Popular Music Matters: Essays in Honour of Simon Frith*, Routledge.

MENGE, Johannes (1989): *Videoclips: Ein Klassifikationsmodell*, In: Wulff, H. J. (ed.): Film und Fernsehwissenschaftliches Kolloquium, Berlin, pp. 189–200.

MIKOS, Lothar (1993): *Selbstreflexive Bilderflut. Zur kulturellen Bedeutung des Musikkanals MTV*, in: medien praktisch, (17).

MIRONOV, Vladimir (2006), *Modern Communication, Culture & Philosophy*, in: Philosophy Now (54), pp. 18–19.

MORITZ, William (1994): *Bilder-Recycling. Die Wurzeln von MTV im Experimentalfilm*, in: Hausheer, Cecilia/Schönholzer, Annette (eds.): Visueller Sound: Musikvideos zwischen Avantgarde und Populärkultur, Zyklop, Luzern pp. 26–45.

MÜLLER, Eggo (2009): *Where quality matters: Discourses on the art of making a YouTube video*, in: Snickars & Vonderau (eds.), YouTube Reader, Stockholm, National Library of Sweden. pp. 126–139.

MÜLLER, Renate & BEHNE, Klaus-Ernst (1996), *Wahrnehmung und Nutzung von Videoclips*, in: Forschungsbericht Institut für Musikpädagogische Forschung, Hochschule für Musik, Theater und Medien Hanover; (6).

NEUMANN-BRAUN, Klaus (ed.) (2004): *Viva MTV! Popmusik im Fernsehen*, Suhrkamp, Frankfurt.

PINK, S., & LEDER MACKLEY, K. (2013*): Saturated and situated: expanding the meaning of media in the routines of everyday life*, in: Media, Culture & Society, 35(6), pp. 677–691.

POPE, Rob (2002): *The English Studies Book – An Introduction to Language, Literature and Culture*, London, Routledge.

RAILTON, Diane & WATSON, Paul (2011): *Music Video and the Politics of Representation*, Edinburgh University Press.

RAPPE, Michael (2010): *Under construction – Kontextbezogene Analyse afroamerikanischer Popmusik*, Dohr, Cologne.

RECKWITZ, Andreas (2000)*: Die Transformation der Kulturtheorien. Zur Entwicklung eines Theorieprogramms*, Velbrück Wissenschaft.

RECKWITZ, Andreas (2014 [2012]): *Die Erfindung der Kreativität. Zum Prozess gesellschaftlicher Ästhetisierung*. Berlin, Suhrkamp.

REDHEAD, Steve et al. (eds.) (1997): *The Clubcultures Reader – Readings in Popular Cultural Studies*, Blackwell Publishers Ltd.

REHBACH, Simon (2018): *Medienreflexion im Musikvideo – Das Fernsehen als Gegenstand intermedialer Beobachtung*, transcript, Bielefeld.

Reichertz and (2012): Abduktion, Deduktion und Induktion in der qualitativen Forschung, in: Steinke, et al., 2012.REICHERTZ, Jo (2012): *Abduktion, Deduktion und Induktion in der qualitativen Forschung*, in: Steinke et al. (eds) (2012): Qualitative Forschung, Rowohlt, Reinbek.

RESCH, Magnus et al. (2018): *Quantifying reputation and success in art*, in: Science, Vol. 362, Issue 6416, pp. 825–829.

RICHARDSON, John (2012): *An Eye for Music – Popular Music and the Audiovisual Surreal*, Oxford University Press.
RICHARDSON, John et al. (eds.) (2013) *The Oxford Handbook of New Audiovisual Aesthetics*, Oxford University Press.
ROGERS, Holly (2014): *Twisted Synaesthesia – Music Video and the Visual Arts*, Sound of Art, pp. 384–388.
RÖSSNER, Michael/UHL, Heidemarie (eds.) (2012): *Renaissance der Authentizität? Über die neue Sehnsucht nach dem Ursprünglichen*, transcript, Bielefeld.
RÖTTER, Günther, (2000): *Videoclips und Visualisierung von E-Musik*, in: Kloppenburg & Budde (eds.): Handbuch der Musik im 20. Jahrhundert. Vol. 11: Musik multimedial –Filmmusik, Videoclip, Fernsehen, Laaber, pp. 259–294.
SÁNCHEZ-OLMOS, Cande & VIÑUELA, Eduardo (2017): *The Musicless Music Video as a Spreadable Meme Video: Format, User Interaction, and Meaning on YouTube*, in: International Journal of Communication: n° 11, pp. 3634–3654.
SCHADE, Henriette (2018): *Soziale Bewegungen in der Mediengesellschaft*, Springer Fachmedien, Wiesbaden.
SCHLEMMER-JAMES, Mirjam (2006) *Schnittmuster – Affektive Reaktionen auf variierte Bildschnitte bei Musikvideos*, Lit Verlag, Hamburg.
SCHMID, Wolf (2013), *Implied Reader*, Paragraph 11, in: Hühn et al. (eds.): The living handbook of narratology. Hamburg: Hamburg University Press.
SCHMIDT, Axel et al. (2009): *Viva MTV! Reloaded. Musikfernsehen und Videoclips crossmedial*, Nomos, Baden-Baden.
SCHMIDT, Siegfried J. (2008): *Der Medienkompaktbegriff*, in Münker/Roesler (eds.): Was ist ein Medium?, Suhrkamp, Frankfurt am Main, pp. 144–158.
SHORE, Michael (1985): *The Rolling Stone Book of Rock Video*, Quill, New York.
SIN, Jeong-Wong (2014): *Du bist, was du hörst – Musiklabels im als Wegweiser im digitalen Zeitalter*, Campus Verlag, Frankfurt; New York.
STOKES, Brenton (2016): *Acoustic Ecology and the Death of the Music Video*, Berklee.
STRAW, Will (1988): *Music video in its contexts: popular music and post-modernism in the 1980s*, in: Popular Music, Vol. 7, No. 3, Music Video and Film (Oct., 1988), pp. 247–266.
STRAW, Will (2018): Music Video in its Contexts: 30 Years Later. Volume, 14:2(1), p. 187a–192a. https://www.cairn.info/revue-volume-2018-1-page-187a.htm.
STRAUB, Jürgen et al. (2007): *Handbuch interkultureller Kommunikation und Kompetenz: Grundbegriffe – Theorien – Anwendungsfelder*, Springer.
TAPSCOTT, Don (1994): *The Digital Economy- Promise and Peril in the Age of Networked Intelligence*, McGraw-Hill.
THOMA, George et al. (2010): *The Interactive Publication – The Document as a Research Tool*, in: Web Semantics, 2010 July 1; 8 (2–3), pp. 145–150.
THOMPSON, John B. (1990): *Ideology and Modern Culture – Critical Social Theory in the Era of Mass Communication*, Cambridge, Polity Press.
TOFFLER, Alvin (1980): *The Third Wave*, Bantam Books.
TURINO, Thomas (1999): *Signs of Imagination, Identity, and Experience: A Peircian Semiotic Theory for MusicAuthor(s)*, in: Ethnomusicology, Vol. 43, No. 2 (Spring - Summer, 1999), University of Illinois Press on behalf of Society for Ethnomusicology, pp. 221–255.

UNGER, Michael (2015): *The Aporia of Presentation: Deconstructing the Genre of K-pop Girl Group Music Videos in South Korea*, in: Journal of Popular Music Studies, Volume 27, Issue 1, pp. 25–47

VERNALLIS, Carol (2004): *Experiencing Music Video: Aesthetics and Cultural Context*, Columbia University Press.

VERNALLIS, Carol (2011): *Storytelling on the ledge – Lady Gaga's Paparazzi and Telephone*, in: Iddon, Martin & Marshall, Melanie (eds.) (2014): Lady Gaga and popular music: performing gender, fashion, and culture, New York, Routledge.

VERNALLIS, Carol (2013): *Unruly Media: YouTube, Music Video, and the New Digital Cinema*, Oxford Scholarship Online.

VERNALLIS, Carol (2013): *Music Video's Second Aesthetic?*, in: Richardson et al. (eds.) The Oxford Handbook of New Audiovisual Aesthetics, pp. 438–465.

VERNALLIS, Carol et al. (2018): *Introduction: APES**T (APESHIT) Beyonce and Jay-Z at the Louvre*, in: Journal for Popular Music Studies.

VIEREGG, Sebastian (2008) *Die Ästhetik des Musikvideos und seine ökonomische Funktion: Ein Medium zwischen Kunst und Kommerzialität*, VDM Verlag, Saarbrücken.

WEIBEL, Peter (1987): *Von der visuellen Musik zum Musikvideo*, in Bódy, Veruschka & Weibel, Peter (eds.): Clip, Klapp, Bum. Von der visuellen Musik zum Musikvideo, Dumont, Cologne, pp. 53–164.

WEIß, Matthias (2007): *Madonna revidiert – Rekursivität im Videoclip*, Reimer, Berlin.

WENZEL, Ulrich (1999): *Pawlows Panther – Zur Rezeption von Musikvideos zwischen bedingtem Reflex und zeichentheoretischer Reflexion*, in: Neumann-Braun, Klaus (ed.) (1999): Viva MTV! – Popmusik im Fernsehen, Suhrkamp, Frankfurt, pp. 45–73.

WHITELEY, Sheila & RAMBARRAN, Shara (eds.) (2016): *The Oxford Handbook of Music and Virtuality*, Oxford University Press.

WILSON, Thomas (1970): *Normative and Interpretive Paradigms in Sociology*, in: Douglas (1970): Understanding everyday life. Toward the reconstruction of sociological knowledge, Aldine, Chicago, pp. 57–79.

WINTER, Rainer (2010): *Der produktive Zuschauer – Medienaneignung als kultureller und ästhetischer Prozess*, Halem, Cologne.

YEH, Sonja (2013): Anything goes? – *Postmoderne Medientheorien im Vergleich; die großen (Medien-) Erzählungen von McLuhan, Baudrillard, Virilio, Kittler und Flusser*, transcript, Bielefeld.

YOON, Kyong (2019): *Digital Mediascapes of Transnational Korean Youth Culture*, Routledge.

YOUNG, James O. (2010): *Cultural Appropriation and the Arts*, John Wiley & Sons.

Online sources

https://www.artsy.net/article/artsy-editorial-golden-age-black-music-video (accessed February 2nd, 2019)
https://arxiv.org/abs/1905.12245 (acc. February 14th, 2019)
http://www.bbc.co.uk/newsbeat/article/11626592/lady-gaga-beats-justin-bieber-to-youtube-record (acc. January 30th, 2019)
https://www.billboard.com/articles/business/8511114/taylor-swift-me-music-videos-digital-age-economics (acc. February 14th, 2019)
https://www.billboard.com/articles/news/6867252/vfx-artist-yaron-yeshinski-coldplay-beyonces-hymn-for-the-weekend-video (acc. June 16th, 2019)
http://www.blackdogfilms.com/15396/interview-director-ben-mor-talks-coldplay-beyonce-and-the-making-of-hymn-for-the-weekend/ (acc. June 16th, 2019)
https://www.businessinsider.de/tech/tiktok-wird-inzwischen-oefter-heruntergeladen-als-whatsapp-2019-9/ (acc. June 19th, 2020)
https://colorcodedlyrics.com/2018/05/bts-bangtansonyeondan-fake-love (acc. July 18th, 2020)
https://www.complex.com/pigeons-and-planes/2017/10/boy-pablo-everytime-youtube-algorithm-interview (acc. September 9th, 2019)
http://www.dazeddigital.com/artsandculture/article/8250/1/romain-gavras-takes-a-journey-to-the-end-of-the-night (acc. July 10th, 2020)
https://diymusician.cdbaby.com/music-promotion/how-to-make-quality-video-content-quickly-and-cheaply/ (acc. July 29th, 2020)
https://edition.cnn.com/2018/03/22/us/sacramento-police-shooting/index.html (acc. September 15th, 2019)
https://www.fastcompany.com/40401628/kendrick-lamar-wants-to-stay-humble-but-this-is-a-video-to-brag-about (acc. July 8th, 2020)
https://genreisdead.com/ (acc. July 16th, 2019)
http://hq.vevo.com/white-paper-influential-music-videos-beauty-style/?lang=gb (acc. September 12th, 2019)
https://i-d.vice.com/en_us/article/qvn4qw/this-choreographer-brought-the-african-diaspora-to-childish-gambinos-this-is-america (acc. September 15th, 2019)
https://www.instagram.com/p/Bkc_rJJg27q/ (acc. September 25th, 2019)
https://medium.com/@pulsefilms/why-music-videos-are-still-so-important-views-from-inside-the-industry-ebaa7d4758d2 (acc. March 15th, 2019)
http://www.mtv.com/news/articles/1633772/20100311/lady_gaga.jhtml (acc. March 18th, 2019)
https://news.harvard.edu/gazette/story/2019/11/new-harvard-study-establishes-music-is-universal/ (Acc. July 3rd, 2020)
https://www.newyorker.com/culture/culture-desk/kahlil-josephs-emotional-eye (acc. April 21st, 2019)
http://www.nbcnews.com/id/15196982/ns/business-us_business/t/google-buys-youtube-billion/#.WsOs_38uDIU (acc. March 11th, 2019)

https://www.npr.org/2016/02/07/465901864/cultural-appropriation-in-pop-music-when-are-artists-are-in-the-wrong (acc. June 12th, 2019)
http://www.nypress.com/article-21128-going-gaga.html (acc. April 22nd, 2019)
https://www.nytimes.com/2019/01/30/arts/music/grammy-awards-music-video.html?fbc lid=IwAR3xk6zCzIIJ8j1jwpR0_ssPswEgnuF19mmVXY5gLWap51SWqB4Jj_i5F24 (acc. September 15th, 2019)
https://www.nytimes.com/2019/06/14/opinion/youtube-algorithm.html (acc. August 7th, 2019)
https://openlab.fm/news/artists-interview-tobias-gremmier! (Acc. August 4th, 2020) https://petapixel.com/2017/03/03/latest-camera-sales-chart-reveals-death-compact-camera/ (acc. August 9th, 2019)
https://proxymusic.club/2018/07/08/james-merry-bjork-utopia/ (acc. August 4th, 2020)
https://www.riaa.com/u-s-sales-database/ (acc. February 3rd, 2019)
https://www.riaa.com/medium-five-stubborn-truths-youtube-value-gap/ (acc. August 23rd, 2019)
https://www.rollingstone.com/music/music-lists/the-30-sexiest-music-videos-of-all-time-202547/ (acc. September 4th, 2019)
https://www.rollingstone.com/music/music-news/on-the-charts-bts-become-first-k-pop-act-to-reach-number-one-629174/ (acc. June 27th, 2020)
https://www.shortlist.com/entertainment/music/kendrick-lamar-the-saviour-of-hip-hop/79605 (acc. July 9th, 2020)
https://www.statista.com/chart/19854/companies-bts-share-of-south-korea-gdp/ (acc. August 9th, 2020)
https://thebiglead.com/2018/04/11/best-music-videos-of-all-time-ranking-top-50/ (acc. September 4th, 2019)
http://theconversation.com/the-false-feminism-of-kendrick-lamars-humble-75596 (acc. July 9th, 2020)
https://theculturetrip.com/asia/south-korea/articles/the-biggest-budget-k-pop-videos-from-korea/ (acc. July 4th, 2020)
https://www.theguardian.com/music/2016/jul/28/how-pop-music-video-got-weird-again (acc. February 5th, 2019)
https://www.theguardian.com/music/2016/sep/28/solange-new-album-q-tip-lil-wayne-kelly-rowland-a-seat-at-the-table (acc. September 15th, 2019)
https://www.thenewamerican.com/culture/item/17311-influential-beats-the-cultural-impact-of-music (acc. August 8th, 2019)
https://time.com/5561466/lil-nas-x-old-town-road-billboard/ (acc. June 19th, 2020)
https://twitter.com/bjork/status/925346387780362240/photo/1 (acc. August 4th, 2020)
https://twitter.com/DBtodomundo/status/993965662941925376 (acc. September 15th, 2019)
https://twitter.com/MileyCyrus/status/1145818700114792449 (acc. October 11th, 2019)
https://twitter.com/MileyCyrus/status/1146041040928944128 (acc. October 11th, 2019)
https://www.vulture.com/2018/05/what-it-means-when-childish-gambino-says-this-is-ame rica.html (acc. September 16th, 2019)
https://www.washingtonpost.com/news/arts-and-entertainment/wp/2018/05/07/this-is-ame rica-breaking-down-childish-gambinos-powerful-new-music-video/ (acc. September 16th, 2019)

Bibliography

https://web.archive.org/web/20131103182155/http://www.inaglobal.fr/en/music/article/k-pop-story-well-oiled-industry-standardized-catchy-tunes (acc. June 27th, 2020)

https://www.whosampled.com/sample/346515/Jamie-xx-Gosh-DJ-Ron-MC-Strings-Unbroadcast-%27One-in-the-Jungle%27-Pilot/ (acc. July 7th, 2020)

http://www.worldbank.org/en/news/infographic/2016/05/27/india-s-poverty-profile (acc. June 16th, 2019)